Praise for *Predictive Analytics for the Modern Enterprise*

Reporting what happened is no longer enough to be competitive in today's business world. Predictive analytics are the basis for looking beyond the immediate and preparing your company for the future.

—*Christopher Gardner, Business Intelligence Analyst,*
University of Michigan

Nooruddin Abbas Ali provides a great blend of technical and practical information, giving many real-life examples along the way that are easy to follow. It's a great read if you are interested in making a difference with your company's data.

—*John Oliver, Data Scientist*

Nooruddin masterfully navigates the intricacies of predictive analytics, captivating readers with each paragraph. His clear explanations demystify various aspects of predictive analytics, making it more accessible to a wider audience.

—*Muzammil Shamim, Systems Engineer*

Predictive Analytics
for the Modern Enterprise
A Practitioner's Guide to Designing
and Implementing Solutions

Nooruddin Abbas Ali

Beijing • Boston • Farnham • Sebastopol • Tokyo

Predictive Analytics for the Modern Enterprise

by Nooruddin Abbas Ali

Copyright © 2024 Nooruddin Abbas Ali. All rights reserved.

Published by O'Reilly Media, Inc., 1005 Gravenstein Highway North, Sebastopol, CA 95472.

O'Reilly books may be purchased for educational, business, or sales promotional use. Online editions are also available for most titles (*http://oreilly.com*). For more information, contact our corporate/institutional sales department: 800-998-9938 or *corporate@oreilly.com*.

Acquisitions Editor: Michelle Smith	**Indexer:** WordCo Indexing Services, Inc.
Development Editor: Angela Rufino	**Interior Designer:** David Futato
Production Editor: Elizabeth Faerm	**Cover Designer:** Karen Montgomery
Copyeditor: Audrey Doyle	**Illustrator:** Kate Dullea
Proofreader: J.M. Olejarz	

June 2024: First Edition

Revision History for the First Edition

2024-05-20: First Release

See *http://oreilly.com/catalog/errata.csp?isbn=9781098136864* for release details.

The O'Reilly logo is a registered trademark of O'Reilly Media, Inc. *Predictive Analytics for the Modern Enterprise*, the cover image, and related trade dress are trademarks of O'Reilly Media, Inc.

The views expressed in this work are those of the author and do not represent the publisher's views. While the publisher and the author have used good faith efforts to ensure that the information and instructions contained in this work are accurate, the publisher and the author disclaim all responsibility for errors or omissions, including without limitation responsibility for damages resulting from the use of or reliance on this work. Use of the information and instructions contained in this work is at your own risk. If any code samples or other technology this work contains or describes is subject to open source licenses or the intellectual property rights of others, it is your responsibility to ensure that your use thereof complies with such licenses and/or rights.

978-1-098-13686-4

[LSI]

Table of Contents

Preface

The predictive analytics market has experienced remarkable growth over the past decade. This trend is expected to continue, as the market's value is projected to surge from $10.5 billion in 2021 to $28.1 billion by 2026. This expansion is being propelled by an increase in automation across industries, the widespread adoption of Internet of Things (IoT) devices, and the advent of high-speed 5G internet connectivity. Enterprises, recognizing the value of processing vast datasets and forecasting future scenarios, are leveraging predictive analytics to gain a competitive edge and bolster revenue streams. Moreover, the COVID-19 pandemic has further underscored the significance of predictive analytics, with organizations now turning to it for strategic planning, operational optimization, and cost savings.

In this era of data-driven decision making, predictive analytics has become an operational imperative. Data professionals today find themselves more intricately linked with business objectives than they ever were before. It is against this backdrop that this book was crafted, aiming to furnish data professionals with the requisite background, tools, and best practices for conceptualizing, implementing, and operationalizing predictive analytics. Through a blend of industry use cases and comprehensive hands-on examples, this book seeks to empower practitioners to navigate the intricacies of predictive analytics with confidence and precision.

Due to the vast nature of predictive analytics, numerous resources delve into its specific frameworks, use cases, coding examples, or mathematical foundations. Yet it remains a challenge to find a book that seamlessly integrates these aspects into a cohesive narrative accessible to learners. Amid this landscape, there is a noticeable absence of literature that explores the latest cloud service providers' key accelerators driving the adoption of AI and machine learning (ML) in today's enterprises. As data professionals, we grapple with the challenge of meeting the ever-growing demands of the business, often without adequate technical literature that aligns with our needs.

This book seeks to bridge these gaps by offering a layered approach to understanding and implementing predictive analytics within enterprises. Drawing upon the most prevalent frameworks and technologies and contextualizing industry disruptions of the past decade, the book aims to equip data professionals with the tools to not only address business requirements but also advocate for data-driven transformations that directly impact the bottom line. Through a blend of practical insights and strategic guidance, this book endeavors to empower readers to navigate the evolving landscape of predictive analytics with confidence and proficiency.

Who Is This Book For?

The primary audience for this book is data professionals and technical managers who want to learn the scientific foundation for predictive analytics and its application in today's enterprise. The book will allow readers to navigate the life cycle of developing predictive analytics capabilities using multiple frameworks, techniques, and platforms. Readers can further hone their understanding of predictive analytics via industry-leading examples that are relevant today. The book is designed to be simple but not basic; comprehensive but not complex. If you are looking for a book that you can pick up on the go to start learning about predictive analytics, this one's for you.

I assume no prior knowledge on the part of the reader except for a basic understanding of programming in Python, a high-level understanding of foundational mathematics, and a high-level understanding of Amazon Web Services (AWS).

How This Book Is Organized

The book establishes what predictive analytics is, why organizations use it, and how it can be used for business problem-solving. This book consists of nine chapters and one appendix.

Chapter 1, "Data Analytics in the Modern Enterprise", introduces predictive analytics through relatable everyday scenarios, offering an accessible entry point for readers with minimal prior knowledge. It traces the historical evolution of data analytics and presents the tools and frameworks available for enterprise implementation.

Chapter 2, "Predictive Analytics: An Operational Necessity", explores the organizational shift toward data-driven strategies, addressing common challenges and showcasing successful implementations across vertical industries.

Chapter 3, "The Mathematics and Algorithms Behind Predictive Analytics", delves into the mathematical foundations of predictive analytics, covering statistics, linear algebra, and ML algorithms.

Chapter 4, "Working with Data", focuses on data preprocessing nuances and the end-to-end predictive analytics pipeline.

Chapter 5, "Python and scikit-learn for Predictive Analytics", provides hands-on learning with Python libraries, facilitating basic predictive modeling and prediction tasks.

Chapter 6, "TensorFlow and Keras for Predictive Analytics", explores TensorFlow fundamentals, including linear regression and deep neural networks.

Chapter 7, "Predictive Analytics for Business Problem-Solving", examines practical applications of predictive analytics in retail, entertainment, and finance, including fraud detection, price optimization, and recommendations.

Chapter 8, "Exploring AWS Cloud Provider Services for AI/ML", explores AI/ML services by AWS, discussing cloud strategies and tools including AWS SageMaker and Amazon Forecast for ML pipelines and time series forecasting.

Chapter 9, "Food for Thought", provides a recap of what was learned in the book and extends into a few additional use cases. It concludes with a discussion about the social impact of predictive analytics.

As the book is geared toward a wide audience, I wanted to make sure I am able to guide you in navigating the book in a way that is most conducive to learning. Hence, you will find symbols in different sections of the book to indicate the type of content you can expect to find there (see Table P-1).

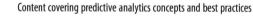	Content covering predictive analytics concepts and best practices
	Heavy technical content (possibly with some code)
	Heavy mathematical content (all mathematical content is intended to enhance the learning experience; as such, a deep understanding of it is not required to work your way through the concepts and examples in the book)

Table P-1. Chapter guide (content categorization for readers)

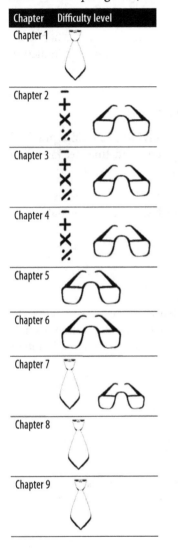

Chapter	Difficulty level
Chapter 1	
Chapter 2	
Chapter 3	
Chapter 4	
Chapter 5	
Chapter 6	
Chapter 7	
Chapter 8	
Chapter 9	

Conventions Used in This Book

The following typographical conventions are used in this book:

Italic
    Indicates new terms, URLs, email addresses, filenames, and file extensions.

`Constant width`
    Used for program listings, as well as within paragraphs to refer to program elements such as variable or function names, databases, data types, environment variables, statements, and keywords.

`Constant width bold`
    Shows commands or other text that should be typed literally by the user.

`Constant width italic`
    Shows text that should be replaced with user-supplied values or by values determined by context.

 This element signifies a tip or suggestion.

 This element signifies a general note.

 This element indicates a warning or caution.

Using Code Examples

Supplemental material (code examples, exercises, etc.) is available for download at *https://github.com/paforme/predictiveanalytics*.

If you have a technical question or a problem using the code examples, please email *support@oreilly.com*.

This book is here to help you get your job done. In general, if example code is offered with this book, you may use it in your programs and documentation. You do not need to contact us for permission unless you're reproducing a significant portion of the code. For example, writing a program that uses several chunks of code from this book does not require permission. Selling or distributing examples from O'Reilly books does require permission. Answering a question by citing this book and quoting example code does not require permission. Incorporating a significant amount of example code from this book into your product's documentation does require permission.

We appreciate, but do not require, attribution. An attribution usually includes the title, author, publisher, and ISBN. For example: *Predictive Analytics for the Modern Enterprise* by Nooruddin Abbas Ali (O'Reilly). Copyright 2024 Nooruddin Abbas Ali, 978-1-098-13686-4."

If you feel your use of code examples falls outside fair use or the permission given above, feel free to contact us at *permissions@oreilly.com*.

O'Reilly Online Learning

O'REILLY® For more than 40 years, *O'Reilly Media* has provided technology and business training, knowledge, and insight to help companies succeed.

Our unique network of experts and innovators share their knowledge and expertise through books, articles, and our online learning platform. O'Reilly's online learning platform gives you on-demand access to live training courses, in-depth learning paths, interactive coding environments, and a vast collection of text and video from O'Reilly and 200+ other publishers. For more information, visit *https://oreilly.com*.

How to Contact Us

Please address comments and questions concerning this book to the publisher:

O'Reilly Media, Inc.
1005 Gravenstein Highway North
Sebastopol, CA 95472
800-889-8969 (in the United States or Canada)
707-827-7019 (international or local)
707-829-0104 (fax)
support@oreilly.com
https://www.oreilly.com/about/contact.html

We have a web page for this book, where we list errata, examples, and any additional information. You can access this page at *https://oreil.ly/predictive-analytics*.

For news and information about our books and courses, visit *https://oreilly.com*.

Find us on LinkedIn: *https://linkedin.com/company/oreilly-media*.

Watch us on YouTube: *https://youtube.com/oreillymedia*.

Acknowledgments

I had tremendous support from so many amazing people throughout my journey of writing this book. A big thank-you goes to everyone who believed in me, cheered me on, and helped make this book possible. I would especially like to thank the following people.

First, I would like to thank my family: my lovely wife, Fatema, for her love and unwavering faith in me and whose understanding and support made this book possible; my parents, Abbas Ali and Khatoon, without whom I would not be who I am today; my lovely boys, Burhanuddin and Hussain, who make my world a little bit better every day; and my sisters, Tasneem, Zahra, and Umme Salma, for always believing in me.

I would also like to thank my friends and colleagues who cheered for me throughout this journey.

O'Reilly has been an absolute pleasure to work with. A big thank-you goes to Angela Rufino for her continuous guidance, understanding, and support. Thank you also to Michelle Smith for believing in me and to Elizabeth Faerm for all her support.

Thank you to Christopher Gardner, George Mount, John Oliver, Chester Ismay, and Tobias Zwingmann for reviewing the book and supplying numerous helpful recommendations and insightful remarks. You have indeed made this book better. Thank you for the time you invested and the interest with which you provided the reviews.

Lastly, I am tremendously thankful to all the incredible data professionals who continue to produce amazing research and literature to further the predictive analytics realm.

## CHAPTER 1

Data Analytics in the Modern Enterprise

When you were growing up, did you ever wonder why you had to study history in school? I did. But it wasn't until I was much older that I realized history's importance. Understanding how things were in the past and where they are now allows us to build on them and anticipate what is to come next—and, in some cases, to also *influence* what is to come next. As I'm writing this, there is a lot of buzz about AI and machine learning (ML). But how did we go from simple calculations to chatbots conversing coherently with humans?

From statistical extrapolation of sales figures to planning stocks based on predicted sales, enterprises have come a long way. This journey from *data producing* to *data consuming* and finally *data driven* is what I explore in this chapter. First, I will delve into the details of how data analytics has evolved over time, what predictive analytics is at its roots, and what its place is in the analytical world. Then, I will discuss its role in data modeling and ML and the tools available today that can help you with data modeling and ML.

The Evolution of Data Analytics

If you still like shopping in person, you know that shopping is as much about the experience as it is about the actual purchase. Experienced sales professionals understand this. What separates the good salespeople from the great ones is their ability to effectively read customers, ask them questions, and understand and direct them toward a successful sale.

The moment you enter a shop you are eyed by a salesperson on the floor. Once they have established that you are not just window-shopping, they approach you politely and ask what you're looking for. The good ones will direct you to that section, but the great ones will ask you a second and maybe a third question. Let's imagine such a conversation:

You (Y): "I am looking for a formal shirt."

Great Salesperson (GS): "Awesome, let me help you with that. May I ask what occasion you are shopping for in order to help you better?"

Y: "Oh, it's the annual sales kickoff at our office, and I want to look sharp."

GS: "Thanks for sharing that. Since it's for a formal gathering, might I recommend blues and pinks or something in classic white?"

Y: "Classic white is more my jam."

GS: "Excellent choice. Let me show you our collection of formal white shirts."

Y: "Great!"

GS: "Since this is for a formal meeting, would you be open to looking at some formal trousers? I have some really great ones in khaki that will complement the shirt you've chosen."

Y: "I wasn't planning on it, but let's have a look."

GS: "Might I suggest the slim-fit ones? Perhaps you should try the combination first, before you make up your mind."

Y: (After putting on the trousers and shirt) "I like it. It looks good."

GS: "I couldn't agree more."

Y: "Great, that will be all then."

GS: "Sure, let me help you with that. Before you change back into your clothes, can I just ask you for one final indulgence? There's a new collection of lightweight formal shoes that I feel will complete the look you're going for. I can quickly bring you a pair in your size, and you can try them on and see how you feel about them."

Y: "I'm really not looking for shoes, but I can spend another minute, I guess."

GS: "Awesome, how about this beige pair with a touch of maroon…"

Most of us are all too familiar with going into a clothes store to buy one thing and ending up buying three. The same concept applies whether you are buying a car, hunting for furniture, or shopping for groceries. While the order might change, the fundamentals remain the same: read the customer, ask questions, understand the requirement, and direct the sale.

Now let's step into the world of ecommerce. Think Amazon, eBay, or your favorite local ecommerce store. Open the app or the website and you have stepped into their shop. The platform is your very "smart" salesperson. In most cases, it already knows your name, your age, where you live, and your preferences, because of your purchase history. Based on all this, the platform personalizes your experience. This could involve a multitude of things, from color themes to targeted product placement to discount codes for your favorite brands. The idea is to show you more of what you are likely to buy. Now imagine a physical store transforming to your preferences as you enter it. This level of personalization in the sales process is unprecedented in the brick-and-mortar world of shopping. As you search, filter, and browse the mobile app, your actions are the equivalent of your body language in person. What categories are you browsing? How much time did you spend on a particular item? Are there any items that you have added to your cart? These and many other metrics are constantly being evaluated to provide you with a unique shopping experience, make the next sale, increase the size of your shopping cart, and compel you to come back later for more.

The next time you are shopping online, notice the "Frequently bought together," "Customers who viewed this item also viewed this," and "What other items do customers buy" sections. These are all examples of personalization of content based on your activity history, the behavior of users similar to you, and demographics, among other things. The platform understands your needs, interacts with you, and directs you. At this point, you are probably wondering one of two things: "What does this have to do with predictive analytics?" or "Why don't we stick to the great salesperson instead of these heartless platforms?" The answer to the first question comes much later in the book, but I will try to answer the second question right now.

Imagine a physical store that has virtually unlimited capacity in terms of the products it can sell, somewhat like a magic store that can keep growing (Figure 1-1). Now imagine you have a genie that can sift through all these products to get you what you want in a matter of seconds. The genie is your friend and knows your likes and dislikes. The genie is also friends with other genies and therefore knows what people similar to you are buying these days. The really good genies can find you the best price for what you are looking for. Shopping at this magic store gives you magic coins that you can use to buy other things. When you're finished shopping you don't need to wait in a queue at the checkout counter. You just say the word and the items are paid for. Last but not least, you don't need to carry those shopping bags home. The genie will get them to your home in a jiffy.

Wouldn't that be great? Now stop imagining, because what I just described is your everyday ecommerce platform. Add to that same-day delivery, easy returns, and being able to shop from the comfort of your bedroom 24/7, and you'll never want to go back to shopping at a mall again.

But did all this happen overnight? Of course not. As early as the late 19th century, governments started collecting census data. They wanted to know more about the population so that they could plan for taxation, food distribution, and army recruitment, among other things. Fast-forward a few decades and the same data was being used to figure out where to build the next road or how to optimize power distribution. Governments realized that subsequent collections of data could be compared with previous collections to understand population growth and help with planning.

Figure 1-1. The magic store

Now consider that industrial workers have been clocking in and out of work long before computers were invented. While the primary reason for this form of data collection was to calculate workers' daily wages, business owners later realized they could use this data for further analysis—comparing, for example, the production efficiency of two different factory locations or figuring out optimal workforce timing to maximize production. At the time, the main sources of data were the workforce, inventory, and revenue (Figure 1-2).

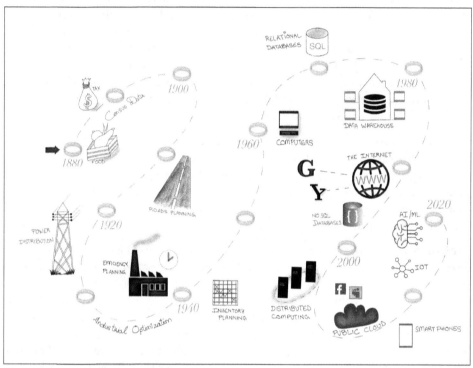

Figure 1-2. Data analytics timeline

With the advent of computers, the way in which data was collected, stored, and processed was profoundly impacted. While the first computers were mainly focused on computation, soon they were being used to not only process information, but store it as well. Some years later, information storage moved from flat files to databases. While there were a few initial attempts to build databases, a clear breakthrough occurred in the early 1970s in the form of relational databases.[1] *Relational databases* allowed users to store data in the form of entities and relationships, while optimizing for storage. Most of them initially supported Structured Query Language (SQL). This standard language allowed users to easily explore and manipulate (relatively) large amounts of data stored in relational databases. Common data sources soon expanded to include employee, operational, and financial data in these databases. Organizations

---

1 Kenneth D. Foote, "A Brief History of Analytics" (*https://oreil.ly/APzLK*), Dataversity, accessed September 20, 2021.

could extract monthly revenue reports or find the total sales of a certain product during a particular season.

As the internet became mainstream, computers became connected to each other and users began interacting with their own computers as well as with other computers on the World Wide Web. The dot-com boom saw the advent of search engines like Yahoo! and Google that were collecting large amounts of HTTP information and data on user click rates. Searching everything on the web was not the same as querying a structured database. Hence, companies came up with a different breed of databases. Developers needed a better way to handle data that was neither as well structured as an enterprise application nor centralized in a single location or enterprise. This family of databases came to be known as *noSQL*.

The need to search eventually gave birth to search engines. Governments wanted to store and process census data with genealogical references, and that led to graph databases. Large amounts of logging data for click streams led to time series databases. These databases were as different from each other as they were from relational databases. However, they were meant for their niche use cases and were designed for storing and processing large amounts of data.

Around this time, organizations realized they needed to collect all the data in the different databases and bring it together in the form of a centralized decision-making system. This was the origin of what we know as *data warehouses* today. Simply put, data warehouses brought data in from multiple sources, transformed it, and made it available to business users for analysis and decision making. As the data grew, so did the infrastructure requirements for data warehouses, to the point that it was no longer economically feasible to invest in these mammoths. This gave rise to horizontally scaling *distributed storage* and *processing frameworks* that allowed data collection and processing at unprecedented scales.

Somewhere between relational databases and distributed frameworks, organizations started utilizing data to drive businesses. *Business intelligence* (BI) practices evolved, and several tools were created to allow businesses to drive actionable insights from their data. Furthermore, organizations started to analyze large datasets to identify different patterns so that they could predict customer and business needs. While the internet opened up the world of data, processing these large amounts of data required significant investment in terms of compute and storage infrastructure. This meant that only very large organizations and governments could really tap into the true power of data. Public cloud providers such as Amazon Web Services (AWS), Google Cloud Platform (GCP), Azure, and Alibaba Cloud removed the entry barriers to collecting, transforming, and analyzing large sets of data. Infrastructure investment moved from a capex (capital expenditure) model to an opex (operational expenditure) model, and we saw further optimizations in compute and storage subsystems.[2,3] New data sources today include social media platforms, mobile user data, and Internet of Things (IoT) data, among others. Since infrastructure is commoditized, any organization (big or small) is able to process large amounts of information to make data-driven decisions.

Ever-improving connectivity and democratization of infrastructure have allowed for tremendous advancements in the fields of AI and ML in the past decade. AI/ML is now being used to map the stars in the universe, build robots, power self-driving vehicles, predict fraud in financial transactions, and build interactive chatbots for companies, among many other applications. While there was a clear distinction between operational and analytical workloads, these lines are now blurring. Data-driven decision making dictates that data analysis is no longer a sidecar running batch reports. It is an integral part of the daily operations of any modern enterprise. The journey from punch cards to AI has been long and arduous and is a culmination of the continued work and dedication of some of the most brilliant minds in history.

Different Types of Data Analytics

You can think of data analytics as the (art and) science of talking to your business. It helps us understand our business better by giving us insights into what happened in the past, what might be happening right now, and why certain things might have happened. Armed with this information, analytics can also help us (within scientific probability) gauge what is likely to happen and figure out what to do next. Organizations employ several data analytics practices to collect, process, analyze, and store their data (Figure 1-3). Depending on the literature that you are referring to, these might vary; however, the ones that appear in most places are the following:

- The past (and present):
  - *Descriptive analytics* helps us understand what happened.
  - *Diagnostic analytics* helps us identify why something might have happened.
- The future:
  - *Predictive analytics* can help us determine what might happen next.
  - *Prescriptive analytics* is about what we can/should do next.[4]

---

2 Capital expenditures are large expenses that organizations undertake, usually for multiple years.

3 Operational expenditures are smaller operational expenses that are usually related to the daily requirements of running a business.

4 Catherine Cote, "What Is Predictive Analytics? 5 Examples" (*https://oreil.ly/tEV38*), Harvard Business School Online, accessed October 26, 2021.

My frequent use of terms such as *might* and *likely* is deliberate. It does not mean we are talking about something scientifically inaccurate. It's to drive home the point that most of what we are discussing is based on scientific probabilities. Therefore, it's important not only to understand the data and its conclusions but also to be able to figure out the level of accuracy of our deductions.

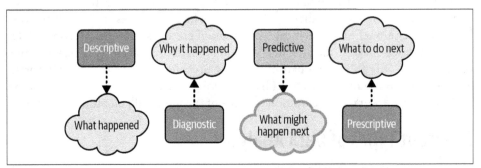

Figure 1-3. Types of data analytics

Descriptive Analytics

I'm baffled by the amount of time my doctors spend browsing and typing on their computers versus talking to me. And what really grinds my gears is that I can't see what they are doing.

Let's analyze a typical medical appointment. The nurse (or assistant) asks for your name and identification. This gives them access to your registration details and medical history. Then, they ask you to accompany them to an exam room where they ask you the reason for your visit. They check your weight, height, blood pressure, and any known allergies, and then you patiently wait to see the doctor. Once the doctor arrives, they usually ask you about your symptoms, when they started, their frequency, and their intensity. You can think of this entire phase as historical and current data collection.

After this, there is a bit (or a lot) of computer time involved (depending on the doctor), at the end of which the doctor either gives you a potential diagnosis or recommends further tests. Medical professionals have access to medical data that is classified by age, demographics, gender, and predisposition to other medical conditions, among other things. For example, they can check your height and weight and plot you on a body mass index (BMI) chart to see whether you are in the healthy range. They can check your blood pressure and see whether you are at risk for hypertension. They can combine these results to see whether you are at risk for heart disease. You can think of this as trend analytics that allows them to map your health.

Recording and understanding your blood pressure and other health metrics is part of descriptive analytics. However, mapping these metrics to make predictive conclusions about your health goes beyond the realm of such analysis.

Another great example of data analytics and trend analysis can be found with streaming platforms such as Netflix, Amazon Prime, and OSN+. While the details of implementation and the accuracy of results might vary, most of these platforms collect large amounts of user activity data to understand the content users are watching in various demographics and during a certain time period. This data is then analyzed to make recommendations to users in various geographies and age groups on currently trending content. The data can be further processed to understand what kinds of content, genres, and actors, among other things, are being favored by audiences at this time. This can help with decision making with regard to continuation of existing contracts, future productions, and marketing campaigns.

Descriptive analytics involves analyzing historical and current data to understand the trends around what has happened. Various techniques are used to understand these trends. You can aggregate or roll up the data into averages of large datasets. You can drill into details of the data, take a slice of the data (e.g., Netflix usage) to understand the most-watched series in a particular month, or further dice the data by creating smaller datasets from larger ones. As we have already seen, this will not only allow trend analysis for better decision making, but also help identify outliers for detecting anomalies. We saw a more personalized example of this in the medical use case. However, heavy use of prescriptive analytics can also be found in other verticals, such as automated fraud detection in the financial industry.

Diagnostic Analytics

Once we understand what happened (or is happening), the next logical step is to figure out why it happened. Diagnostic analytics answers this question. The analysis can be in the form of a root cause analysis, or it can involve analyzing trends to understand the relationships between different but seemingly related occurrences. Diagnostic analytics can be used to draw better conclusions about why something happened.

It is important to differentiate causality from correlation. Two (or more) items can be correlated if a relationship can be established in the way they change. In statistical terms, two variables are *positively correlated* if they both move together in the same direction. This means that if one increases, the other increases with it. Two variables are *negatively correlated* if they move in opposite directions. However, this does not mean that one is causing the change to the other. For example, the rainy season is often called gloomy weather. That means some people feel sad or depressed when it rains. We can conclude that there is a correlation between rainy weather and individuals feeling down. But the conclusion that rain causes depression would be incorrect.

Scientifically speaking, exposure to sunlight releases a hormone called serotonin in the brain. Serotonin is known to be associated with boosting mood and helping with focus. Hence, a more logical conclusion would be that the lack of sunlight results in reduced energy levels among the masses. Diagnostic analytics aims to understand the relationships between variables and trends to establish correlation and causation.

Diagnostic analytics can be performed manually, as in the preceding example where we analyzed the relationship between rain and people's mood; by using regression (e.g., determining the relationship between marketing spend and the total sales of an item in retail to identify important ranges and outliers); or by using data analysis tools such as Microsoft Excel. Going back to the medical use case, if a doctor has established that a patient has hypertension, they would then strive to understand why the patient has hypertension. When doing so, they have access to tools such as common questions to ask, common causes of hypertension, and complications related to hypertension. This analysis helps the doctor get to the root cause of the problem for which hypertension is the symptom. While medication can help a patient keep their blood pressure in check, every doctor will tell you that the proper way to do that is for the patient to make lifestyle changes that address the root cause of their high blood pressure.

Looking back at the Netflix example, once Netflix has figured out what titles are the most watched in a month, it would want to understand why this is the case. For example, it might realize that in the summer months the titles from the animation genre are the most watched. A root cause analysis might uncover that this is because most school-age children are at home in the summer. Over time, such an analysis can be automated and fed into Netflix's decision-making process with regard to planning and launching new titles and continuation (or discontinuation) of older ones.

Predictive Analytics

Predictive analytics is a branch of data analysis that deals with using historical and current data to predict future events. We have not yet created machines that can predict the future. However, we are inching toward a distant future that just might allow us to do that. Coming back to reality, the predictions could be a simple binary; that is, the likelihood of something happening or not. Or they could be more complex, such as predicting a selling price of fuel that optimizes profits based on location and weather conditions. Predictive analysis can be done the old-school way, by analyzing data manually; or it can be done using predictive data modeling and ML. It is one of the most critical data analytical practices employed by organizations to collect, process, and analyze their data. The idea is to use data to understand the business better and produce actionable insights that will lead to prescriptive analytics.

As we talk about the various forms of analytics, it is important to understand that organizations are at different stages in their analytics journey. These broad categories mostly feed into each other and will usually have some form of overlap. When working with deep technology, it often helps to go back to the business problem you are trying to solve and then to figure out the best way to achieve the solution. Just as you would not use a tank to kill a fly, it's not always better to use the most complex analytics solution.

Now let's discuss the details of the business problem that predictive analytics helps solve, the different technologies that data analysts and organizations can leverage, and how to set up predictive analytics for various use cases. Continuing with our medical use case, if the doctor learns that their patient has high blood pressure caused by a high-stress lifestyle, the doctor will more often than not investigate other factors contributing to the patient's high blood pressure. For example, a patient who is overweight and has high levels of cholesterol along with hypertension is at a high risk of developing heart disease. This prediction can help the doctor treat the patient's hypertension as well as develop a holistic approach to improving the patient's overall health.

Businesses like Netflix take this one step further. By understanding customer behavior on the platform, Netflix can predict what the customer is likely to watch next. Content personalization is one of the major use cases for predictive analytics that we'll dig much deeper into in later chapters. Simply put, companies such as Netflix may analyze what kind of content the user watches, how much time they spend on the platform and on different categories, and their age group to determine, using predictive modeling, what kind of content the user is likely to watch. If you were to observe the content on different Netflix profiles within the same household, you would realize that the recommended content varies among the profiles. This is because of deep content personalization, which caters to users' individual needs and preferences. If Netflix were only using descriptive analytics for personalization, we would see very similar content across users within the same geography.

Prescriptive Analytics

Prescriptive analytics is the last leg in data-driven decision making. It helps businesses determine what is the optimal next step. To answer the question of what to do next, businesses evaluate multiple variables to chalk out the best next course of action. Like other forms of analytics, prescriptive analytics can be manual, via analytical tools; or it can be automated, using algorithms.

When we address a problem, we are working with a certain set of limitations and constraints. A problem might have more than one feasible solution. If these solutions are limited in number, it is easy to go through them one by one to figure out which one produced the best outcome within the given constraints. There are, however, some problems that are unsolvable, and for those, one needs to relax the limitations and constraints to solve them. Of the solvable problems, there are those that are *optimally solvable*, meaning we can say with mathematical certainty that a particular solution is the best. Optimization techniques that help achieve this include linear, nonlinear, and stochastic mathematical programming.

But when a method can provide a solution but we are unable to confirm that it is the best feasible solution, the problem is understood to be *heuristically solvable*. This means we end up with better solutions, but we cannot confirm whether one of them is the best solution. Heuristic problem-solving can include simulation modeling.[5] Simulations can be thought of as computer representations of real-world scenarios. While the simulation is a representation of reality, it is nearly impossible to capture all the nuances and variables of the real world. However, it is still very effective at estimating outcomes based on current conditions or potential future actions. For example, a model can simulate the spread of a disease across a certain geography with reasonable accuracy so that preventive or corrective actions can be taken in advance.

Going back to our patient who is likely to develop heart disease, the doctor would probably conduct a few more tests and interviews to determine the best course of action. Note that the course of action is dependent not only on our prediction of the patient developing heart disease, but also on the limitations and constraints of the patient and the doctor. These limitations can be financial, such as the kind of insurance the patient has; or they can be medical, such as other conditions that might prevent the patient from taking certain medications. Based on this, the doctor puts together a treatment plan that is optimized for the patient.

You may ask what Netflix (or other companies) could still do that it hasn't already done. It figured out what a user is most likely to watch, so why not just propose that content? Well, if the business problem it was trying to solve was to ensure that it showed content the viewer is likely to watch, and if the accuracy of its prediction was high enough, this would be one feasible solution. However, there are many other questions Netflix needs to answer. For example: "If we push the exact content that we predicted, will it maximize the time the user spends on the platform?" "If we maximize this time, will it translate into increased revenue?" "Are we trying to maximize revenue?" "Are we trying to increase the user base?" "What content needs to be pushed to optimize sponsors?" And so on. Based on this, the platform can attempt to find the most optimized content that should be pushed to the user.

---

5 Dursun Delen, *Prescriptive Analytics: The Final Frontier for Evidence-Based Management and Optimal Decision Making* (Pearson FT Press: Upper Saddle River, NJ, 2019).

Knowledge Acquisition, Machine Learning, and the Role of Predictive Analytics

When driving, your natural reaction when you see a pedestrian is to slow down. The decisions of whether to stop or continue driving and what is a safe distance to be from the pedestrian depend on a number of factors. Is it a child, adult, or senior citizen? Are they looking down at the pavement or looking at the road, waiting to cross? What does their body language tell you? Is there a pedestrian crosswalk in sight? These are just some of the many questions the mind considers and for which it computes the answers to predict the behavior of the pedestrian and decide accordingly.

This process is based on knowledge. In this case, such knowledge is mostly acquired during your initial training from a driving instructor, academic training, and practice. But does your learning stop once you acquire a driver's license? Probably not. As you continue to drive, you keep learning and improving your skills by exploring different terrains, driving at different times of the day, experiencing different traffic conditions, and so on; hence the term *experienced driver*. This seemingly trivial activity helps us understand some of the types of knowledge we acquire:

- Knowledge we are born with (instincts and behaviors)
- Knowledge we gain from institutions, books, conversations, and the internet (learning from the experiences of others)
- Knowledge we acquire from our own experiences
- And more

Our dependence on machines is ever increasing. From simple, everyday tasks such as buying groceries to complex tasks such as driving from point A to point B, we see the use of machines everywhere. There are smartphones, smart vacuums, smart cars, and even smart refrigerators. We are surrounded by them. If a machine (and by "a machine" I mean anything programmable) needs to survive, it is no longer enough for it to just keep doing what it does best. There is an inherent need for the machine to acquire knowledge.

Machine learning is the human attempt to imitate the process of learning and improving in machines. In machine learning, algorithms are trained to make predictions. You can think of these predictions as being as simple as a true-or-false classification such as whether an email message is or isn't spam, or as complex as a guess about the effective lifespan of a piece of industrial equipment. These predictions form the basis of actionable insights that eventually drive business decisions. But how do machines actually learn? Consider the following:

Decision process

This takes in the input values, applies a bunch of recipes, and then attempts to make predictions using patterns within the data.

Error function

This assesses the prediction for its accuracy. When known examples are available (mostly in the form of historical data), the error function can help evaluate whether the prediction was correct, and if it wasn't, how far off the prediction was from the actual values.

Optimization

This takes the known examples and the predicted values and tweaks the model (we will talk about what this tweaking means later) to minimize the divergence between them. This process can be automated and continuous to allow the model to achieve a certain level of accuracy.[6]

What I just described is known as *supervised learning*. Supervised learning uses labeled datasets (often known as training data) to train algorithms. Think of these labels as useful tags about the training data. For example, a large sample of data about tumor classification can be used to train an algorithm to predict whether a tumor is malignant or benign. The decision process makes predictions, the error function uses the labels to figure out the error of its ways, and then the optimization function adjusts the algorithm to minimize the difference between the predictions and the labels.

As you might have guessed, the other type of learning in machines is called *unsupervised learning*. It is used when we do not have access to labeled data. An algorithm helps identify relationships and patterns in the data without any external help (such as historical data or user input). But what happens if you have only a small amount of labeled data? In such cases, an approach known as *semi-supervised learning* is used. This approach uses a smaller labeled dataset with a much larger set of unlabeled data during training. That combination allows the algorithm to learn to label the unlabeled data and then produce predictions. Then there is *reinforcement machine learning*, where the model is not trained using labeled data. Rather, the algorithm learns similar to how a child learns new things: using trial and error, and mostly using rewards to reinforce successful outcomes and punishment to minimize failures. This feedback to the algorithm allows it to learn from its own experiences.[7]

The democratization of machine learning in the past couple of decades, for business analysis and for decision making, has been the driving force behind industry

---

6 "What Is Machine Learning (ML)?" (*https://oreil.ly/Go-GB*), Berkeley School of Information, last updated February 2022.

7 "What Is Machine Learning (ML)?" Berkeley School of Information.

disruptors and allowed companies to achieve unprecedented growth in record time. Circling back to where we started, the argument boils down to how programmable machines acquire and consume data. Drawing a parallel to what we discussed earlier:

- Machines can be programmed with a set of models to operate with.
- They can learn from historical and current data to constantly optimize their operational models (training and machine learning).
- They can learn from experience.

Where the machines have a leg up on us is in their ability to efficiently collect, analyze, and consume very large amounts of data in a very short span of time. Add to this autonomous machine-to-machine communication, and we effectively have a hive where each individual entity is constantly learning and improving from the past and present experiences of others, thus forming the foundation of ever-improving data-driven decision making powered by predictive analytics.

To make data-driven decisions, enterprises need to achieve the following:

- Collect and store large amounts of data from various data sources
- Preprocess this data to:
  — Ensure that the data is collected (or adjusted) for the business context of the problem they are trying to solve
  — Clean, classify, and label the data (when applicable)
- Use the data to understand the history and current state of the business:
  — What happened/is happening
  — Why it happened/is happening
- Use the data to predict the future of the business
- Use these predictions to make data-driven decisions

And they need to do all of that in a loop.

Predictive analytics sits at the heart of this process, driving how a business continuously acquires knowledge through data, training, and experience. It helps convert raw data into knowledge that can then be used to make predictions about the future of the business. So, what are some questions that companies might try to answer?

- Business question: A hospitality chain would like to understand how much staff it should deploy in each of its locations based on the season and the weather.
  — Needed prediction: How many guests can the chain expect in each of its locations?

- Business question: A logistics company would like to understand how much stock of each product it should maintain for the coming season.
  - Needed prediction: What are the expected sales for each product for the coming season?
- Business question: An electricity provider would like to determine how much energy should be generated for the upcoming cycle.
  - Needed prediction: How much power will consumers utilize for the given block in the upcoming cycle?

Without accurate predictions, businesses risk miscalculating these key matrices. If the logistics company were to overstock products, it would run into unwarranted space and labor expenses, not to mention unsold items expiring or becoming obsolete. Likewise, if it were to underestimate product demand, it would result in loss of potential sales and decreased customer satisfaction. Similarly, overproduction of energy is wasteful and overallocation of staff is a waste of human resources; both translate into an unnecessary financial burden on the business. And not being able to produce enough energy or not having enough staff would directly impact the customer experience. Accurate predictions of these metrics are undoubtedly an operational necessity and a key component of data-driven decision making.

Tools, Frameworks, and Platforms in the Predictive Analytics World

Enterprises have leveraged analytics for a long time, and that is not about to change anytime soon. If anything, analytics is becoming more mainstream day by day. We live in a world where competition is fierce and time is a very expensive commodity. Hence, enterprises are continuously looking for new ways to reduce their time to market for new services and are in a continuous cycle of improving customer experience to stay ahead of the competition. Analytics is one of the tools they employ to better understand their business and their customers and to make relevant changes more quickly.

Enterprises understand that competitive advantage cannot be bought but needs to be developed. One of the most common open source technologies out there for building big data analytics systems is Hadoop. Hadoop, at its core, is a distributed storage system that allows users to store very large datasets across a distributed architecture. Usually coupled with Hadoop is MapReduce, which helps process these large datasets across this distributed architecture.

Though based on a whitepaper that came out of Google, Hadoop is an open source project often known as Apache Hadoop, released around the 2005–2006 time frame. Since then, this ecosystem has evolved both for the better *and* arguably for the worse.

Real-time processing requirements are now supported by the Spark and Flink projects. Additionally, abstraction layers have evolved on top of MapReduce, such as Pig (for SQL), and nonrelational database functionality is supported by the likes of HBase running on top of Hadoop. Organizations tend to build these platforms either on premises or in the cloud in a self-managed fashion. There are, of course, third-party vendors that have developed expertise and tools around Hadoop, and they offer their own versions and add-ons. There are also fully managed versions from cloud providers and third-party vendors that are ready to consume and are offered in a software as a service (SaaS) model.

But this is not a book about Hadoop or general analytics, so this is the extent to which we will talk about these subjects. (If you want to learn more about the Hadoop ecosystem, SimpliLearn Solutions (*https://oreil.ly/5L9Ou*) offers a great learning resource.) Instead, we will delve deeper into predictive analytics and the languages, libraries, and services needed to develop predictive functionality within organizations.

Languages and Libraries

We'll start with Python. *Python* is an object-oriented programming language that has taken the world by storm. Its object-oriented nature makes code easy to traverse and understand, and its dynamic variable binding capability means your variables need not be declared but are automatically assigned datatypes based on the value assigned to them, a process known as dynamic binding, as shown in the following code:

```
X  = 10;
print("Value of X is:", end = " ");
print(X);
print("Type of X is:", end = " ");
print(type(X)); #The variable type binding automatically becomes integer
print("X + 10 = ", end =" ");
print(X + 10); #You can do integer addition on X
print("");
X = "ABC"; #X is now assigned the value "ABC"
print("Value of X is:", end = " ");
print(X);
print("Type of X is:", end = " ");
print(type(X)); #The variable type binding automatically becomes string
print("X + 10 = ", end =" ");
print(X + str(10)); #Addition results in string concatenation

Value of X is: 10
Type of X is: <class 'int'>
X + 10 = 20

Value of X is: ABC
Type of X is: <class 'str'>
X + 10 = ABC10
```

These attributes make Python ideal for rapid application development, thereby optimizing developer productivity and reducing time to market for new functionality. Python allows you to develop packages and modules so that code can be modular and reusable. Python also boasts more than 100,000 libraries that allow users to do all forms of data processing and data visualization.[8] One very famous library that will be a major part of our discussions is TensorFlow.

TensorFlow provides an open source library for performing detailed numeric computations. It was developed by Google and was released to the general public in 2015. On top of the library, TensorFlow provides the tools and community support that allow development of applications that can leverage machine learning. Google built TensorFlow in C++, but TensorFlow provides libraries in C++ as well as Python and JavaScript for developing applications.[9] In this book, you will learn how to leverage TensorFlow libraries in Python to utilize, train, and test ML models. We will work with prediction functions that can push out results to operational applications. We'll also look at further advancements with TensorFlow 2.0 and the model-training API in Keras.

Services

While TensorFlow with Python gives us a strong foundation in machine learning and its use for predictive analytics, it's worthwhile to also explore AI/ML services from major public cloud providers. For the purposes of this book, we will be working with the services from AWS and GCP.

AWS services

We will start with AWS SageMaker. *SageMaker* is a fully managed service from AWS geared toward machine learning. It caters to the entire ML life cycle, as it allows you to develop and train ML models and then deploy them for production use. Sage-Maker supports the Jupyter Notebook platform for easy data exploration and analysis. You can quickly get started with commonly used algorithms or bring your own algorithms for further customization. This service is for those who like to get their hands dirty with ML and want to customize their development according to the needs of their application.

At the other end of the spectrum are users who want to stand on the shoulders of giants (the likes of Amazon). To that end, *Amazon Personalize* is a fully managed service that allows developers to build applications that focus on personalizing the user experience. This can be via product recommendations and ranking or via customized

---

8 Mehedi Hasan, "The 30 Best Python Libraries and Packages for Beginners" (*https://oreil.ly/kG_uE*), ubuntu-pit.com (*https://www.ubuntupit.com*), last updated November 12, 2022.

9 "TensorFlow" (*https://oreil.ly/3RYOw*), Wikipedia, accessed February 22, 2024.

marketing specific to user activity and preferences. The platform does not require a lot of ML knowledge, as it does most of the legwork for you. Everything from deploying the needed infrastructure to processing data, selecting the optimal ML models, training, and then eventually deploying the models is handled by the platform. All developers need to interact with is the API and its integration with their business applications. While Amazon is a retail behemoth, the service can be used for other industry verticals such as streaming and online entertainment services.

A similar service that focuses on a different aspect of the business is Amazon Forecast. *Amazon Forecast* is a fully managed service that allows businesses to use their historical time series data to help them develop their demand forecast. Think about being able to understand the demand for various products and services in advance and planning inventory and resource allocation accordingly. Similar to Amazon Personalize, Forecast requires little to no knowledge of machine learning and is able to do all the heavy lifting so that businesses need only worry about feeding it historical data and then consuming API-based demand forecasts. In addition to historical data, Forecast can integrate with local weather data to further fine-tune the accuracy of the predictions. While it is abstracting the complexity away from the developers, it gives them visibility into monitoring matrices so that they can continuously gauge the accuracy of forecasted predictions.

Amazon Lookout for Equipment caters to the realm of predictive maintenance, one of the important use cases of predictive analytics. It follows the same theme as the Personalize and Forecast services, taking the complexity of identifying, building, and training ML models for predictive maintenance away from the users. It uses industrial sensor data as input for training, as well as real-time analytics to identify potential faults and failures in the future. This allows industries to perform predictive maintenance and avoid huge costs incurred due to unforeseen downtime or industrial accidents.

When we work with data in AWS there are a number of underlying services that help glue everything together. Many of these services are beyond the scope of this book. The three that we will cover here are AWS Lambda, AWS Kinesis, and AWS S3.

AWS Lambda allows you to write serverless code for applications. In our case, we will mostly be writing code for data processing. *AWS Kinesis* allows ingestion, processing, and analysis of streaming data in real time. Think about time series IoT data flowing from industrial equipment or heartbeat data from mobile applications. *AWS S3* is the object storage service provided by AWS. S3 will be used across data pipelines from ingest to classification and also to store analyzed results. It is a globally distributed and highly available service that offers an economical solution for storage and processing of large datasets.

GCP services

As analytics becomes more mainstream, it is imperative for organizations to have a multicloud strategy. Like their operational applications, analytics platforms need to avoid vendor lock-in. Hence, we will explore the services from GCP that can assist us in our predictive analytics journey. While there seems to be a bit of overlap among the GCP services, we will explore how they augment each other to help enterprises build effective predictive analytics platforms.

Vertex AI is the first of the services that we will explore. It is a fully managed ML platform that allows for building, training, and deploying ML models easily. Similar to what we saw with the Amazon services, the Vertex AI platform requires little to no ML knowledge. It acts as a central repository for all your ML models while providing strong integration with vision, video, and natural language processing (NLP) APIs for cognitive analytics integration. It also provides integration with open source AI/ML platforms, such as Spark, and with GCP's data services, such as BigQuery and Dataproc. Furthermore, it integrates with common ML frameworks such as TensorFlow, scikit-learn, and PyTorch, and it works across the entire life cycle of creating, training, tuning, deploying, and monitoring ML models.

AutoML is another service from GCP geared toward the use of ML models for analytics. As its services overlap somewhat with the services provided by Vertex AI, we will explore the use of AutoML for automatically building and deploying ML models based on structured data. AutoML also provides other services based on image, video, and text analysis that can act as data sources along with predictions from the ML models for decision making via prescriptive analytics.

As the name suggests, *Timeseries Insights API* is a fully managed service provided by GCP that allows you to process large amounts of time series data in real time for anomaly detection trend forecasting. This service can be used in applications such as financial fraud analysis (e.g., detection of fraudulent credit card transactions) and industrial predictive maintenance. It is well integrated with Google Cloud storage to allow for seamless storage and processing of company data.

BigQuery is the final GCP service that we will explore. It is Google's data warehouse as a service with built-in machine learning and business intelligence capabilities. I will cover predictive modeling using BigQuery ML in detail in later chapters. Other interesting features of BigQuery include multicloud data analysis for data sources in AWS and Azure, and analytics on geospatial data.

Conclusion

There are a large number of open source ML frameworks and other analytics services available from cloud providers and third-party vendors. It would take more than an encyclopedia to cover everything. That is not the approach I am taking with this book. My goal is for you to look at the prevalent frameworks and services as a representative subset and understand in detail how they can be used to practically build applications that operationalize predictive analytics. This will allow you to learn the finer details of predictive analytics and will give you a baseline that you can then port to other frameworks and platforms.

## CHAPTER 2

Predictive Analytics: An Operational Necessity

Anyone who is part of an enterprise understands that analytics is no longer a sidecar. As we discussed in Chapter 1, the scope of analytics has expanded far beyond weekly and monthly reports or batch processing of multiyear data to build strategic plans. Today analytics is used in everyday applications. When you browse a hotel booking website and it tells you there are only two rooms left in the category you are looking at, this is an example of operational analytics. Another example is when a recommendation engine on an ecommerce website displays photos of other items that people who bought the item you are looking at also bought. Predictive analytics is no exception to this. Analytics is no longer analyzing things after the fact. It is about processing data in flight, learning from it, and in certain cases, providing feedback that the business can use in real time.

The Move from "Data Producing" to "Data Driven"

When it comes to understanding the nature of data, I like to break the topic down into its subcomponents. You've likely heard of the term *data pipeline*, but what does a data pipeline actually entail? Let's start with where the data originates: in producers.

Most legacy enterprise application data was produced when end users and services interacted with the application or fetched data from other applications using hardcoded integrations—for example, a travel agent booking a flight for a customer on an interface that was directly interacting with a mainframe computer, or a bank teller onboarding a customer at a branch with the data entry going into a core banking system after manual verification. As businesses were usually driven by person-to-person interactions, the touchpoints where a person could actually interact directly with the business were limited.

This is no longer the case. Today a user can interact with business services using a multitude of methods. For example:

- A web interface, using their browser; think Amazon.com
- A mobile application, using their phone and tablet; think Booking.com
- Aggregation services that combine services from multiple providers; think eBay.com

However, users are no longer the only data producers. Data is also being produced by devices. For example, cell phones constantly share a plethora of information with applications, including location data, browsing history, and audiovisual data. Internet of Things (IoT) devices are constantly sending keepalive heartbeats and monitoring metrics to industrial and commercial management platforms. Data from the sea and from the far depths of the universe is being collected and analyzed (though not for enterprise applications). And there are applications that can easily feed data into other applications, thanks to advancements in messaging and integration technologies. You can see how the number of data producers, and consequently the volume of data, has exploded in the past couple of decades, hence the term *big data*.

Now, consider everything that produces data as being on the left side of a spectrum, with our enterprise application taking all the data in, storing it, and processing it. On the right side of the spectrum are the "consuming" applications that pull the data from our application. These consumers can be other enterprise applications, business intelligence (BI) tools for business dashboarding and reports, or AI/ML platforms that need to pull the data to train their ML models. The consumers can be part of the same organization or a different organization; think of an airline flight-tracking application that pulls data from local weather centers to understand the impact of the weather on the arrival and departure times of particular flights. A seemingly trivial but important aspect of this communication is that data can flow both ways. An ML application may pull training data from an application, but then push back a trained model. Or an application may pull data from multiple sources, correlate it, and produce insights that the business can act on. Considering these aspects, Figure 2-1 depicts a high-level but mostly complete picture of what a potential data pipeline could look like.

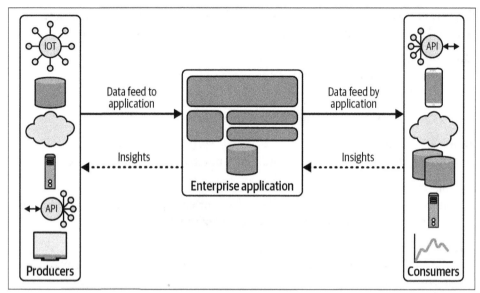

Figure 2-1. Data pipeline

The subtle thing to realize here is that even though our enterprise application is at the heart of this discussion, that's only because of the lens through which we are viewing it. Between producers, our application, and consumers, there is an application at each of these layers. As such, applications are constantly creating, producing, and sharing data with users, services, and other applications. Going one level above these applications represents one or more enterprise business services. So, it becomes clear that enterprise services depend not only on their end customers for data, but also on a number of other services and applications.

The question, then, is why do we need to gather all this data? To answer that question, consider that an ecommerce business takes its user interaction data, combines it with its purchase history and demographic profile, and predicts what its customers are most likely to buy. Similarly, a flight-tracking application takes weather data into consideration, and processes it in conjunction with historical data and other parameters to predict what time a specific flight will land. Likewise, a hotel booking app makes sure to tell the customer whether a room is in high demand, to shorten the purchasing decision cycle.

As you can see, businesses are no longer just *data producing*; they are now *data driven*. Traditionally, it was enough to pull out monthly or quarterly reports, analyze them, and build a strategy for the future. However, now enterprises need to understand data and react in near-real time to tactically influence the outcome of the business. Customer behavior, customer click rate, and customer experience are all part of this business effort to ensure that customer interaction is effortless, enjoyable, decisive, and repetitive. Some of the reasons you would want to do this include:

Customer acquisition
Make it super simple for new customers to sign up.

Recommendation engines
Figure out what the customer is likely to buy/consume next.

Transaction time
Reduce the time it takes for a customer to purchase a product or service.

Automation
Automate classification of a business item; for example, is an email spam or not, or is the banking transaction fraudulent or legitimate.

Inventory management
Use daily sales forecasting to estimate the inventory that needs to be maintained in each location.

While some of these use cases are more about customer experience and ease of acquisition, most of them require some form of analysis, other than batch analysis, to forecast or predict an outcome to either save or make more money for the business. This analysis is not something that happens in the background weekly, monthly, or yearly. It is happening on an hourly or daily basis, and it has a direct impact on the business.

Challenges to Using Predictive Analytics

Effective use of predictive analytics in an organization requires a holistic approach to the paradigm. Although it might be possible to start with one use case to test the waters with predictive analytics, the journey from data producing to data driven warrants changes at several touchpoints across an organization. An end-to-end approach to business transformation for this purpose is definitely something that should be studied and implemented, but that is beyond the scope of this book. Having said that, I would like to share my learnings in this area so that they can be used as building blocks for a much larger transformation initiative.

Embracing predictive analytics requires changes at three layers:

- People
- Data
- Technology

People

With people, wherever there is change, challenges will follow. I've found that one of the more creative ways for getting employees to embrace change is to ask them what they think is their organization's greatest asset.[1] The answers will vary, but usually they will include the organization's employees, reputation, service, product, and customers. If the same is true in your organization, you need to start educating your employees on the importance of data. They need to understand that data is not just information produced by the organization's applications; it is a huge asset that, when utilized properly, can make a significant impact on the business's bottom line.

It's imperative that whenever managers talk about services and applications they are proactively thinking about the data and its use to the business. But the education should not stop there. An IT engineer needs to appreciate the importance of data and plan for efficient data pipelines and data consolidation. When building applications, developers need to keep in mind the fact that the data produced by the application should be easily consumable by others, and vice versa. I'm using this example in the context of predictive analytics, but this shift in mindset applies to the overall realm of analytics, as well.

Predictive analytics, like most good things in life, takes time, effort, and money to implement. However, unlike buying a subscription to Netflix, where it is immediately obvious (for the first month at least) why you are paying for it, when it comes to predictive analytics the benefits are not so "in your face." Therefore, it's important for any organization to understand why it is going through this exercise and what it will get out of it.

In technical terms, understanding the organizational pain or opportunity and calculating the return on investment (ROI) of such an initiative will ensure its longevity and eventual success. The organizational pain or opportunity will help you understand the problem you are trying to solve or the opportunity you are trying to capture and the time and money associated with it. It will also help define the criteria required to gauge the success or failure of the initiative. Considering the many layers of change needed on an organizational level, a well-defined business case backed by a positive ROI will ensure the right amount of organizational support at different levels.

Another long-term consideration (though not strictly people-related) is to have processes in place for the introduction, development, changes, and sunsetting of business applications. As the scope of predictive analytics grows within an organization, changes to the application landscape will have a direct impact on the data pipeline.

---

1 Ron Klimberg and B.D. McCullough, *Fundamentals of Predictive Analytics with JMP*, Second Edition (Cary, NC: SAS Institute, 2017).

Since the data pipeline is now directly (or indirectly) linked to the business's bottom line, these changes should be regulated like any other business-level change.

Data

Everything in the predictive analytics world revolves around data. However, when you set out to implement predictive analytics, there are a number of data-related challenges that you need to keep in mind. Organizational data that is relevant to the business is hardly ever sitting in one place. As organizations evolve organically, so does their application landscape. This means related data ends up sitting in data silos. These silos are often a result of organic (and not-so-well-planned) growth. However, human factors such as office politics and other bureaucratic reasons can also prevent teams from sharing data with each other. Technical reasons such as lack of a microservices-based approach, integration API services, and granular authentication and authorization controls can also hamper healthy data sharing between departments within an organization. One of the key aspects of solving the data problem is to ensure that the data can be collected, stored, and shared in a scalable and secure manner. In short, the data needs to be powered by a platform that is:

- Agile enough to handle different types and structures of data
- Scalable enough to handle very large volumes of data from throughout the organization
- Secure enough to ensure that the data can be tracked and made accessible to authorized users and services

 We will talk about the nuances of working with data in Chapter 4.

Of course, these problems increase exponentially if you are trying to gather data at a group level across multiple suborganizations. In this case, the data silos can result in several challenges:

- Incomplete data (e.g., transaction data without customer details)
- Duplicate data (e.g., the same customer exists across multiple business lines as independent customers)
- Relevant data access not being available to departments (e.g., marketing is unable to utilize new inventory information to send personalized offers to customers)

All of this leads to dirty data. It's a misnomer that *dirty data* only refers to data that is erroneous or incomplete. Dirty data can also result from nonstandardization, duplication, and lack of relationship. Another aspect of dirty data that is particularly relevant to predictive analytics is that it is misleading. This can be a result of an established bias when the data was created. For example, consider a company with primary operations in the United States that is expanding into Europe. Since most of its customers are in the United States, a predictive analytics model trained with this data could end up learning that US prospects are more likely to become customers than European prospects. These are some of the data challenges that organizations have to deal with before they can embark on their predictive analytics journey.

Technology

Bringing into one place large amounts of data from across the organization requires a significant investment in the research, design, implementation, and operations of IT infrastructure and technology. Add to this the complex nature of training (perhaps also building) and implementing predictive analytics models, and you can see that a significant investment needs to be made in both hardware and software infrastructure to make this a reality.

Even if your organization has addressed the cultural and technological aspects of implementing predictive analytics, you still need people who understand data modeling and machine learning. You also need people who understand and can manipulate data in creative ways to make it available to the business, and you need people who can create a successful marriage between the technical and business sides of the data. These individuals include data scientists, data engineers, and business consultants, among others. This is a niche skill set that is hard to come by and even harder to retain.

Here is where cloud providers, such as AWS, Azure, GCP, and Alibaba Cloud, along with a few data companies, come in. They provide solutions while lowering the technical requirement for organizations to start using predictive analytics. While these solutions are evolving rapidly, how much (or how little) one needs to know to consume these services, and whether they actually provide market differentiation for consumers, is up for debate.

The last piece of the puzzle that I want to discuss is the feedback loop and its importance as a component in the practice of predictive analytics. Imagine that you have a prediction machine that will tell you about the future, but you are not allowed to proactively make any changes in your life to influence the future. The only purpose of this machine is to put you in a state of worry, and possibly helplessness, as you await the inevitable. Predictive analytics without a feedback loop into the business is similar to this machine. You can predict a lot of things, but you really don't take any actions to influence your business.

Hence, it's imperative to understand that predictive analytics needs to feed directly back into the business operations. This feedback can be manual or in near-real time. However, as organizations mature, they automate most of the training and analytics and feed these insights directly back into the business. For example, a stock-planning report that is run every month could help forecast purchase requirements for the next month or quarter. However, the pace of analysis and action can be much faster when deciding whether to approve or reject a loan application based on how likely the requester is to pay off the loan in due time. Irrespective of the pace, this loopback is an essential component to move an organization from data producing to data driven.

As I move from the case for predictive analytics to real-world examples, I want to share an important observation with you. While we had the mathematics and the will behind predictive analytics long before we saw practical use cases, the key barrier to entry was access to resources.

People, data, and technology are the three resources that are crucial for the successful practice of predictive analytics. However, imagine being a small startup trying to implement predictive analytics prior to the era of the public cloud. If your startup was already struggling with budgets, you would need to invest large amounts of money on infrastructure to support predictive analytics. This is on top of the infrastructure you'd need for operating the business. Such an investment would occur in the form of capital expenditure, but when making a business decision on where to spend money, predictive analytics usually loses to applications that are required to run a business's daily operations. If by some means you were able to source the infrastructure, setting up and maintaining large, open source data warehouses, data lakes, and the like would be an operational nightmare. Your other option would be to add more to your capital expenditure budget for expensive commercial-off-the-shelf (COTS) applications.

Cloud providers offered a new paradigm by commoditizing the infrastructure, software, and services needed to launch a business. A small organization could start with as little as a $100 monthly expenditure and could gradually grow to millions of dollars in cloud spending. Cloud providers allowed businesses to convert all their capital expenditure to operational expenditure so that they were not blocked by large investment requirements when it came to IT infrastructure and software. As the business grew, it could fine-tune its spending and walk away at any point without incurring a loss in unused investment. Since cloud providers were built for multiple customers, they brought groundbreaking innovation in infrastructure as well as in distributed architectures, data solutions, AI, and ML. This meant that smaller companies could pick up these services and consume them without having to invest millions of dollars up front in developing something from scratch.

All this commoditization allowed companies to do much more with limited budgets, and so sidecars such as predictive analytics now had a chance. Access to top-of-class resources became financially viable for smaller companies, while earlier this was only true for large enterprises. This is one of the reasons we have seen incumbents being disrupted in multiple industries from car manufacturing to entertainment and from banking and finance to healthcare.

Vertical Industry Use Cases for Predictive Analytics

Predictive analytics is used by many vertical industries to gain a competitive advantage. We see the use of predictive analytics from customer segmentation to service personalization and from business process optimization to targeted marketing and sales. In this section, I'll discuss some scenarios across a few industries where predictive analytics is making a difference. While the implementation of such projects takes significant planning, execution, and maintenance, with the entry barriers to predictive analytics removed by the hyperscalers there is no reason why any organization should not be able to adopt and improve on the success of these existing use cases.

 All the use cases discussed in this book are based on material and research that is publicly available. The details I provide represent my interpretation of these use cases; they do not represent, in any way, shape, or form, the official understanding, content, or views of the organization being discussed. Due to this and to the constantly evolving nature of technology, the specifics mentioned in the book might be different from what is currently implemented in production for these use cases.

Finance

When applying predictive analytics in any industry, your only limitation is your creativity. Though finance is no exception, it does have its nuances. Contrary to the likes of an ecommerce business, the stakes when predicting for finance could be significantly higher for individuals. An incorrect prediction on whether a loan applicant is likely to pay back their loan could mean the difference between the applicant being able to buy a house or not. Compare this to a recommendation engine proposing an incorrect item for a customer's next buy. This doesn't mean predictive analytics should not be used. It very much should be, but with better controls and better human-machine amalgamation.

Algorithmic credit scoring of customers is a unique but hugely successful use case of predictive analytics in China. When Alibaba launched its ecommerce business in China, it developed what was at the time a financial arm of the company to allow buyers and sellers to transact securely over the internet. Later, this financial arm (now known as Ant Group) became a separate entity, and at one point it was rumored to be one of the largest financial institutions in the world.

Of the numerous financial services that Ant offers to its customers, a few are related to loans and microfinance. In this regard, Ant faced a couple of challenges. To determine which were good loans and which weren't, it needed a way to score its potential and existing customers. However, China did not have a centralized credit scoring system like the United States and many parts of Europe do. Alibaba realized that it was sitting on a wealth of data for more than 1 billion customers in China. Ant decided to tap into the power of data to estimate its customers' credit scores (Figure 2-2).

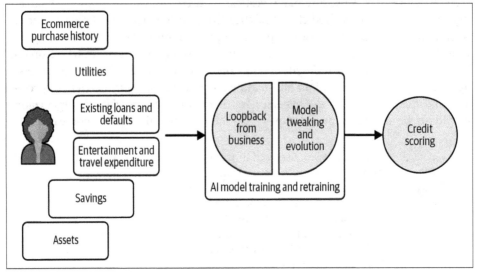

Figure 2-2. Ant Group credit scoring example

The company gathered its best minds to build, train, and continuously optimize complex financial AI models. According to *MIT Technology Review*, Ant "assesses a person's creditworthiness based on his or her spending history and other data including friends' credit scores."[2] This allowed Ant to build a system that could operate independent of any external party, and could also handle mass volumes of business due to the automated nature of algorithmic credit scoring. The company was able to integrate the system into its many financial services, such as micro and macro loans, and was able to offer it as a service to other financial institutions.

Another use case comes from Chase Bank. In 1996, Chase Manhattan Corporation merged with what was the second largest bank at that time, Chemical Banking Corporation, to form what would be the largest bank in the United States.[3] As a result of

---

2 Will Knight, "Meet the Chinese Finance Giant That's Secretly an AI Company" (*https://oreil.ly/ZRvGW*), *MIT Technology Review*, June 16, 2017.

3 Encyclopedia Britannica. "The Chase Manhattan Corporation" (*https://oreil.ly/C6f6Z*). *Encyclopedia Britannica*. November 11, 2011.

the merger, the bank had a lot more customers than before. More customers equals more business, but it also means more risk. The home loan department had millions of mortgages to deal with, and while each mortgage had been individually classified in terms of risk, the bank faced an unprecedented challenge with such a large number of mortgages being offered by a single entity. Therefore, it became imperative to reevaluate the risks of default and of early payment on these loans (early payment means the bank misses out on interest revenue).

It became abundantly clear to the bank that it could not redo a manual risk assessment for millions of mortgages, so it turned to predictive analytics to build and train models that would allow the bank to continuously perform micro-risk assessments on existing and new mortgages. Such an assessment done in the traditional way would be prone to human error and be both time and cost prohibitive. With predictive analytics, the bank could classify and reclassify these loans and identify all the small risks so that it could take corrective and preventive measures. Eventually, the bank went a step further and used predictive analytics to estimate the future values of these mortgages, which enabled it to make better decisions on which mortgages it should keep and which ones it should sell to other banks.[4]

Another interesting use case from the finance industry is from 2018, when Citigroup launched its AI-based Payment Outlier Detection, which it has since launched in 90 countries.[5] The solution was created by Citi's Treasury and Trade Solutions business, which used advanced ML algorithms to automatically detect outliers in customer payments based on clients' past payment activity. This meant payments could be sent to the customer for approval or rejection, before crediting beneficiary accounts. This was a step up from the typical rule-based fraud detection engines, as the platform used statistical models for pattern creation and outlier detection. While the model was being trained with large amounts of historical data, it could be applied to individual customer profiles for pattern recognition. Also, the model was constantly learning from ongoing client payment activity to predict fraudulent transactions more accurately via outlier detection.

These are just some examples. There are additional use cases around budgeting, targeted marketing, and resource allocation, among others, that all rely on historical data to train models that can help direct business decisions.

---

4 Eric Siegel, *Predictive Analytics, Revised and Updated* (Hoboken, NJ: Wiley, 2016).

5 "Citi Payment Outlier Detection Launches in 90 Countries" (*https://oreil.ly/9lcaV*), Citigroup Inc., June 26, 2019.

Healthcare

If you thought the stakes were high for predictive analytics in the finance world, consider healthcare. Here, the stakes are even higher in certain use cases because we're talking about a direct impact on the health of individuals and entire populations. Nonetheless, the adoption of predictive analytics is growing in healthcare. Consider the following:

- Who is prone to developing which disease, and how likely are they to develop the disease?
- Which treatment is likely to be most effective?
- What is the likelihood of a patient following their treatment plan (medication, tests, and follow-up visits)?
- Who is at risk of being readmitted to the hospital soon after they are discharged?

While capturing these details is beyond the scope of this book, I'll discuss a few representative use cases. It's important to understand that what we are discussing here is *predictive*, meaning what might happen in the future and the probability of it happening. This is not the same as *diagnostic*, which is based on medical tests and their results to detect and confirm a present medical condition.

We'll start with cardiovascular disease (CVD), a disease of the heart and/or blood vessels that can lead to conditions such as stroke, angina (chest pain due to blood flow problems to and from the heart), heart attack, and heart failure. A good cardiologist will likely spend a large amount of time profiling their patient. First, they'd gather basic information, such as the patient's age, gender, weight, and recent bloodwork results. Then, they'd ask questions to understand the patient's lifestyle, such as whether they smoke or consume alcohol, their dietary habits, and any previous surgeries they may have had. Next, they'd ask about existing conditions, such as hypertension and diabetes, and their existence on the maternal and/or paternal side of the patient's family. The cardiologist would combine this information with the results of medical tests to assess the patient's health. Since curing a disease is more expensive in time and money for the patient and the cardiologist than preventing the disease, both would work toward preventing the disease from occurring. There are well-established risk indicators in the medical world (e.g., the Framingham risk models) that allow for predicting a person's 10-year risk of developing CVD and CHD (coronary heart disease). In 2020, Johnson & Johnson, in collaboration with Apple, launched a virtual clinical study to understand how the ECG App along with its irregular rhythm notification feature for the Apple iPhone and ECG-enabled smartwatch can help with early detection of atrial fibrillation (A-fib).[6] A-fib is typically difficult to detect early and can be a leading cause of stroke. The aim of this trial was to understand whether the risk of stroke could be detected early enough to engage individuals in timely preventive interventions or life-saving interventions from medical professionals.

Another chronic disease in which the fundamental contributors (and hence the risk factors) are well appreciated is diabetes. Diabetes is a global problem, and in 2021, approximately 537 million people worldwide between the ages of 20 and 79 were living with it. It's estimated that one out of two adults has undiagnosed diabetes. Type 2 diabetes, which is the most common, happens when the body becomes resistant to insulin or does not produce enough insulin, causing blood sugar levels to rise. Type 1 diabetes is when the pancreas produces little to no insulin.

With diabetes, early detection is key, and this is where predictive analytics can help. Similar to CVD, there are several risk factors that can contribute to diabetes. These can include a person's first-degree relatives with a history of the disease, as well as the person's weight, gender, and ethnicity. Also, predisposition to diseases such as hypertension as well as unhealthy lifestyle choices in terms of activity and food could be contributing factors. Monitoring of blood glucose levels and blood pressure could be effective input metrics for risk scoring for diabetes.[7] While Type 1 diabetes is not preventable, Type 2 diabetes can be prevented in high-risk individuals with timely interventions based on lifestyle changes.

Preventive healthcare is a win-win for both employers and employees when it comes to chronic illness. It allows employers to save millions of dollars on health plans that would have been needed if preventable chronic diseases among employees went unchecked. And it allows for a much healthier workforce and improves the lives of the individual employees. Several organizations provide preventive healthcare solutions today. For example, Changing Health is a UK-based organization that provides a digital platform offering behavior change programs in Type 2 diabetes prevention, Type 2 diabetes management, and weight management.[8] In the United States, Omada Health provides a prevention program that identifies prediabetics and offers them a plan to prevent or limit the risk of chronic diabetes. These programs are based on behavioral change (lifestyle changes), educating individuals about the disease, monitoring (via remote devices), referrals, and medication adherence management.

---

6 "Johnson & Johnson Launches Heartline, the First-of-its-Kind, Virtual Study Designed to Explore if a New iPhone App and Apple Watch Can Help Reduce the Risk of Stroke" (*https://oreil.ly/cTArj*), Johnson & Johnson, February 25, 2020.

7 "About Diabetes: Facts & Figures" (*https://oreil.ly/AjUFy*), International Diabetes Federation, December 9, 2021.

8 "Digital Behavior Change at Scale" (*https://oreil.ly/TofB3*), Changing Health Ltd.

Omada claims to have saved participants more than $1,000 annually in gross medical costs while also improving their overall health.[9]

Predictive analytics is also used to help pharmaceutical companies target their sales and marketing campaigns. Predictive models can help identify potential patients based on parameters such as centralized health records, insurance data, and practitioner visits, among other things. The data can also help report on the existence and volume of patients in specific areas for aiding in resource planning on top of targeted sales and marketing campaigns. This approach helps patients get timely and high-quality healthcare, helps healthcare professionals with diagnoses, and potentially decreases overall healthcare costs for patients.

Some other use cases of predictive analytics in healthcare include, but are not limited to, mental health management, falls (prediction, detection, and avoidance), sepsis detection, and identification of high-risk population segments for targeted campaigns and testing.

Automotive

There is a growing consensus that Tesla is more of a data company than an electric car manufacturer. While arguably other car manufacturers had made technological advancements in this space long before Tesla came into being, Tesla was able to create the full loop of data generation, collection, training, and feedback. As a result, the automotive industry has seen an uptake of predictive analytics in the past decade.

Tesla launched its first electric car in 2008. While everyone was focused on commercializing an electric car, Tesla had something more up its sleeve. It had sensors all over its cars and was constantly collecting data from these sensors. This data was then pushed to its servers, where the company would analyze the data and draw conclusions on how to improve its cars. One of the outcomes of this analysis was that Tesla was able to detect problems with its cars even before the car owners did. Tesla was able to tell owners things like when their car was overdue for service and when an owner could expect to repair or replace a certain part in the future. This allowed owners to take corrective actions earlier to avoid expensive maintenance. It also assisted Tesla with resource and inventory planning at the regional and subregional levels. Such data-driven planning helped avoid over- or understocking and timely service delivery to customers. The company once fixed an overheating issue caused by power fluctuations using an OTA (over the air) update.[10] While Tesla will ask owners to

---

9 "Changing Mindsets to Change Health" (*https://oreil.ly/L-aHS*), Omada Health, January 1, 2023.

10 Vikram Singh, "Tesla: A Data Driven Future" (*https://oreil.ly/xxQnV*), Digital Innovation and Transformation, Harvard Business School, March 23, 2021.

bring in their car for major repairs, the ability to fix software problems OTA is unprecedented in the automotive space.

BMW also uses predictive maintenance, but in a more traditional sense. Sensor data from vehicle production machines is collected and sent to the cloud via a gateway. This data is then analyzed using statistical and predictive AI algorithms to determine the current state of the machines and provide guidance on when maintenance will be required on certain parts. This method is more efficient than the traditional rule-based approach that works on fixed schedules, as the predictive method considers the current running state of the machine when making maintenance decisions. This results in a sustainable approach that can gauge when a piece of machinery requires maintenance.

Preventive maintenance also allows for anticipating faults before they occur and taking corrective action to avoid unplanned downtimes. Since a lot of the sensor input is standardized, BMW is able to roll out predictive analytics across departments and regions. In the BMW body shop, a welding gun performs approximately 15,000 spot welds per day. Downtime of any of these guns could result in significant delays in production, which translate into direct cost.[11] Similarly, when it comes to vehicle assembly, predictive analytics helps ensure that conveyors don't suffer from unplanned downtimes. Data from these conveyors in certain locations is sent for analysis 24/7. Predictive modeling then helps perform anomaly detection to identify potential technical issues before they turn into production problems.

Going back to Tesla, another innovative use of data is its assisted driving (later self-driving) capability. Sensors and cameras all around the car constantly capture information about the surroundings. This information is used to make driving decisions based on terrain, traffic lights, pedestrians, and other factors. While the decision making and the use of the corresponding models happen in real time on the car, the actual training of these models happens in the cloud. Data from all the different Tesla vehicles is uploaded to Tesla servers, where it is then used to train Tesla's ML models. Trained models are then pushed down to the cars and are used for driving. Self-driving cars are not an exclusive predictive analytics use case. There's a lot more going on to power self-driving cars. From a data perspective, we are looking at complex AI/ML model creation and training as well as predictive and prescriptive analytics. From a terrain perspective, there is complex vision analysis in the form of cognitive analytics, and all this is powered by a symphony of cloud and edge computing.

One of the biggest pain points for car manufacturers is product quality and recall management. Quality teams can utilize historical data to predict the quality of

---

11 BMW Group, "Predictive Maintenance: When a Machine Knows in Advance That Repairs Are Needed" (*https://oreil.ly/mHBj9*), press release, August 5, 2021.

products. This allows them to not only estimate whether and when these parts are likely to fail, but also take corrective action to prevent failures that could lead to expensive recalls and extensive reputation damage. The ability for systems to capture both structured and unstructured data helps consolidate information from multiple data sources to build a complete picture of what is happening post-sale. Data from social media channels can be combined with customer service center data, along with data on sales of different parts and shipping information, to help manufacturers understand what parts are failing and where, as well as predict when they can expect a corresponding recall. Data-driven forecasting capability allows manufacturers to act before authorities get involved. This helps them avoid expensive fines and improve customer satisfaction. Depending on how extensive these models are and what kind of data is flowing into them, they can predict immediate part failure(s) post-sale and provide predictions for defects down the line that might result in warranty claims. Such information can be effectively used by parts suppliers in prototype planning, inventory optimization, and supply chain and recall management.

Predictive analytics is all about predicting with a certain degree of accuracy the likelihood of future events. This allows automotive manufacturers and suppliers to take proactive measures that help the organization save time and money and improve customer satisfaction, thus protecting and improving their brand value. As the world moves from manual to automatic and analog to digital, we can think of ourselves as driving large mobile computers. The more things are software-driven, the more data they generate. This plethora of data, if used correctly, is the foundation of data-driven business.

Entertainment

Netflix took the streaming world by storm. It started as a movie rental business in 1997, where you could subscribe to a monthly service online and choose movies from an online catalog; these movies would then be mailed to you. Once you watched the movies, you could mail them back and get another set of chosen films. However, in 2006, Netflix offered a $1 million prize to any team that could improve, by more than 10%, its recommendation system that was responsible for predicting a user's movie preferences based on previous rental data.[12] This was the beginning of Netflix's journey into the data space.

The competition was won by a team known as "BellKor's Pragmatic Chaos." In 2007, Netflix started offering its subscribers the option to stream their selected movies directly to their homes via the internet. This became the primary mode of business for Netflix. Soon we saw a race for streaming services from Hulu, Disney, Amazon Prime, HBO, and many others. One thing to note here is that this race included both

---

12 "Netflix" (*https://oreil.ly/-C-ub*), Wikipedia, accessed February 27, 2024.

the incumbent players, such as Disney and HBO, and new players, such as Hulu and Amazon Prime. This was only made possible because cloud computing removed the entry barriers to several vertical industries in terms of infrastructure, software, and analytics, as we discussed in the previous section. As Netflix competed with a few of the largest names in the industry (i.e., HBO and Disney) and giants such as Amazon, it had still managed to maintain its lead in the movie streaming industry. Of the many business practices, one of Netflix's key differentiators is its superior recommendation engine.

Recommendation is the core of the Netflix product that we see today. Recommendations are used in many different aspects of the business. Like in most recommendation systems, the data that Netflix potentially has access to includes:

- What users have watched
- How users interact with the service

While rating prediction is fundamental to figuring out what content an individual user will select next, recommendations are also being used for:

- Personalized ranking (not just overall rating of the content)
- Page generation (what content makes up the user's home page)
- Search (the content displayed in search results)
- Image selection (what images to use for content display)
- Messaging (notifications and messages sent to individual users)[13]

In principle, this means every user on Netflix has a hyper-personalized experience that is tailored to their preferences (Figure 2-3).

However, relevance to the user is only one part of the story. Netflix would have realized it was building a recommendation system that was working with a limited time budget. In simple terms, the user had a limited span of time in which they would evaluate their options and select what they wanted to view next. This meant that in addition to the relevance to the user, Netflix also needed to consider the evaluation cost of what it was displaying. For example, a user might decide to watch something popular just based on its title, but for other items, they might want to see the trailer, maybe consider the cast, and in some cases look at third-party reviews of the content. Each of these items adds to the evaluation cost of that content, and when curating the user library, Netflix needed to balance relevance and evaluation cost to optimize the experience within each user's time constraints.

---

13 "Recommendations" (*https://oreil.ly/XWCLT*), Netflix Research, January 1, 2022.

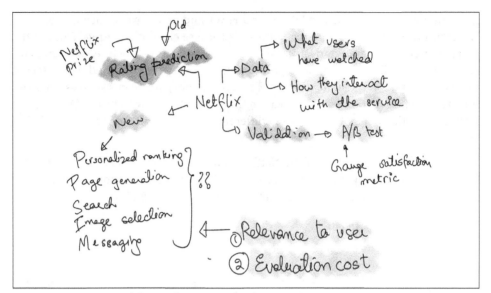

Figure 2-3. Nuances of the Netflix recommendation engine

In addition, Netflix had to consider the personalities of individual users that were difficult to generalize or categorize on a mass scale. Different users have different preferences and usually need a recommendation when they cannot decide for themselves what they want to watch. These unique human elements make designing a recommendation engine all the more challenging.

Figure 2-4 shows Netflix's use of recommendations. The components of the Netflix product that are potentially using recommendations shown in Figure 2-4 are as follows:

- The first video, displayed at the top of the home page (1).
- Videos sequenced in the "Continue Watching" section (7).
- Videos sequenced in the "New Releases" section (5).
- How the different strips of content need to be displayed (4 and 6). For example, should "New Releases" be on top of "Continue Watching"?
- Personalized messages and notifications to users (3).
- The content to be displayed as part of the Search functionality (2).[14]

14 Harald Steck, et al., "Deep Learning for Recommender Systems: A Netflix Case Study" (*https://oreil.ly/n_grJ*), *AI Magazine*, September 1, 2021, 7–18.

Figure 2-4. Netflix use case recommendations

The recommendation system needs to determine which videos to display on the home page. However, the home page can be split into many subsections. With trial and error, research, and a lot of A/B testing, the Netflix team would realize there was no silver bullet when it came to figuring out the model for recommendations. While some models worked well with one task, a completely different ML model might be needed to be used for others. By breaking down the problem into smaller subtasks, models could potentially be optimized for each task individually, with a targeted end goal of ensuring the long-term satisfaction of individual users, which is tied to customer retention on the platform. Users who are not satisfied can unsubscribe from the service at any point in time.

Like most recommendation systems, Netflix would have been working with the user information, the item (video) information, and user-item interactions from the past. When comparing deep learning models versus well-tuned non-deep learning approaches, the team realized that if they added to this data additional context on the user-item interaction, the deep learning models started showing much promise in terms of accuracy and performance versus their non-deep learning counterparts.

There are some challenges to keep in mind when working with recommendation systems based on user-item interactions:

- User-item interactions are not randomly distributed. They are specific to each user.
- If an interaction has not happened yet, there are a couple of possibilities:
  - The user is genuinely not interested in that content.
  - The interaction might happen in the future.
- Observed data is very sparse. Users spend most of their time watching content and not selecting it.
- There is a large popularity skew, especially for extremely popular content (e.g., *Squid Game*).
- There are only a few active users and a large number of less active users.

This leads to a couple of interesting questions:

- How to recommend unpopular items to individual users?
- How to accurately recommend items to less active users?
- How to recommend newly added content (without any user-item interaction data)?

While I have discussed the importance of feedback from predictive analytics into operational systems, there are some interesting observations when building a recommendation practice (Figure 2-5).

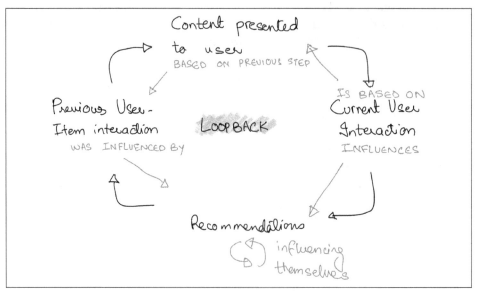

Figure 2-5. Recommendation loopback

If the content to be recommended is based on the user's previous interaction with the system, and if the previous interaction was influenced by a suggestion from the recommendation engine, then by extension what we present to the user influences not only their choices but also what we recommend to them. This creates a self-serving loop where the recommendation engine is feeding back to itself and it is not clear whether this is based on user preferences or whether it is a self-fulfilling prophecy. Therefore, one of the challenges was to figure out how to break this feedback loop.

The core of the recommendation engine is to figure out which videos to display to users. Netflix used a combination of approaches when attacking this problem. The first approach was to treat all content as a "bag of items." In other words, all videos are placed into a figurative "bag" with no consideration for the sequence with which the user played the videos. This approach assumes that the impact of time balances out in the long term, and hence the idea is to target the user's long-term interest by using such an approach.

Netflix found interesting results when using autoencoders for this task. An *autoencoder* is an artificial neural network that uses unsupervised learning with several hidden layers that have nonlinear activation functions. Autoencoders are trained in a recommendation system using user interaction data (which videos did the user play in the past [binary 0/1]), and some continuous values such as the duration for which the user played a video. Other generalizations of the autoencoder were also tested in the form of a deep *feed-forward model*: while the input to the model was the user's play history, the output could be something much simpler, such as predicting the most recent video the user played. This would allow Netflix to cater to current (versus long-term) user interests while accounting for popularity trends in content.[15]

The other approach was to consider sequential models. Several deep sequential models were adapted from NLP. While in NLP the idea is to predict the next word, in this case the models needed to predict the next video the user would interact with. Several approaches, among them n-grams, recurrent neural networks, and transformer architectures, were tested as part of this research. I briefly mentioned earlier that the teams realized deep learning models showed a lot of promise when context was added to the user-item interaction. One example of such context is time. Consider the following scenarios:

- Children are likely to watch more content in the afternoon.
- Different days of the week can dictate different preferences.
- Content needs to consider different holidays (e.g., Eid, Christmas, New Year's Day).

---

15 "Recommendations" (*https://oreil.ly/XWCLT*), Netflix Research, Netflix, January 1, 2022.

One way to add the context of time was to use *discretization of time*, or transforming the interaction timestamp into the day of the week, week of the month, or month of the year. While this provided better generalization, the gains in terms of predictability and performance were limited. The second approach was to use continuous raw data—for example, when was the video last interacted with versus what is the time right now. When using the continuous approach, the recommendations showed massive increases in accuracy.[16]

While I anticipate that the Netflix team is continuously innovating on the recommendation engine, they shared a few learnings that are worth mentioning:

- Traditional recommendation systems that are well tuned are comparable in performance to their deep learning counterparts, especially when only using user-item interaction as input.

- Deep learning can improve accuracy when considering additional parameters such as time in the context of the interaction and input data from images, videos, and text.

- Deep learning can help prevent overfitting of models on short-term preferences so that longer-term customer satisfaction can be achieved.

Conclusion

Predictive analytics is serving business needs across several vertical industries. The scope of predictive analytics goes far beyond traditional batch analytics. Predictive analytics started as a complement to existing business practices. The idea was to provide competitive advantage in vertical industry landscapes versus traditional incumbents. However, companies such as Tesla and Netflix have effectively harnessed the power of predictive analytics and deep learning to disrupt the incumbents in their respective industries and become market leaders on a global scale. In this chapter, we discussed a few prominent use cases of predictive analytics. However, its scope extends to other vertical industries, including insurance, retail, communications, and government, to name a few.

---

16 Ibid.

CHAPTER 3

The Mathematics and Algorithms Behind Predictive Analytics

As humans, we are constantly learning. Our experiences are the teachers that shape the way we think and how we live our lives. This process of continuous learning extends beyond one individual, and as a species we continue to evolve from a biological and an intellectual standpoint. This collective learning has allowed us to find cures for deadly diseases, build airplanes, explore interstellar space, and observe far-off galaxies.

As part of this intellectual evolution, we built computers to help us in our daily lives. Today we use computers in almost every aspect of our lives. But even before computers, there was math all around us. Mathematics is everywhere, and with enough understanding and effort you can arguably represent any scenario as a mathematical problem. Hence, mathematics is often referred to as a universal language.

It is no surprise, then, that mathematics forms the foundation of computer science, from binary data representation at the hardware level to software programming and machine learning (ML) algorithms. In this chapter, we will explore statistics and linear algebra in relation to predictive data analytics. Then, we will extend this discussion to develop a better understanding of regression, decision trees, and a few other models used in machine learning and predictive analytics.

Statistics and Linear Algebra

Statistics is the art (or science) of collecting numeric data, understanding and representing that data, and drawing conclusions from it. Compare this to the way we defined predictive analytics in Chapter 2, where we use historical and current data to predict future events. The stark similarity between the two is not a coincidence, as the fundamental mathematics that powers predictive analytics involves statistical analysis of large amounts of data as well as other forms of applied mathematics, including (but not limited to) linear algebra, probability, and calculus.

In this section, I will not be delving into the statistics behind various algorithms used in predictive analytics. Rather, I will explain the concept behind some of the fundamentals used in the field so that the next time you interact with predictive analytics it is something relatable and not black-box science fiction.

Let's start with a very simple problem. Imagine you are the owner of a grocery store and you have 100 items to sell. You want to find the answers to the following questions:

- How much of each item do I sell each month?
- Which items sell the most (and least) in a particular month?
- What are my average overall sales per month?
- How am I growing my sales month over month?

All of these questions can be answered by collecting, processing, and analyzing your sales data. Statistics allows you to process this data to derive insights that will help your business. The data can be represented visually or in the form of reports for analysis. Following are some of the insights you can obtain from this analysis:

- Which items contribute the most to revenue, and how do I maintain and improve their sales?
- Which items contribute the least, why is this the case, and what do I do next?
- How is the business doing overall in terms of revenue month over month, and how can I set up business targets for specific timelines and then build a plan that helps achieve those targets?

Now imagine that the business has grown from a grocery store to a grocery chain and then to a conglomerate. Obviously, the amount and complexity of the data generated by the business would have increased significantly. Some of the questions we'd now ask would remain the same: for example, "How do I grow my business?" But others would be added over time; for instance: "Why is one location performing better than another?" or "How should I effectively distribute my inventory to fulfill the needs of the business?" To answer these questions, statistics provides us with the following set of tools:

Mean

Gives the average of a frequency distribution of values. In our earlier example, it would help answer the question about average sales.

Median

The value that sits at the middle of a frequency distribution of values such that there is an equal probability that an observation would fall above or below it. Looking at our retail example, median would help us understand the typical selling price for something without being influenced by outliers.

Mode

Represents the most frequently occurring observation. In our example, it would apply to answering the question about the most-sold item.

Standard deviation

Helps us understand how dispersed our distribution is when compared to the mean value. For our earlier example, it could help us study how revenue compares across our stores.

Here's a simple example. If the total sales of mangoes in a particular month are represented by Y, the price per mango is a constant c, and the number of mangoes sold is represented by T, the revenue generated by selling Y mangoes in one month can be represented by the following equation:

$$Y = c \times T$$

There is a direct dependency between the revenue generated and the number of mangoes sold; that is, the more mangoes you sell, the more money you make. But business questions are hardly as simple as the preceding one. Rather, a business might ask its analysts to determine how much of each item it should stock in each of its warehouses. If the stock needed is represented by Y, what are some things that can impact this number?

X = How much of each item do we already have in stock?
A = What is the shelf life of that item?
B = How much of each item do we expect to sell in each location?

B1 = What is the average sale of each item?
B2 = What is the seasonal impact on the sale of this item next month?
B3 = Are there any specific events that can impact the sale of this item?

And so on. Did you notice how with B we are trying to predict how many items we would sell in each location?

This is by no means a comprehensive list of questions, but rather a representative subset of questions that a business might encounter during inventory planning. Mathematically speaking, these dependencies can be represented as different equations, with some of these variables having interdependencies. With some background in mathematics, we all know that solving a single equation with a known and an unknown variable is a trivial task. However, consider the following equations:

$$X = cY + Z$$
$$Z = kX + m$$
$$Y = 2Z + iX$$

In these equations, the letters c, i, k, and m represent constants. As mathematics students, we know that as the number of equations and variables increases, it becomes more time-consuming to solve them. This is where linear algebra comes to our rescue. Before we go into specifics, let's try to build our understanding of the correlation between equations and data analytics.

Going back to our grocery example:

- Market cost of each mango = \$0.2
- Margin = 10%
- Fixed revenue (irrespective of total sales) per month = \$20
- Number of mangoes sold per month = N
- Total revenue in dollars per month = R

We can represent the total revenue as a function of N:

$$R = (0.2N) \times 1.10 + 20$$
$$R = 0.22N + 20$$

This equation is plotted in Figure 3-1.

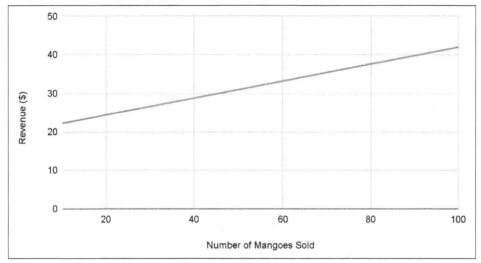

Figure 3-1. Plot showing revenue versus number of mangoes sold

Using this graph, we can quickly figure out how many mangoes we would need to sell to reach a particular revenue target. While this is great for simple analysis, real-life business questions could be more complex. Let's take a hypothetical example in which the profit per month is a function of the number of mangoes sold such that:

Profit(USD) = 100 − (0.8 × number of mangoes sold)
$$P = 100 - 0.8N$$

We can also figure out the sweet spot where we can maximize both monthly revenue and profit (see Figure 3-2).

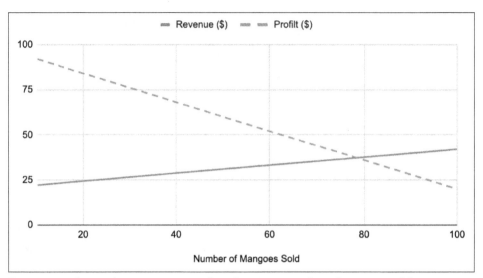

Figure 3-2. Plot analyzing revenue and profit versus number of mangoes sold

The graph tells us that our sweet spot is between 70 and 80 mangoes. Using calculus, we can solve the following set of equations to get that exact number:

$$R = 0.22N + 20$$
$$P = 100 - 0.8N$$

At the sweet spot, $R = P$.

This gives us three equations where we can solve for N:

$$0.22N + 20 = 100 - 0.8N$$
$$1.02N = 80$$
$$N = 78.4$$

Of course, we can't sell 0.4 mangoes, but the math does tell us that we need to sell around 78 mangoes to achieve the result we need. If we continue to add variables into the mix, we also need to add more equations, and the more we add, the more difficult it will be to solve them. An area where linear algebra helps with this is the use of matrices to represent equations. Take a look at the following set of equations for the problem we are trying to solve:

$$2x + 5y + 2z = -38$$
$$3x - 2y - 4z = 17$$
$$-6x + y - 7z = -12$$

Ref: Standard Matrix Multiplication

$$\begin{bmatrix} a & b & c \\ d & e & f \\ g & h & i \end{bmatrix} \begin{bmatrix} x \\ y \\ z \end{bmatrix} = \begin{bmatrix} K \\ L \\ M \end{bmatrix}$$

where:

$$ax + by + cz = K$$
$$dx + ey + fz = L$$
$$gx + hy + iz = M$$

The three equations can be presented as the following matrix:

$$\begin{bmatrix} 2 & 5 & 2 \\ 3 & -2 & 4 \\ -6 & 1 & -7 \end{bmatrix} \begin{bmatrix} x \\ y \\ z \end{bmatrix} = \begin{bmatrix} -38 \\ 17 \\ 12 \end{bmatrix}$$

Now that we have the equations as matrices we can manipulate the matrices to solve for x, y, and z. There are several methods to do this, and going into detail on each method is beyond the scope of this book. Instead, we'll look at one example using row echelon form.

To work with matrices (in the context of solving equations) the following conditions need to apply:

- Any matrix manipulation should preserve the solution.
- We should be able to reverse the manipulation to come back to the original state.

A few manipulations can help us:

- The order of the equations can be changed in the matrix.
- We can multiply both sides of the equations with a nonzero constant.
- We can multiply any equations with a nonzero constant and then add it to another equation.

As long as we follow these rules, we'll preserve the solution. It is noteworthy to understand that all of these operations are reversible.

Let's try to solve our three equations using row echelon form. The first step is to represent the equations as a combined matrix:

$$\begin{bmatrix} 2 & 5 & 2 & -38 \\ 3 & -2 & 4 & 17 \\ -6 & 1 & -7 & 12 \end{bmatrix}$$

Step 1: Multiply equation 1 by −1.5 and add it to equation 2. Multiply equation 1 by 6 and add it to equation 3.

The resulting matrix is:

$$\begin{bmatrix} 2 & 5 & 2 & -38 \\ 0 & \frac{-19}{2} & 1 & 74 \\ 0 & 1 & 16 & -126 \end{bmatrix}$$

Step 2: Multiply equation 2 by $\frac{32}{19}$ and add it to equation 3.

The resulting matrix is:

$$\begin{bmatrix} 2 & 5 & 2 & -38 \\ 0 & \frac{-19}{2} & 1 & 74 \\ 0 & 1 & \frac{13}{19} & \frac{-26}{19} \end{bmatrix}$$

Step 3: Using the third row, you can conclude the following:

$$0 \times x + 0 \times y + \frac{13}{19} \times z = \frac{-26}{19}$$
$$z = -2$$

Step 4: Substitute z in row 2 to get y:

$$(0 \times x) - \left(\frac{19}{2} \times y \right) + (-2) = 74$$
$$y = -8$$

Step 5: Substitute y and z in equation 1 to get x:

$$(2 \times x) + (5 \times (-8)) + (2 \times (-2)) = -38$$
$$x = 3$$

While we were able to solve the preceding equations by using manipulations, not all equations can be solved in this way. For example, sometimes there is no unique solution to the equations, and other times there can be an infinite number of solutions. We won't go into those cases here. Instead, the idea here is for you to see how linear algebra helps solve equations, how these equations represent real-life problems for which we are seeking solutions, and therefore that linear algebra can be used for analyzing real-world data. Note that this is just a simple use case for linear algebra. Linear algebra has several applications in machine learning, among them loss functions in linear regression, regularization, and support vector classification. I'll go through a number of these applications in this book.

Regression

So far, I've discussed how real-world problems can be expressed as mathematical equations and how an understanding of statistics and linear algebra helps in solving these equations and drawing real-world conclusions from the solutions. Now let's go a step further and try to understand how to predict future values from historical data.

Let's assume we are trying to predict the value of something that can be represented by the letter Y. I'll call Y the *dependent variable*. Y could be anything, from the stock price of a certain asset at a given time to the amount of lemonade sold by a stand on a given day. Let's also bring one more variable in and call it X. I'll call X the *independent variable*. X could be something like the day of the week or the average temperature during the day.

The variable distribution for this example is shown in Table 3-1.

Table 3-1. Variable distribution

X	Y
3	2
5	13
10	24
11	27
12	23
17	30
20	41
22	50
23	52
25	49
30	65

Table 3-1 represents real-world values that we've observed. We can plot these values, as shown in Figure 3-3.

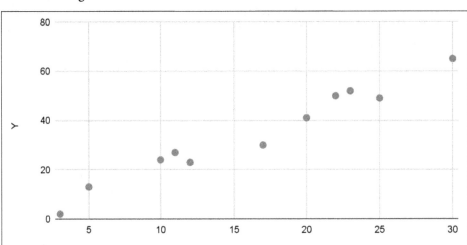

Figure 3-3. An independent variable plotted against a dependent variable

At first glance, we can make a few observations. The value of Y increases with the value of X, and the increase in the value of Y is proportional to the increase in the value of X. Now, if someone were to ask us to predict the value of Y when the value of X is 40, we would need to extrapolate the data to guess what the potential value of Y could look like. This extrapolation is depicted in Figure 3-4.

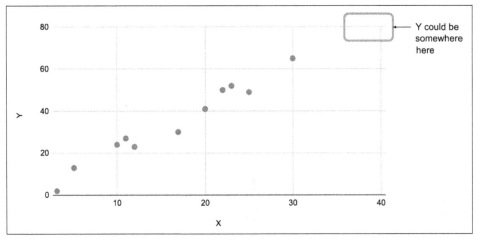

Figure 3-4. Predicting Y

To make this a bit more scientific, rather than depending on our power of observation, we can draw a line through our historical observations and predict the values of Y based on the line in Figure 3-5.

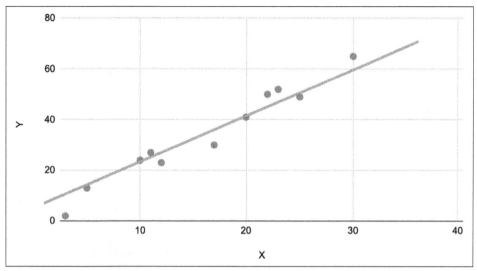

Figure 3-5. Prediction line roughly fitting the observations

The line in Figure 3-5 looks like a good fit and could give a reasonable prediction for the value of Y, not only for larger values but also for values in between observed values, such as X = 28. The line can be represented by the following equation:

$$Y = c + sX$$

In the preceding equation, c is the y-intercept (when X = 0) and s is the slope of the line. However, take a look at Figure 3-6.

All three lines seem to fit some of the observations. Now we have three equations:

$$Y = c + sX$$
$$Y = c_1 + s_1X$$
$$Y = c_2 + s_2X$$

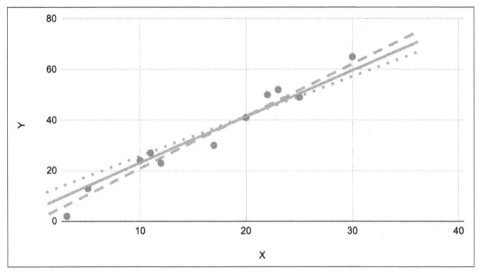

Figure 3-6. Multiple possibilities for a prediction line

How do we choose the best fit for our predictions? The statistical process of under-standing the strength and nature of the relationship between a dependent variable (Y) and one or more independent variables (X_1, X_2 ... X_n) is known as *regression*.

What Is Regression Analysis?

The use of regression for forecasting (or prediction) is called *regression analysis*. We will continue to use the preceding example to build further concepts. However, please understand that in real life, the datasets are much larger, and regression analysis is usually performed by a computer program.

The first question that comes to mind is how do we decide which line is the best fit for our analysis. To gather this data, scientists use a *loss function*, which is a measure of the accuracy of a prediction model that tells us which is the best line that fits our observations. There are multiple ways to evaluate the loss function. Let's start with Figure 3-7.

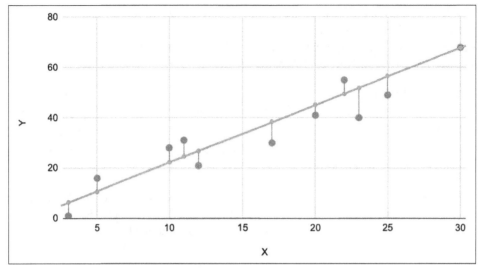

Figure 3-7. Loss function

The loss function does the following:

- It finds the difference between the observed values (Y) and the predicted values (Y'). The predicted value is the value of Y on the line, when the value of X is the same as the one used for the observation:

$$Y_i - Y_i'$$

- It squares all the differences:

$$\left(Y_i - Y_i'\right)^2$$

- It sums all the squared differences:

$$\sum_{i=1}^{N} \left(Y_i - Y_i'\right)^2$$

- It takes the average of the sum of the squares of all the differences:

$$\frac{1}{N} \sum_{i=1}^{N} \left(Y_i - Y_i'\right)^2$$

The higher the difference is between the observed and predicted values, the higher the average will be. Computer programs will work to find a model (fitting of the line) that minimizes the loss function. The method we used here is known as mean squared error (MSE). Note the following regarding MSE:

- It doesn't matter whether the observed value is less than or greater than the predicted value. The formula only cares about the difference. (Squaring the difference will get rid of any negative values.)
- If the difference between an observation and the corresponding prediction is large, it is penalized (as this difference is squared).

Since MSE is a square of the differences, its unit is also a square of the unit of Y. To get an error value with the same unit as Y, root mean squared error (RMSE) is often used. RMSE can be easily obtained using the square root of MSE:

$$\sqrt{\frac{1}{N}\sum_{i=1}^{N}\left(Y_i - Y_i'\right)^2}$$

Another method for calculating the loss function is mean absolute error (MAE). While the general idea is the same, instead of squaring the difference between the observed and predicted values, MAE takes an absolute of the difference:

$$\left|Y_i - Y_i'\right|$$

Hence, the final formula is:

$$\frac{1}{N}\sum_{i=1}^{N}\left|Y_i - Y_i'\right|$$

When using MAE, note the following:

- It doesn't matter whether the observed value is less than or greater than the predicted value. The formula only cares about the difference. (The absolute function ensures that the difference is always positive.)
- If the difference between an observation and the corresponding prediction is large, it is not penalized more than the actual value of the difference.

Observations that are significantly different from their predicted values are referred to as *outliers*. It's important to identify outliers, because they might not fit the population (the dataset) and can cause many problems during regression analysis (e.g., increasing the value of a loss function that might otherwise fit well with the rest of the observed population).

Now that you have a basic understanding of regression analysis, let's take a look at some regression techniques.

Regression Techniques

Several types of regression techniques are used to define predictive analytics models. In this section, we will discuss linear, polynomial, and logistic regression. We will look at how they are used and the different considerations and limitations of each.

Linear regression

The most common type of modeling technique that you will come across is linear regression. Linear regression is used to understand the relationship between a dependent variable (Y) and one or more independent variables (X_1, X_2 ... X_n). This is why I used a linear regression example to take you through the fundamentals of regression analysis in the previous section.

Figure 3-8 depicts a simple linear regression analysis to find a best-fit straight line to represent our observed population. As discussed earlier, this line can be represented by

$$Y = c + sX$$

where:

Y is the dependent variable.
X is the independent variable.
c is the y-intercept (the value of Y when X = 0).
s is the slope of the line (the factor by which Y changes for every 1-unit increase of X).

This line represents the prediction line. Often, an additional variable is added to this. We'll call this variable e. The e variable represents the error between the observed value and the predicted value. So, if the observed value is Y_o, it can be represented by:

$$Y_o = c + sX + e$$

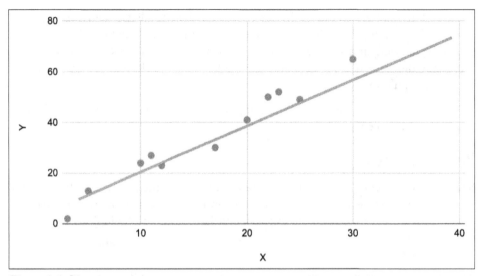

Figure 3-8. Linear regression

Please note that while c and s are constants, Y_o, X, and e are variables and will change for each observation. Simple linear regression only deals with one independent variable. When there is more than one independent variable, it is known as multiple linear regression. Multiple linear regression can be represented as follows:

$$Y = c + s_1X_1 + s_2X_2 + s_3X_3...s_nX_n$$

In the preceding equation:

Y is the dependent variable.
X_n is the independent variable(s).
c is the y-intercept (the value of Y when $X_n = 0$).
s_n is the slope of the line (given that all other variables remain constant, the factor by which Y changes for every 1-unit change of X_n).

There are a few important points to keep in mind regarding linear regression:

- The dependent variable can be *continuous*. That means it can take any numerical value between two observations. For example, a person's height could be 170 cm or 180 cm or somewhere in between; hence, height is a continuous variable. Or, the dependent variable can be *discrete*, which means it can only take a specific value. An example would be a variable representing the observation of an event occurring: if the event occurs, the observation is 1; otherwise, it is 0.

- The independent variable(s) can also be continuous or discrete.

- There must be a linear relationship between the dependent and independent variables.

- Linear regression is sensitive to outliers that can influence the prediction line and hence the prediction values.

- There should be no *autocorrelation* between observations. Autocorrelation usually occurs in time series data; observations that occur closer in time are likely to be more similar to each other compared to observations that occur farther apart in time. For example, if a dataset contains continuous samples of average daily temperatures, it is likely that the average temperature on day 1 is more similar to the average temperature on day 2 than it is to the average temperature on day 30. In this case, the data is autocorrelated.

- If there is more than one independent variable, there should not be any correlation between them. This is called *multicollinearity*. When this occurs, it is difficult for the model to determine which correlated variable is causing a change in the value of the dependent variable. Hence, one or more of those variables are redundant and should not be used.

- The *residual* is the difference between the observed value and the predicted value. A standardized residual is the ratio of the residual divided by the estimated standard deviation of the residual. If the variation between the predicted value and the observed value is constant, the model is a good fit for the training dataset. To determine whether a model meets this criterion, we can plot the standard residuals against the predicted values. If the corresponding scatterplot does not show a pattern and is randomly distributed around zero, this model fulfills *homoscedasticity*. This is demonstrated by the first scatterplot in Figure 3-9. In the second scatterplot in that figure, the standard residuals are fanning out, which means the variance in the residual is changing. This is an example in which the model does not fulfill the condition of homoscedasticity, because the variances of the residuals are equal or similar.

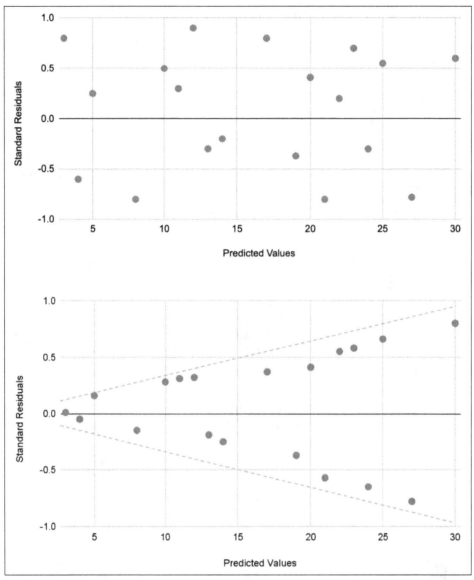

Figure 3-9. Homoscedasticity

A model's residuals should follow a normal distribution. This can be checked easily by plotting standardized residuals on a histogram. If the histogram is not skewed, the residuals are following a normal distribution (Figure 3-10). In simple terms, you have most of your residuals distributed equally around a mean value, and as the variation increases, the number of values decreases to provide a normal distribution.

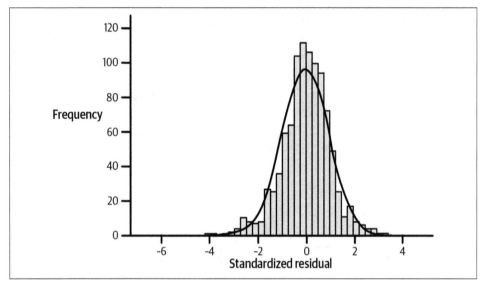

Figure 3-10. Normal distribution of standardized residuals

Polynomial regression

Not all relationships between dependent and independent variables will be linear. When a relationship is nonlinear it cannot be represented by a straight line and instead will be represented by a curve. In statistics, this means that in the regression equation, the power of the independent variable is greater than 1. A polynomial regression model can be represented by the following equation:

$$y = b_0 + b_1 x^n$$

where:

y is the dependent variable.
b_0 is the y-intercept when x is zero.
x is the independent variable.
b_1 is the coefficient of X.
n is greater than 1.

The following is a more generalized representation of a polynomial regression equation:

$$y = b_0 + b_1 x + b_2 x^2 + b_3 x^3 + \ldots + b_n x^n$$

In Figure 3-11, the graph on the left uses simple linear regression to model a dataset, and the graph on the right uses polynomial regression to obtain a better fit line for the dataset. If the dataset is arranged such that there is a nonlinear relationship between the dependent and independent variables, we should use polynomial regression.

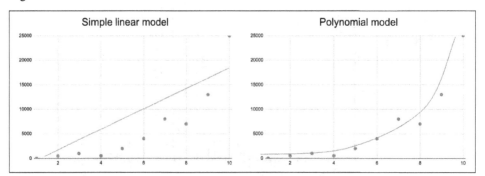

Figure 3-11. A simple linear model (left) and a polynomial model (right)

Polynomial regression can be multivariate as well. A second order multiple polynomial regression can be expressed as the following:

$$y = b + b_1 x_1 + b_2 x_2 + b_{11} x_1^2 + b_{22} x_2^2 + b_{12} x_1 x_2$$

For simplicity, I have not shown the error terms in the preceding equation.

Here are some points to keep in mind when using polynomial regression:

- The relationship between the dependent and independent variable(s) can be linear or curvilinear. (Note that polynomial regression is a special case of linear regression.)
- The residuals of a model should follow a normal distribution.
- If a scatterplot of residuals versus predicted values does not show uniform randomness but is following a pattern, the model is most likely underfitted.
- In multivariate polynomial regression, independent variables should not be dependent on each other.

- It might be tempting to use a higher-degree polynomial (X^4 instead of X^2) to fit the training data better and reduce the error between the observed and predicted values. However, this might lead to overfitting (Figure 3-12). Plotting the regression line against the data will help visualize what is going on. Overfitted models tend to behave strangely when extrapolated, so it is a good idea to look at how the model is behaving toward the edges.

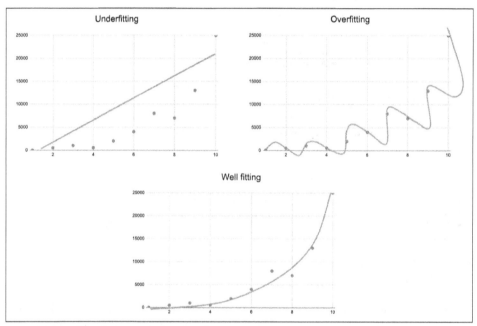

Figure 3-12. Overfitting in polynomial regression

Logistic regression

Logistic regression is often used to solve classification problems. There are many types of logistic regression. *Binary logistic regression* allows you to model the probability of a discrete output. In most cases, this output is a binary 0 or 1 (representing true or false). Binary logistic regression could be used to classify, for example, whether an email is spam or not or whether a tumor is malignant or not. *Multinomial logistic regression* can classify the output in three or more categories, where the order of the categories is not important. An example could be figuring out the voter preference in an election with three or more candidates. *Ordinal logistic regression* also deals with three or more categories for classification; however, these categories are ordered. An example would be predicting the popularity rating of an Airbnb rental based on its location and number of bookings, where the rating from lowest to highest can be from 1 to 5. Figure 3-13 shows an example of logistic regression.

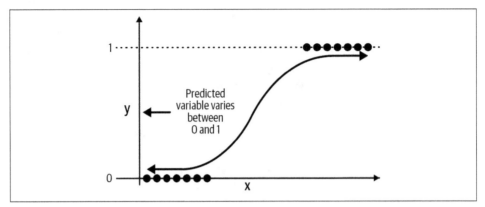

Figure 3-13. Logistic regression

Let's understand the derivation of calculating the probability of an event using logistic regression:

- *p* is the probability of an event occurring.
- 1 − *p* is the probability of an event not occurring.
- *Odds* = *p*/(1 − *p*) represents the odds of the event occurring versus the event not occurring.
- The logit function is defined as the natural log of the odds = *ln(Odds)* = *ln(p/(1 − p)* = *logit(P)*.

Logistic regression assumes that there is a linear relationship between the log odds (*Logit(P)*) and the independent variables. For simplicity, let's assume one independent variable:

- *Y* = *mX* + *c* represents a simple linear equation with one independent variable and one dependent variable.
- In our case, the dependent variable is the log odds or *Logit(P)*.

Hence:

$$Logit(P) = mX + c$$

$$ln\left(\frac{p}{1-p}\right) = mX + c$$

Simplifying, we get:

$$\frac{p}{1-p} = e^{mX + c}$$

$$p = \frac{e^{mX + c}}{1 + e^{mX + c}}$$

$$p = \frac{1}{1 + e^{-(mX + c)}}$$

The formula can be extended to the following for multiple independent variables:[1]

$$P = \frac{1}{1 + e^{-(c + m1X1 + m2X2 + m3X3 + ...mnXn)}}$$

Keep the following points in mind when using logistic regression:

- Independent variables should not be correlated with each other.
- There should be a linear relationship between the log odds and the independent variables. This is not the same as probability, which is defined by a logistic function of the independent variables.
- The accuracy of logistic regression results improves with large samples.

R-squared and P-value

Additional useful terms used in regression analysis are *R-squared* and *p-values*. R-squared tells us how well a regression line estimates actual values. In other words, it's a measure of the degree to which the independent variables explain the variation in the dependent variable. Let's look at how R-squared is calculated by working through a simple example.

We start with the actual values of the data, and we find its mean (Figure 3-14).

---

1 This equation is based on the derivation from Ashish Kumar and Joseph Babcock, *Python: Advanced Predictive Analytics* (Birmingham, UK: Packt Publishing, 2017).

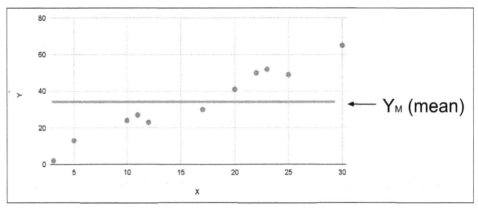

Figure 3-14. R-squared (mean)

Then we calculate the distance from the actual values to the mean (Figure 3-15).

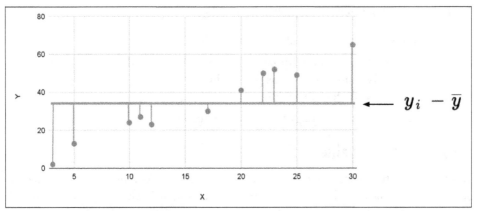

Figure 3-15. R-squared (difference of observed values from mean)

If we were to add these numbers together, we would get zero. So instead, we square all the values and then add them up:

$$\sum_{i=1}^{N}(y_i - \bar{y}_i)^2$$

Now we calculate the distance of the predicted values on the regression line from the actual values (Figure 3-16).

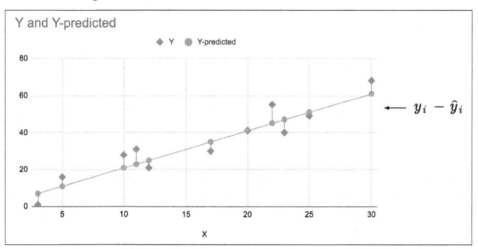

Figure 3-16. R-squared (difference of predicted values from actual values)

Once again, when we add these numbers together we get zero. Instead, we can square all the values and then add them together:

$$\sum_{i=1}^{N} (y_i - \hat{y}_i)^2$$

R-squared is calculated as follows:

$$R^2 = 1 - \frac{\sum_{i=1}^{N} (y_i - \hat{y}_i)^2}{\sum_{i=1}^{N} (y_i - \bar{y}_i)^2}$$

The value of R-squared will range between 0% and 100%. As the predicted values get closer to the actual value, the value of R-squared will approach 100%; conversely, as the predicted values move away from the actual value, the value of R-squared approaches 0%. Take the example of the price of a house. An R-squared value of 0.9 (or 90%) would mean that 90% of the variance of the dependent variable (i.e., the price of the house) is explained by the independent variable(s) (e.g., congestion and location).

With multivariate regression, which we will discuss shortly, the value of R-squared remains the same or increases every time we add a new independent variable, even though there might not be any correlation between the newly added independent variable and the dependent variable. In such cases, Adjusted R-squared is used, which penalizes the addition of new variables that do not improve the existing model.

R-squared is completely dependent on the sample (the training data). So, while it can tell you how well your model will perform for your training data, it does not really give you any indication of how the model will perform when used on a different or larger dataset. This is where p-value comes in.

P-value works in tandem with the coefficients of the independent variable(s) in your linear regression equation and determines whether there is a statistically significant relationship between the independent variable and the dependent variable. In multivariate regression, there will be a p-value associated with every coefficient of an independent variable. A p-value of <0.05 means the independent variable is a good addition to the model. Larger p-values indicate that the independent variable does not affect the model, and changes in the independent variable aren't correlated with changes in the dependent variable.

P-values cannot be used to establish significance in nonlinear regression models. This is because the variation in the dependent variable is dependent not only on the coefficient of the independent variable, but also on the value of the dependent variable. In other words, the change in the dependent variable per unit of change in the independent variable depends on where you are on the curve. Plotting the model against the dataset and domain knowledge comes in handy when evaluating the significance of nonlinear regression models.

Selecting a Regression Model

Since there are a number of regression techniques and numerous corresponding derivatives, it can sometimes be challenging to determine which approach is best when trying to solve a particular problem. In this section, I will provide some food for thought when selecting a regression model and validating its correctness.

Following are some factors to consider when selecting a regression model:

- Explore the data to understand the nature of the relationship between the independent and dependent variables. If the relationship is linear, a linear model would be a better fit. If the relationship is nonlinear, start with a polynomial model. If the regression model is underfitting, consider a polynomial option to get to an optimal fit.

- Understand whether the dependent variable is continuous (e.g., the weight of a person) or discrete (e.g., obese versus nonobese). If it is discrete, evaluate logistic regression.

- Are there multiple independent variables? If so, evaluate *stepwise regression*, a technique that allows for automated selection of independent variables without the need for human intervention.[2] This is done by adding and dropping independent variables one at a time. The selection is done by observing certain statistical indicators.

- Are the independent variables correlated with each other? Linear, polynomial, and logistic regression aren't good candidates for correlated independent variables. When independent variables are dependent on each other, the model ends up with redundant variables, and it becomes difficult to determine which of these variables has a real impact on the dependent variable and which is just a codependence on another independent variable. Evaluate ridge regression or lasso regression in such cases.[3,4]

- Is the sample size small? Logistic regression is less likely to be accurate in this case and hence is not a good candidate.

The validity of the model can be checked by doing the following:

- Divide the data between the training and validation groups. SMSE, the simple mean squared difference between the observed and predicted values, can be used as a measure for the prediction accuracy.

- Use R-squared and Adjusted R-squared to understand how well the model fits the training data.

- Use p-values in linear regression to establish the significance of the independent variable(s).

---

2 Amar Sahay, *Applied Regression and Modeling* (New York: Business Expert Press, 2016).

3 A.K. Md. Ehsanes Saleh, Mohammad Arashi, and B.M. Golam Kibria, *Theory of Ridge Regression Estimation with Applications* (Hoboken, NJ: Wiley, 2019).

4 Sunil Ray, "7 Regression Techniques You Should Know!" (*https://oreil.ly/ldUWl*), Analytics Vidhya, August 14, 2015.

- Use plotting (when possible) and domain knowledge, both of which are of utmost importance when interpreting the efficacy of a regression model.

- When using a polynomial model, be aware of overfitting. Observing how the model behaves at the edges can help identify overfitting.

Note that this is by no means a comprehensive guide on getting to the best possible regression model. The idea here is to raise the right questions that will assist with the decision process of selecting and evaluating a regression model. Like in most fields, there is no alternative to domain knowledge and experience.

Decision Trees

The whole idea behind predictive analytics is to anticipate (or estimate) future outcomes of one or more metrics. These insights into the future allow businesses to take intelligent actions that directly impact the bottom line. It is a cardinal component to data-driven decision making. A very valuable tool in our analytics toolbox is *decision trees*. Decision trees are a simple but effective form of multivariate analysis. Not only can they be a substitute for regression analysis, but they can also be used in tandem with it to assist at various stages.

Let's start with a simple classification problem to understand the basic concept behind decision trees. In this example, we want to predict whether a potential loan applicant is high or low risk based on their current annual salary and their average account balance over the past six months. Table 3-2 shows historical data based on previous loan candidates.

Table 3-2. Risk classification based on average account balance

Salary ($)	Average account balance ($)	Risk classification
60,000	10,000	High risk
45,000	100,000	Low risk
80,000	2,000	Low risk
100,000	20,000	Low risk
35,000	4,000	High risk
75,000	30,000	Low risk
110,000	10,000	Low risk
68,000	3,000	High risk
12,000	40,000	High risk
40,000	10,000	High risk
42,000	20,000	High risk
47,500	70,000	Low risk
200,000	80,000	Low risk
124,000	5,000	Low risk

There are a few things to understand about the dataset in Table 3-2:

- Salary and average account balance are our independent variables. These can be continuous or discrete (we will cover continuous variables shortly).

- Risk classification is our dependent variable that needs to be predicted. Since this is a classification problem, it has two discrete values: low risk and high risk.

Let's say we came up with the following rules based on our analysis of this data:

- If a customer's current annual salary is greater than or equal to $70,000, they are low risk.

- If a customer's current annual salary is less than $70,000, then:

  — If their average account balance in the last six months is greater than or equal to $60,000, they are low risk.

  — If their average account balance in the last six months is less than $60,000, they are high risk.

This simple algorithm is represented as the decision tree in Figure 3-17.

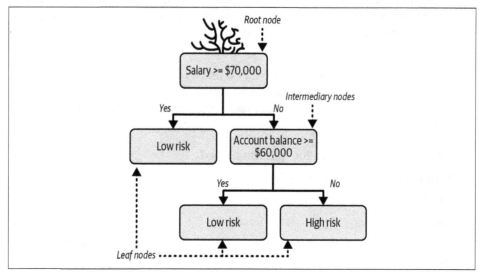

Figure 3-17. Basic decision tree

You might have seen similar structures when dealing with flowcharts. Think of this decision tree as an upside-down tree that starts with the *root node* on top. The data passes through the root node and is split based on the split condition (i.e., salary >= 70,000 in this case). The candidates who have a salary >= 70,000 move to the left of the tree and reach what is known as a *leaf node*. Leaf nodes signal the termination of that branch of the tree and indicate that the required prediction has been reached. Hence, these candidates are classified as low risk.

The decision path for candidates who have a salary <$70,000 moves to the right branch of the tree and reaches another condition in an *intermediary node*. This node has another split condition that needs to be evaluated and hence does not signify the termination of this particular branch of the tree. The data is further split based on the second condition, and then is classified as either low risk or high risk as it reaches the leaf nodes.

While real-world classification problems are much more complex, the example depicted in Figure 3-17 demonstrates a simple model that can be adopted and modified to build an automated customer classification model that can be used to process thousands of applications. What we have built in this example is a *classification tree* in which the predicted output is a discrete class. Another form of decision tree, known as a *regression tree*, can be used to predict continuous values, such as an estimated bank account balance. A common term used in this context is *CART*, which stands for classification and regression trees.

A real-world customer analysis would have a much broader set of independent variables, and the size of the dataset would be much larger as well. As we attempt to define a decision tree for such a scenario, we need to consider the following questions:

- How do we come up with the split conditions?
- How many levels deep should the tree be?
- At what point do we stop splitting?
- Will a trial-and-error approach be feasible?
- Among multiple tree possibilities, how do we decide which tree is optimal for this problem?

To answer these questions, we need to understand the process of training decision trees.

Training Decision Trees

Training the linear regression model is about finding the line that best fits the training data. The process of finding this line is about minimizing the loss function using one of a few methods that we discussed. While the process and parameters of training different types of models vary, the end goal is similar: find a way to train a model that does a good job at predicting the values for the training dataset, ensure that there is no overfitting (i.e., it works well with the training model only), and ensure that it is applicable to the larger (unknown) population of data. Training a decision tree is the process of actually building a tree that not only will fit well with the training data, but that also allows us to make accurate predictions based on the larger population of future (currently unknown) data.

We start at the root node that contains the entire population of the training data. Then, we find a way to split the population such that the split nodes are more congruent than their parent node. This means we want the nodes to become purer as we move down the inverted tree. But a node population can be split in multiple ways. To achieve maximum pure nodes at the shortest depth, we chose splits that maximize the increase in the node purity (Figure 3-18).

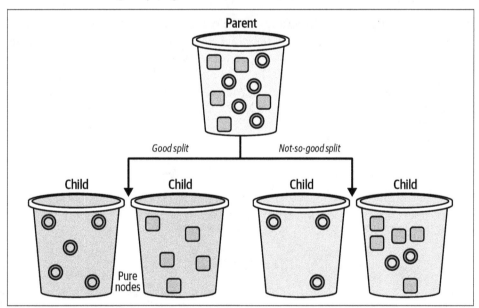

Figure 3-18. Node splitting

For us to be able to maximize the increase in node purity, first we need to find a way to measure it. The first method to measure node purity is to calculate the node *entropy*. Let's say your data is composed of observations $y_1, y_2, y_1...y_n \in Y$, where $P(y_i)$ defines the frequency with which observation i occurs relative to the rest of the set. In this case, the entropy of the set is defined as:

$$H(Y) = \sum_{i=1}^{n} -P(y_i).log_2 Py_i$$

Generally speaking, an entropy is a general decline into disorder, and we are seeking the opposite. The preceding formula will give us lower values for purer nodes. Now we can target splits that will minimize the entropy of the resulting split nodes. There is, however, an edge case in which a system can minimize the entropy of a node with a small set of observations that make it pure, but the rest of the population is split into a much larger (not-so-pure) node. While this makes sense from a single-split perspective, in the larger scheme of the whole tree we have just added an extra split that does not really improve the performance of the tree. To get a more apt metric for splitting, we can use *information gain*.

Information gain compares the entropy of the (parent) node before the split against a weighted sum of the entropy(s) of the child nodes (Figures 3-19 and 3-20). This weight is proportional to the number of observations in the child node. This approach ensures that the impact of the child nodes on the final calculator is tantamount to the number of observations in that node. Hence, a smaller node will have a smaller weight, which would result in a less significant impact on the overall calculation of the information gain (see Table 3-3). For observations $y_1, y_2, y_1...y_n \in Y$, information gain is defined as follows:

Information gain = Entropy of parent node – (Weighted sum of the entropy of child nodes)

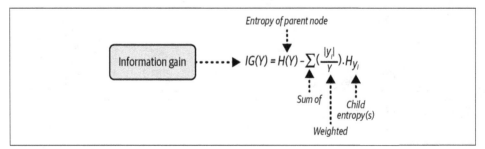

Figure 3-19. Information gain

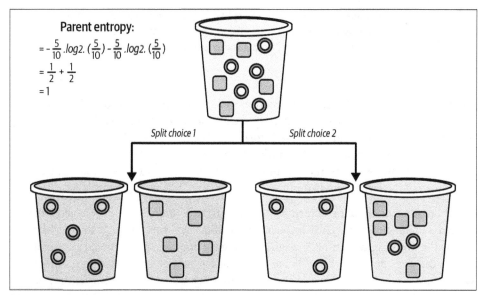

Parent entropy:

$$= -\frac{5}{10}.log2.\left(\frac{5}{10}\right) - \frac{5}{10}.log2.\left(\frac{5}{10}\right)$$

$$= \frac{1}{2} + \frac{1}{2}$$

$$= 1$$

Split choice 1 *Split choice 2*

Figure 3-20. Information gain visualization

Table 3-3. Calculating information gain

Split 1-bucket 1 entropy	Split 1-bucket 2 entropy	Split 2-bucket 1 entropy	Split 2-bucket 2 entropy
$= -\frac{5}{5}.log\,2.\left(\frac{5}{5}\right)$ $= 0$	$= -\frac{5}{5}.log\,2.\left(\frac{5}{5}\right)$ $= 0$	$= -\frac{3}{3}.log\,2.\left(\frac{3}{3}\right)$ $= 0$	$= -\frac{5}{7}.log\,2.\left(\frac{5}{7}\right) - \frac{2}{7}.log\,2.\left(\frac{2}{7}\right)$ $= 0.347 + 0.516$ $= 0.863$

Here is the equation to calculate information gain for split choice 1:

$$= 1 - \left(\frac{5}{10}.0 + \frac{5}{10}.0\right) = 1$$

And here is the equation to calculate information gain for split choice 2:

$$= 1 - \left(\frac{3}{10}.0 + \frac{7}{10}.0.863\right) = 0.497$$

There are many other ways to split the population. However, we are evaluating only a couple of options here to establish a better understanding of the calculation behind entropy and information gain.

For the first split choice, the information gain is 1. This is the best-case scenario because both child nodes are completely pure post-split. This gives them an entropy score of 0. For the second split, the information gain is 0.497. Hence, the algorithm would choose split 1 over split 2. Another thing to note is that even though split 2 has a smaller pure node, the weighted sum in the information gain formula ensures that the impact of the larger set is amplified.

An alternative method to determining the purity of a split in the decision tree is known as *Gini impurity*. Gini impurity of a node can vary from 0 to 0.5, where 0 means the node is pure and 0.5 means it is highly impure. In contrast, the entropy of a node can vary between 0 and 1. For a population of data composed of observations $y_1, y_2, y_1...y_n \in Y$, where $P(y_i)$ defines the frequency with which observation i occurs relative to the rest of the set, the Gini impurity of the set is defined as follows:

$$Gini(Y) = 1 - \sum_{i=1}^{N} P(y_i^2)$$

This process is repeated until we reach the ideal purity of the leaf nodes. Known data is used to train the model (which is the same as creating the tree). The created model is then applied to additional test data to see how well it performs on data that is different from that used to train it. The model is further optimized at this stage (Figure 3-21). Finally, it is ready for use in real-world scenarios to predict future events. Models can be continuously reevaluated and optimized by comparing their predictions to the actual occurrence of events.

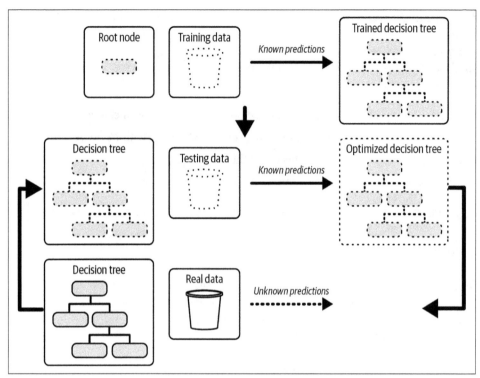

Figure 3-21. Decision tree optimization

Up until now, we have talked about observation data that is discrete and hence can be easily split into categories. However, how are we going to split data that is continuous? I'll explain, using an example:

Country of Origin: {"Pakistan," "USA," "Spain," "Brazil"}
These are discrete values, so we can easily figure out all the possible splits and then optimize based on our purity estimation.

Weight: { 60, 72.5, 77, 80, 100, 102 }
Since weight is a continuous variable, where should we split? For example, between 60 and 72.5, there is an infinite number of split possibilities. Should we split in the middle of each consecutive pair?

Consider a scenario in which the data comprises 2,000 unique data points with country of origin and weight. There are approximately 180 countries in the world, but there can be 1,999 split points for the weight with the 2,000 values in the set. This method does not really scale well for larger datasets. To address this, the k-means clustering algorithm can be used:

1. The k-means algorithm takes a dataset and selects k-random centers.
2. It then creates k-clusters by associating every data point with its nearest mean.
3. The centroid of each cluster becomes the new mean.
4. It repeats steps 2 and 3 until cluster membership is stabilized.

Applying the k-means algorithm on the weight data can result in the following:

{60} {72.5,77,80} {100,102}

What we have effectively done is create discrete sets out of our continuous data, with two possible splits instead of five. This is a rather manageable problem that scales well with larger datasets as it avoids evaluating unnecessary splits, thus speeding up the training process of the decision tree.

Using Decision Trees to Solve Regression Problems: Regression Trees

All the decision tree examples we have seen so far have been related to the problem of classification. Even though we have discussed the possibility of our independent variable (predictor) data being discrete or continuous, the dependent variable (predicted) has always been categorical (e.g., "high risk" versus "low risk") or discrete.

Decision trees can also be used to solve regression problems, such as figuring out the price of a stock. Such decision trees are known as *regression trees*. Regression trees are similar to classification trees, with some differences. Impurity in a regression tree is not measured by obtaining pure nodes. Rather, we choose a split that minimizes the sum of the squared error in the child nodes. This is similar to how we try to minimize the squared error when fitting a regression line during linear regression training.

The error for an observation y_i is depicted by the following difference:

$error = y_i - y_p$

where y_p is the predicted value. However, there is no predicted value while the tree is being created. Hence, the predicted value in this case is defined as the mean value of all the observations that are part of this node:

$$y_p = y_m = \frac{1}{n_c} \cdot \sum_{i \in c} y_i$$

where:

n_c is the total number of observations in the node.

$\sum\limits_{i \in c} y_i$ represents the sum of all observations in the node.

Now, since we are trying to minimize the sum of squared errors (SSE) of the resulting nodes:

$$SSE = \sum_{c \in nodes} \sum_{i \in c} (y_i - y_m)^2$$

Let's understand how we came up with the preceding equation. The equation helps us calculate the sum of squared errors, which we can then minimize to solve regression problems:

1. Find the arithmetic average of the values within each split node (ym).

2. Calculate the error by finding the difference between each observation within the node and the average $(y_i - y_m)$.

3. Square the error $(y_i - y_m)^2$.

4. Sum all the squares in a node $\left(\sum\limits_{i \in c} (y_i - y_m)^2 \right)$.

5. Sum all the squares of all the nodes after the split $\left(\sum\limits_{c \in nodes} \sum\limits_{i \in c} (y_i - y_m)^2 \right)$.

Figure 3-22 is a visual representation of a regression tree and the corresponding visualization of the data.

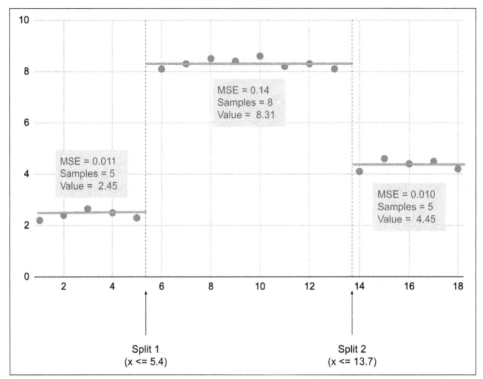

Figure 3-22. Regression (decision) tree

Tuning Decision Trees

A number of real-world considerations need to be accounted for when building decision trees. I will cover a few important ones in this section.

If you were paying attention during the regression discussion, the first consideration will sound familiar: *overfitting*. An overfitted tree is one that has been over-customized for the training data. This means it will work on the training data to a high degree of accuracy, but when it comes to new (unknown) data, these specific customizations might prove to be more of a problem than a value-add. As we saw in the case for regression, an overfitted polynomial graph would pass through most of the training data points but would start acting strangely when extrapolated. Decision trees are similar in that regard. When overfitted, they could contain specific splits for *outliers* (data that does not fit the pattern). Such splits can result in unpredictable behavior when dealing with larger datasets.

A number of techniques can be followed to prevent overfitting in decision trees. The first technique is to evaluate the independent variables (predictors) and figure out which are the most significant ones. The more variables we have, the more rules we will create, and more rules means more splits (larger decision tree). So, reducing the number of predictors can help generalize our approach.

Another technique is known as *early stopping*. Note that as we traverse downward from the root node, the tree becomes increasingly specific as it attempts to improve the purity of the child nodes and the information gain at each step. However, this can eventually lead to splits that are very specific to the training data and can impact the generalized nature of the decision tree. Although we continue to build the tree on the basis of purity and information gain, we set a stopping criterion that can stop even if the child nodes have not achieved 100% purity. Examples of rules that can help with early stopping include the following:

- Define a minimum threshold of information gain. If the algorithm is unable to find a split with an information gain higher than the defined threshold, the tree stops growing.

- Based on experience, stipulate the maximum depth a tree can have, and once it reaches that depth, stop splitting.

- Set a minimum number of observations that can be part of the child node. Once the number of observations falls below the defined number, stop splitting.

So far, we have looked at techniques that help keep the size and complexity of the decision tree in check by taking preemptive measures before or during the creation of the tree. However, what happens if we already have an overfitted tree? For such a scenario, a technique known as *pruning* is used. As the name suggests, it helps reduce overfitting by pruning certain parts of the tree. Similar to early stopping, pruning can be done using a multitude of criteria:

- Generate multiple pruned trees from the overfitted tree and test their efficacy against independent test data. (Note that the test data is different from the data used to train the model.) Do a performance assessment of the various trees and choose an optimal one accordingly.

- Using independent test data, evaluate the number of errors of each node that is not a leaf and compare this with the number of errors if the subtree is not removed. More often than not, the pruned node will perform better without the subtree, and the one that has the highest difference in the number of errors becomes the candidate for pruning. This process stops when pruning the subtree actually results in more errors (i.e., performance gain from pruning becomes negative).

It should be no surprise that, as with regression, decision trees can also suffer from *underfitting*. This can happen especially when using early stopping techniques. Hence, it is important to understand that there is no exact formula of what technique and criteria to use. They will depend on the particular use case, and as such, domain expertise and previous experience would be a huge asset. These techniques can be used independently or in tandem, and if nothing else, trial and error is always a good way of reaching an amicable solution.

Other Algorithms

Now let's discuss a few additional algorithms (modeling techniques) that are used across different use cases of predictive analytics. Random forests, discussed first, build upon the concepts we already discussed regarding decision trees. The other algorithms will also have conceptual elements similar to what we have discussed so far. Note that there are many additional algorithms out there that either are unique or are variations of one or more of the algorithms discussed in this book.

Random Forests

Random forests are fairly straightforward to understand once you grasp decision trees (Figure 3-23). In the previous section, we covered decision trees in some amount of detail. Random forests are an ensemble of decision trees. Simply put, you model a number of decision trees for the same problem. Then, you pass on the data that needs to be classified to these trees and come up with a number of predicted classifications. The final result in classification tasks is often the majority vote among the individual trees. The class with the most votes wins, whereas in regression tasks, the final result is often a simple average of the individual predictions from the decision trees in the forest.

There are a couple of considerations to keep in mind when modeling random forests:

- The independent variable(s) actually have some level of predictive correlation with the dependent variable. We cannot be building random forests using independent variables that have no correlation with the dependent (predicted) variable.

- The decision trees in the forest, and hence the predictions, are uncorrelated (or minimally correlated).

A few techniques can be used when modeling random forests to minimize the correlation between the decision trees comprising the forest. Decision trees are sensitive to the data they are trained with, so they end up with the issue of overfitting on the sample data.

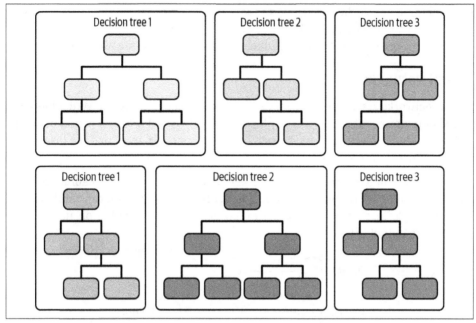

Figure 3-23. Random forest

The simplest way to produce multiple, minimally correlated decision trees is to give them different training data. One common approach to this is to fix a sample size of N, and then feed each tree with a random data sample using replacement. Now that each tree is feeding on a random sample, we also sample the features (independent variables). None of the trees use all the features, nor do they all use the same subset of features for training. Whereas using random samples of data for each tree helps minimize overall error, sampling the features for each tree minimizes the correlation between the decision trees that form the random forest ensemble.

When we are building decision trees we tend to stop at each split and evaluate the independent variables to choose the one that maximizes the purity (or information gain) of the split nodes. At this point, the decision tree has access to all the independent variables to choose from. When modeling a decision tree within a random forest, we can limit the number of random independent variables that the decision tree can use when making the "split decision" (pun intended). When we limit the number of independent variables at each split, some decision trees in the random forest will be able to find splits down the tree, which would not have been possible when considering all the variables. These could potentially be better splits that were previously undiscovered.

Generally speaking, as the number of decision trees in a random forest increases, the variance of the ensemble decreases. For the individual decision trees, the preceding two techniques can be used to reduce their individual variance and minimize overfitting.

Neural Networks

Neural networks are yet another model used in predictive analytics. While there are varied opinions about similarities (or lack thereof) between artificial neural networks (ANNs) and the workings of the human brain, most people agree that the inspiration for neural networks comes from how the brain works.

Similar to the human brain, which can be considered a biological neural network, ANNs are built of neurons, often known as artificial neurons. You can think of neurons as simple machines that take an input, do some computation on it, and then push out an output (Figure 3-24).

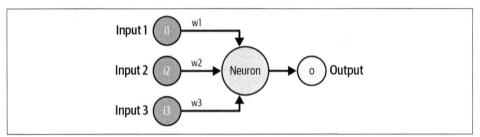

Figure 3-24. Visualizing a neuron

The real fun begins when you start *stacking* these neurons:

- Neurons can take direct input or input from other neurons.
- The output of a neuron can be pushed to other neurons or be the final output leading to a prediction.
- Neurons are built in layers.

Let's go through a few important concepts. Figure 3-25 shows an ANN with multiple layers. The first layer is called the *input layer* and it consists of *passthrough* neurons. These simply pass the input value to the next layer without any processing. The next couple of layers are called *hidden layers* (mostly because they are hidden from the users). The neurons in these layers receive the various inputs, process them, and pass them on to the final layer, known as the *output layer*, which is responsible for generating the predicted output for the ANN.

Each connection represented by arrows in Figure 3-25 carries a certain *weight* (for simplicity, I did not show weights in the figure). These weights determine the importance given by the receiving neuron to the input. These connections are often referred to as *synapses*.

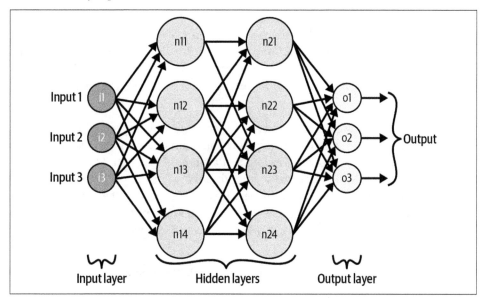

Figure 3-25. Artificial neural network

Consider a single neuron receiving multiple inputs with different weights:

- Let i_n represent the nth input to the neuron.
- Let w_n represent the weight of the synapse for the nth input.
- Let o represent the output of the neuron.

Then the neuron performs the following functions:

- The neuron calculates the weighted sum of all the inputs.
- The neuron passes this on to an *activation function*, which performs some manipulation.
- The activation function outputs o, which is then passed on to the next layer.

This can be mathematically represented as:

$$\sum_{a=1}^{n} i_a w_a \rightarrow [ActivationFunction] \rightarrow o$$

The activation function is responsible for transforming the weighted average received by the neuron. The output of this transformation is then passed on to the next layer. Following is a summary of some commonly used activation functions:

Threshold function

The threshold function takes the input (Figure 3-26). The output of the threshold function is 0 for values below the threshold and 1 for values above the threshold. Due to the way the graph looks, the threshold function is often known as a *step function*. The one limitation that the threshold function has is that the output is nondifferentiating at the threshold value, as there is no changing gradient.

Sigmoid function

This is the same function we discussed in regard to logistic regression in the previous section. The sigmoid function takes the input and outputs a value between 0 and 1. Figure 3-27 shows an example of a sigmoid function. On the left of the figure, the sigmoid function has a smooth curve. This allows it to have a well-defined nonzero derivative at each step. It is a function that defines the gradient of another function; it is a measure of how the gradient of a function changes. This is particularly useful when training the ANN, as we will see shortly.

Rectifier function

The rectifier function is a very simple function that outputs the maximum of the input value versus 0 (Figure 3-28). For every input value greater than 0, it relays the same value. For anything less than or equal to 0, it outputs 0. It is nondifferentiable at 0, as the gradient suddenly changes (as opposed to the smooth curve in the sigmoid function). The rectifier function is also known as a rectified linear unit (ReLU) activation function.

Hyperbolic tangent function

The hyperbolic tangent function is S-shaped and differentiable with varying derivatives at each step, just like the sigmoid function. However, the output values range from –1 to 1 (rather than 0 to 1, as in the case of sigmoid functions). This means the outputs from each layer are normally distributed around 0, which is useful when training the ANN. Figure 3-29 shows an example of a hyperbolic tangent function.

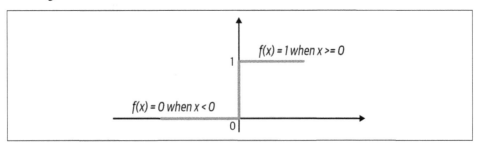

Figure 3-26. Threshold function (step function)

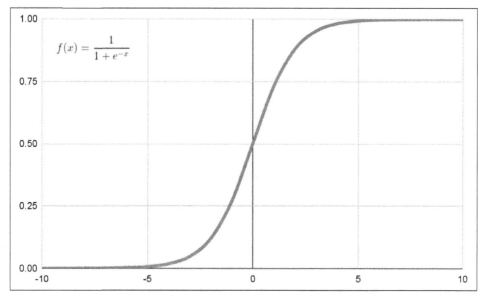

Figure 3-27. Sigmoid function

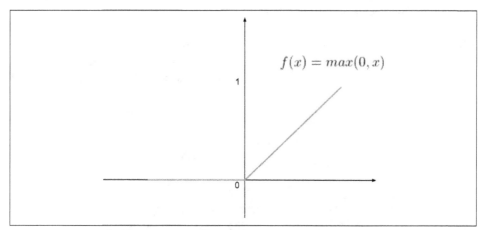

Figure 3-28. Rectifier function

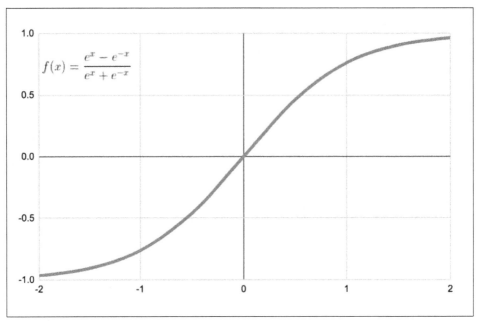

$$f(x) = \frac{e^x - e^{-x}}{e^x + e^{-x}}$$

Figure 3-29. Hyperbolic tangent function

ANNs are commonly used to address classification problems. The classification could be binary, such as an email being spam or not spam or a transaction being fraudulent or legitimate. Figure 3-30 shows a representation of a possible model that could be used for classification.

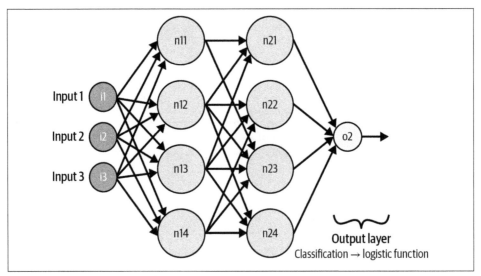

Figure 3-30. ANN for classification

Which Model Fits Best?

When working with multiple models, it is important to understand where one might be a better fit than the others. For example, if you are working with straightforward classification on uncomplicated data that is moderate in size, a random forest would do a good job at addressing this classification problem. On the other hand, if you have a very large dataset with lots of features and high complexity, an ANN would be worth looking into.

You also need to consider the fact that an ANN is computationally more intensive to run than a random forest, and if understanding the model logic is a consideration, a random forest would be a better choice.

Ultimately the best way to determine this is to try out these models and make a choice based on which one performs better and is practically feasible.

The output layers in such an ANN would contain a function to classify the prediction in one of the two classes in the binary set. It is worthwhile to note that ANNs can be used to predict continuous data as well, such as the market price of a property. The model would look similar to that shown in Figure 3-30, but the output layer would not be using a function that outputs binary classification; rather, it would look something like a weighted sum to get to a value prediction.

There is another type of classification problem that is nonbinary. Let's say you want to classify something according to three classes, 1 through 3. In this case, you could use a model such as that shown in Figure 3-31.

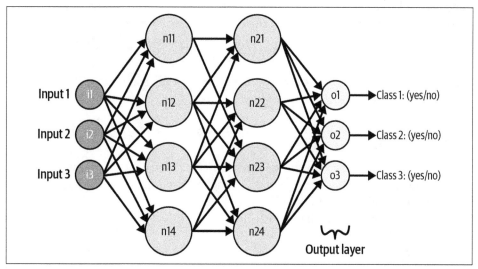

Figure 3-31. ANN for nonbinary classification

Each output node gives a prediction about a specific class for the provided data. The model in Figure 3-31 assumes the classes are not mutually exclusive (i.e., an item could belong to more than one class). Note that in this case, once again each output node could use a function for binary classification. However, if the model is dealing with mutually exclusive categories (i.e., an email is either social or work or advertisement), ANNs use something known as *softmax* (Figure 3-32).

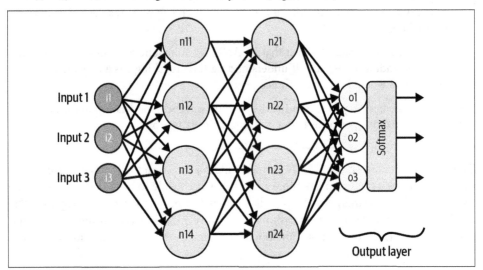

Figure 3-32. ANN for nonbinary exclusive classification

This can be achieved by replacing the individual classification functions for each output node with a shared classification function. The output of each node then represents the estimated probability of the specific class. In this case, we want the sum of all the small probabilities for all the outputs to be equal to one. The probabilities can then be used to perform the specific classification.

The back propagation training algorithm can be used for training ANNs. The back propagation algorithm does the following:

1. First, it passes each training instance to the network and calculates the output of each neuron at each consecutive layer.

2. Next, it calculates the error of the prediction for the network. It does this using a cost function. MSE is a common cost function used in ANNs. This is the same function we discussed previously regarding regression. As a reminder, the formula for the MSE is as follows:

$$\frac{1}{N}\sum_{i=1}^{N}(Y_i - Y_i')^2$$

3. Then, it calculates how much each neuron in the hidden layer contributed to this error. It repeats this for the previous hidden layer and continues until it reaches the input layer. As the algorithm moves backward, it measures the *error gradient* of each connection in the network.

4. It adjusts all the connection weights using the error gradient error calculated in the previous steps to minimize the cost function. This is called *gradient descent*.

5. This process continues until either there is no change in the weights or the amount of change between two passes is smaller than a defined value.

Support Vector Machines

A support vector machine (SVM) is an ML model that is primarily used for binary classification. There are variations of the SVM that can be used to classify more than two categories, and there is one, known as support vector regression (SVR), a machine learning algorithm used for regression analysis. However, so that you can grasp the fundamentals, we will discuss the binary classification problem.

To understand SVM, we will start with the SVM performing a *linear classification* (Figure 3-33).

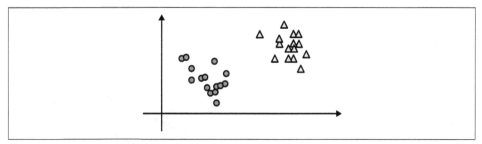

Figure 3-33. SVM linear classification

To classify the data shown in Figure 3-33, we can fit a straight line between the datasets that would split them well. When a straight line can be used to classify the data, it is known as *linear SVM classification*. With that out of the way, let's take a look at the line (Figure 3-34).

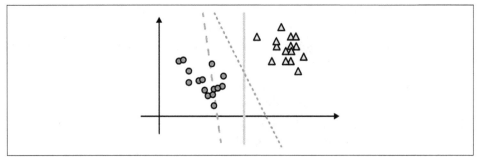

Figure 3-34. Linear SVM classification

Figure 3-34 shows three of the many possibilities to create this classification. Off the bat, it is obvious that the line that goes through the circles is not a good choice, as it fails to properly categorize the data points. However, which is the better line of the remaining two? SVM allows us to figure out the best line in this case. But note that we are assuming x and y as the independent variables, yet the number of independent variables (predictors) could be much higher. For example, if we had three predictors (x, y, and z), this separating boundary would be a plane instead of a line, as shown in Figure 3-35.

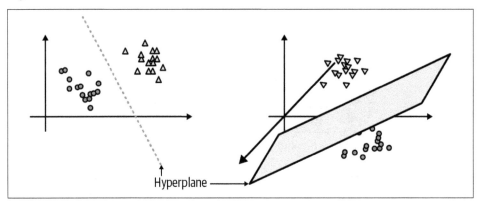

Figure 3-35. SVM hyperplane

This separating boundary is called the *hyperplane*. It gets a bit difficult to visualize this beyond three predictors, but the same concept can be applied with n predictors, where SVM will help find the optimal hyperplane in the n-dimensional space that separates the two categories. SVM does this by maximizing the distance from the closest training observations to the hyperplane. This distance is known as the *margin*. So essentially, SVM maximizes the margin from the closest observations. These observations are known as *support vectors* (Figure 3-36).

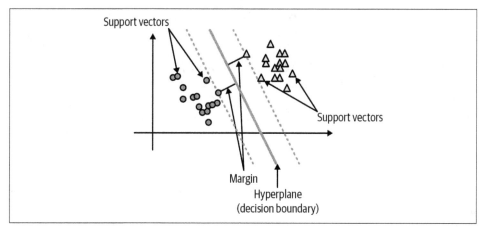

Figure 3-36. SVM margin and decision boundary

Think of the margin as a highway around the hyperplane with no support vectors inside it. It is worth mentioning that adding more support vectors outside the highway has no impact on the decision boundary.[5] The boundary is only impacted if the support vectors on the edge of the highway change. This is usually a small subset of the training sample instances. This behavior is different from regression or neural networks, where the training is based on a greedy algorithm impacted by all instances in the training sample. SVM is hence an optimization model rather than a greedy search. This allows SVM to work with small training samples (as opposed to neural networks) and makes it ideal for problems where the training data is limited. Data in the real world is rarely this clean (Figure 3-37).

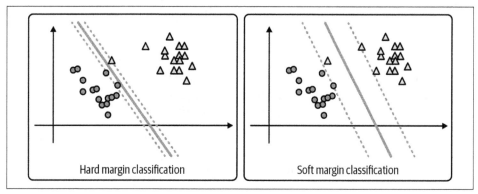

Figure 3-37. SVM hard and soft margin classification

---

5 Aurélien Géron. *Understanding Support Vector Machines* (Sebastopol, CA: O'Reilly, 2017).

In the previous support vectors, we added a new triangle (outlier) sitting very close to the set of circles. If the model were to follow the strict rules of finding the optimal decision boundary, it would end up with the hyperplane shown on the left of Figure 3-37. This is known as *hard margin classification*. Fortunately, there is an alternative, known as *soft margin classification*. Soft margin classification attempts to maximize the highway while keeping the violations (instances inside the highway) to a minimum, as shown on the right in Figure 3-37. This desensitizes the model to outliers and avoids overfitting. While we will discuss nonlinear classification shortly, it is not hard to imagine at this point in our discussion that it would be much more difficult to follow hard margin classification on nonlinear hyperplanes.

So far, we have worked under the assumption that our data can be classified using a linear hyperplane. However, what happens if we need a hyperplane that is nonlinear (Figure 3-38)?

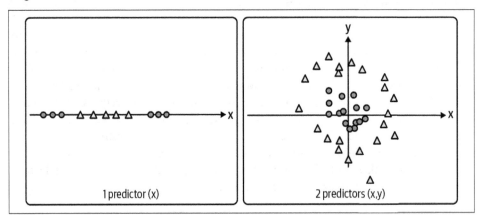

Figure 3-38. SVM nonlinear hyperplane

Even though the two datasets in Figure 3-38 can be split into two groups, it is not possible to split them using a linear hyperplane. (Note that on the left side of the figure, a linear hyperplane would be a dot, and on the right, a linear hyperplane would be a straight line.) However, the data can still be clearly split into two groups.

One approach is to transform the data into a new space. This can be done by adding more *calculated polynomial* predictors. For the diagram on the left side of Figure 3-38, we could do the following transformation:

$$y = x^2$$

where y is the new calculated predictor.

We can do a similar transformation on the diagram on the right:

$$z = x^2 + y^2$$

With the added dimension, the visualization will look like Figure 3-39.

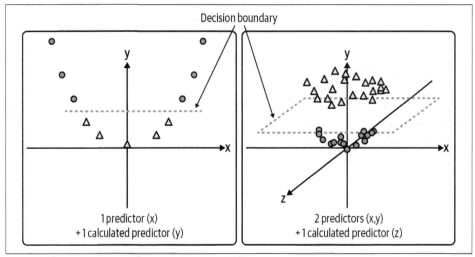

Figure 3-39. SVM calculated predictors

It is evident from the data visualization in Figure 3-39 that we are not able to find a single hyperplane (a line in the first diagram and a two-dimensional flat surface in the second), as a decision boundary between the two datasets. If we map the diagram on the right back to two dimensions, we end up with Figure 3-40.

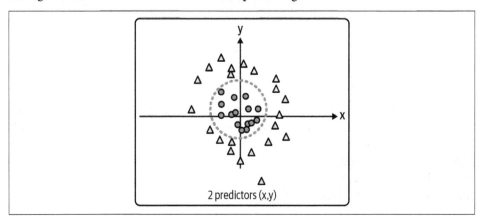

Figure 3-40. SVM two dimensions

As the data distribution gets more complex, we need to move to higher-degree polynomials to get to a workable decision boundary. However, as we move to higher-degree polynomials, the model calculations become more complex, and this has an adverse effect on the performance of our model as it becomes computationally more expensive.

To circumvent this, SVM can implement something called the *kernel trick*.[6] It turns out that, to do its job, SVM does not actually need the higher-degree dimensions. SVM can do it with the dot product of the higher-degree support vectors. Let's say we have two support vectors a and b in the original plane. The transformation ϕ transforms these support vectors into a higher plane, and now we have the transformed support vectors $\phi(a)$ and $\phi(b)$. The kernel trick allows us to express $\phi(a)T\ \phi(b)$ as a function of the original vectors a and b. Since SVM can work with the dot product of transformed support vectors, which can now be expressed as a function of the original support vectors, there is no need to actually calculate the higher-degree vectors. A kernel used in machine learning is a function that will allow the calculation of the dot product $\phi(a)T\ \phi(b)$ only by using the original support vectors a and b without having any knowledge of the transformation function. Some common kernels used in SVM can be found in Table 3-4.

Table 3-4. SVM common kernels

SVM kernel	Kernel expression	Description
Linear	$K(a,b) = a^T b$	Used when the data is linearly separable. Useful when there is a large number of classifications to consider.
Polynomial	$K(a,b) = (\gamma a^T b + c)^d$	Where γ is a constant and d represents the degree of the polynomial. Used for nonlinearly separable data.
Gaussian RBF	$K(a,b) = \exp(-\gamma\|\|\ a - b\ \|\|)^2$	Used for nonlinearly separable data. However, it is capable of handling much higher-degree dimensions (versus the polynomial kernel) due to its use of exponential calculation.
Sigmoid	$K(a,b) = \tanh(\gamma a^T b + c)$	Widely used in neural networks as an activation function. It provides high classification accuracy when used in SVM.

Naive Bayes Classifier

So far, we have discussed many ML models based on different mathematical techniques and formulas. Some of these have been more complex than others. We will conclude this chapter with a very simple yet powerful probabilistic ML algorithm known as the *Naive Bayes* classifier. Naive Bayes classifier refers to a family of algorithms that work on common assumptions. It is a classification algorithm and does what any classification algorithm does: predicts the category of the data, based on a

---

6 Aurélien Géron, *Hands-On Machine Learning with Scikit-Learn, Keras, and TensorFlow*, 3rd Edition (Sebastopol, CA: O'Reilly, 2022).

set of predictors (features). The classification performed could be binary, such as a tumor being benign or malignant, or it could be multiclass, such as predicting the type of plant based on a picture of its leaves.

The algorithm is based on the *Bayes theorem*, which gives us a way to calculate conditional probabilities. Let me take you through some terminology:

- P(A) means the probability of A occurring.
- P(B) means (yes, you guessed it) the probability of B occurring.
- P(A|B) means the probability of A occurring given that B has already occurred.
- P(B|A) means the probability of B occurring given that A has already occurred.

The Bayes theorem states the following:[7]

$$P(A \mid B) = \frac{P(B \mid A).P(A)}{P(B)}$$

The Naive Bayes algorithm makes the following assumptions:

- Each predictor (feature) is independent of the others. For example, if you were classifying email based on words, each word would be independent of the others, so "my dog" would be treated the same as "dog my" without any consideration for language semantics, the context of the words, or their order.
- Each feature contributes equally to the prediction. This means that if you are classifying fruit based on color and size, both of these features would contribute equally to the final prediction (unlike other algorithms, where we can also define weights).

Now that we understand this, let's derive the probability formula:

Let:

y be the classification (independent variable)
X be the predictors (or features), where X = (x_1, x_2, x_3, x_4 ... x_n)

The probability of y given a set of x features that have occurred can be represented by the following:

$$P(y \mid x_1, x_2, x_3 ... x_n) = \frac{P(x_1 \mid y)P(x_2 \mid y)P(x_3 \mid y)...P(x_n \mid y).P(y)}{P(x_1)P(x_2)P(x_3)...P(x_n)}$$

---

7 Allen B. Downey, *Think Bayes*, 2nd Edition (Sebastopol, CA: O'Reilly, 2021), Chapter 2.

Since the denominator of the equation does not change for a given dataset, we can remove it for proportionality:

$$P(y|x_1, x_2, x_3...x_n) \propto P(x_1|y)P(x_2|y)P(x_3|y)...P(x_n|y).P(y)$$

$$P(y|x_1, x_2, x_3...x_n) \propto P(y)\Pi_{i=1}^{n} P(x_i|y)$$

Note that we can be classifying for more than two classes of y. If this is the case, we need to calculate the probability of each and then choose the one with the highest probability.

We end up with the following:

$$y = argmax_y P(y)\Pi_{i=1}^{n} P(x_i|y)$$

Let's use an example to understand this better. Consider the arbitrary dataset shown in Table 3-5.

Table 3-5. Naive Bayes dataset

Email #	Cash	Bank	Won	Friend	Spam
1	1	1	1	0	Y
2	0	0	0	1	N
3	1	1	0	0	Y
4	1	0	0	1	N
5	1	1	1	1	Y
6	1	1	0	1	Y
7	0	1	0	0	N
8	0	0	1	1	N
9	1	0	1	0	Y
10	1	1	0	1	N

The data in Table 3-5 represents about 10 emails, and we are basing our decision on the email being spam based on the occurrence of four words. (Note that this is just for the purposes of this exercise. Normally, a simplified set like this would not be enough to build a decent spam filter.)

Let y represent the classification of an email. Now, assume we have the following email parameters for a new email that we want to classify:

Email #11 contains the words (Cash x 2, Won x 1, and Bank x 1)

The first thing we need to do is calculate the probability of an email being spam or not. We can use any parameter to calculate this, but if we go by our dataset, we have five emails that are spam and five that are not. Hence:

$P(y_{spam}) = 5 / 10 = 0.5$

$P(y_{not\text{-}spam}) = 5 / 10 = 0.5$

Now let's calculate the probability of each word occurring when an email is spam and when an email is not spam. Figure 3-41 shows the frequency distribution for each word.

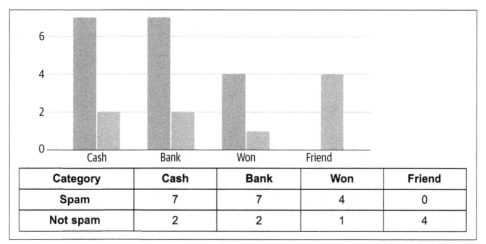

Category	Cash	Bank	Won	Friend
Spam	7	7	4	0
Not spam	2	2	1	4

Figure 3-41. Frequency distribution for email dataset

The corresponding probabilities (likelihoods) for each word occurring given whether the email is spam or not are shown in Figure 3-42.

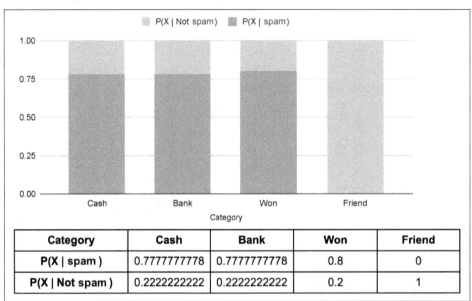

Category	Cash	Bank	Won	Friend
P(X | spam)	0.7777777778	0.7777777778	0.8	0
P(X | Not spam)	0.2222222222	0.2222222222	0.2	1

Figure 3-42. Probability of being spam or not

Our new email has the following attributes:

Cash x 2, Won x 1, and Bank x 1

Hence:

P(SPAM | Cashx2,Bank,Won) α P(y_{spam}) . P(Cash|SPAM)^2 . P(Won|SPAM) . P(Bank|SPAM)

P(SPAM | Cashx2,Bank,Won) α 0.5 x 0.78^2 x 0.8 x 0.78 = 0.19

P(notSPAM | Cashx2,Bank,Won) α P($y_{not\text{-}spam}$) . P(Cash|notSPAM)2 . P(Won|not-SPAM) . P(Bank|notSPAM)

P(notSPAM | Cashx2,Bank,Won) α 0.5 x 0.222 x 0.2 x 0.22 = 0.001

Since the max of the two values is 0.19, we would classify this email as spam.

Now let's look at another email:

Email #12 contains the words (Cash x 1, Won x 1, Bank x 1, Friend x 1)

We will apply the same formulas as before:

P(SPAM | Cash,Bank,Won,Friend) α 0.5 × 0.78 × 0.8 × 0.78 × 0 = 0

P(notSPAM | Cash,Bank,Won,Friend) α 0.5 × 0.222 × 0.2 × 0.22 × 1 = 0.001

Because no spam emails in our dataset contain the word *Friend*, any email that has the word *Friend* would be marked as notSPAM. This is referred to as the *zero frequency problem*. To get around this problem, we can add 1 to each element in our dataset. Our newly transformed dataset looks like Table 3-6.

Table 3-6. Adjusting for the zero frequency problem

Email #	Cash	Bank	Won	Friend	Spam
1	3	2	2	1	Y
2	1	1	1	2	N
3	2	4	1	1	Y
4	2	1	1	2	N
5	2	2	3	1	Y
6	2	3	1	1	Y
7	1	2	1	1	N
8	1	1	2	2	N
9	3	1	2	1	Y
10	2	2	1	2	N

Category	Cash	Bank	Won	Friend
Spam	12	12	9	5
Not spam	7	7	6	9
Category	Cash	Bank	Won	Friend
P(X | SPAM)	0.6315789474	0.6315789474	0.6	0.3571428571
P(X | Not SPAM)	0.3684210526	0.3684210526	0.4	0.6428571429

Now, if we reprocess the same problem again:

Email #12 contains the words (Cash x 1, Won x 1, Bank x 1, Friend x 1)

and if we apply the same formulas as before:

P(SPAM | Cash,Bank,Won,Friend) α 0.5 × 0.63 × 0.6 × 0.63 × 0.36 = 0.043

P(notSPAM | Cash,Bank,Won,Friend) α 0.5 × 0.37 × 0.4 × 0.37 × 0.64 = 0.017

the greater value indicates that this email is also spam.

As you start implementing Naive Bayes algorithms, depending on the problem you are addressing you are likely to run into one or more of the following Naive Bayes classifiers:

Bernoulli Naive Bayes classifier
> This is used in problem statements where the predictors (features) in the dataset can only take binary values. For example, is the fruit red or not? The algorithm is capable of classifying into more than two categories, so you could have a set of apples, oranges, and pears, for instance.

Multinomial Naive Bayes classifier
> This can be used where the predictors are measured with discrete counts, such as the spam example we just looked at. The algorithm uses the frequency of the occurrence of the predictors. Even though the detailed example that we went through was a binary classification (Spam | Not spam), Multinomial Naive Bayes can be used for categorization across more than two categories.

Gaussian Naive Bayes classifier
> This is used when we have predictors that are continuous values rather than discrete categories. In such a case, we assume that the predictor sample has been extracted from a normal distribution (Figure 3-43).

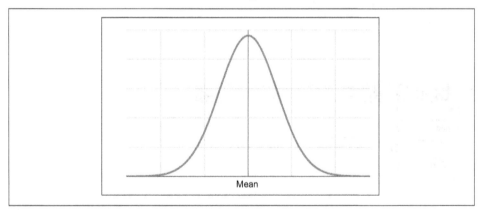

Figure 3-43. Gaussian distribution

The formula for calculating the individual probabilities of the predictors (x_i) changes to the following:

$$P(x_i | y) = \frac{1}{\sqrt{2\Pi \sigma_y^2}} exp\left(-\frac{(x_i - \mu)^2}{2\sigma_y^2} \right)$$

The preceding formula is driven from the probability density function for a normal distribution:

Mean:

$$\mu = \frac{1}{n} \sum_{i=1}^{n} x_i$$

Standard deviation:

$$\sigma = \left[\frac{1}{n-1} \sum_{i=1}^{n} (x_i - \mu)^2 \right]^{0.5}$$

Normal distribution:

$$f(x) = \frac{1}{\sqrt{2\Pi}\sigma} e^{-\frac{(x-\mu)^2}{2\sigma^2}}$$

Note that the preceding probabilities formula is used to calculate the probabilities of individual predictors and not the final classification. Once these probabilities are calculated, they can be plugged into the formula(s) discussed earlier for classification.

The simplicity of the algorithm makes it easy to implement. Of the two conditions we discussed earlier, having independent predictors is usually a challenge in real-life situations. In theory, this would impact the efficacy and performance of the classifier. Having said that, the Naive Bayes classifier is successfully used across many use cases, among them weather forecasting, fraud analysis, and spam detection.

Other Learning Patterns in Machine Learning

There are different types of machine learning. The choice of method is usually driven by what kind of data we are dealing with, how we have obtained it, and how we intend to use it in our specific use case. While the use cases can be distinctly classified into different categories, you should not be surprised to find the same ML algorithms applied to more than one category of learning. Up until now, the majority of our discussions have revolved around the first pattern, known as supervised learning. We start with a training dataset that contains two components:

Features (predictors)
    The data fields used to make predictions (e.g., the age and gender of a penguin)

Labels (predicted)
    The data field that needs to be predicted (e.g., the species of a penguin)

Data that contains both features and labels is known as *labeled data*. Labeled data plays a crucial role in the training of our data model. Once we are satisfied with our data model, we use a test dataset to understand how our model works with previously unseen data. The test dataset also contains both the features and corresponding labels. We employ the model to predict values for the labels and then compare these with the actual values to determine the efficacy of the data model.

Supervised learning refers to the practice of using labeled data to train and test our data models, allowing us to make predictions based on the information provided by these models. This approach applies to both regression and classification problems, which are two common types of tasks within the realm of supervised learning. This kind of learning is widely used in several industries. Predicting flight times based on traffic segmentation and weather conditions, classifying emails as spam, analyzing sentiment in text, weather forecasting, and predicting price fluctuations on commodities are all examples of supervised learning.

In contrast, another type of learning involves starting with unlabeled data. Unlabeled data is utilized without human supervision to uncover previously unknown patterns within a dataset. This particular ML pattern is known as *unsupervised learning*. Several types of unsupervised learning can be applied across various use cases. For creating groups within a dataset based on similarities (or differences), we can use *clustering*. As new data comes in, a trained (clustered) model can be used to identify the cluster that the new data belongs to. Once a cluster is assigned, further analysis can be done on the data (Figure 3-44).

Another form of unsupervised learning commonly used for providing recommendations is known as *association*. This technique builds association rules by understanding the relationships between different entities and how strong the associations are. Unsupervised learning can also be used to reduce the number of features in a dataset without compromising its integrity. This process is known as *dimensionality reduction*.

Unsupervised learning is also widely used in recommendation engines based on a history of interactions. It can be used for anomaly detection for previously unknown patterns in network intrusion systems and fraud detection. Customer segmentation is also a common use case for this pattern. Another problem often solved using clustering is semi-supervised learning. This learning pattern is used to automate the labeling of large amounts of unlabeled data based on a small subset of labeled data.

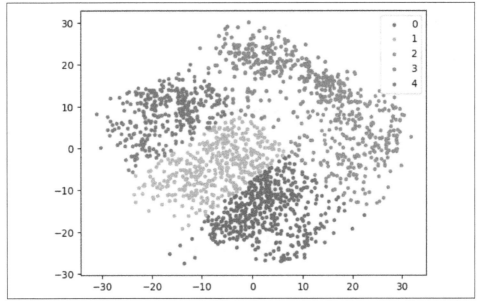

Figure 3-44. Example of clustering with five clusters

Let's explore a few of the algorithms used in unsupervised learning. Earlier in the chapter, we looked at an example of using the k-means clustering algorithm. We saw how it can be used to create groups out of continuous data when training decision trees. The k-means algorithm works by:

1. Selecting k random centers in a dataset (where k is provided as input).

2. Associating each data point with the center that has the minimum distance from it. All data points associated with a center form a group. Hence, we end up with k groups.

3. Moving to the center within each group to minimize the distance from all data points in that group.

4. Repeating steps 2 and 3 until either the center stops moving or the maximum number of iterations (which can also be provided as input) is reached.

Some other examples of algorithms used in unsupervised learning include Gaussian mixture models, frequent pattern growth, and principal component analysis. Further reading on k-means and Gaussian mixture analysis can be found in *Hands-On Machine Learning with Scikit-Learn, Keras, and TensorFlow*, 2nd Edition, by Aurélien Géron (O'Reilly). Material on principal component analysis can be found in *Feature Engineering for Machine Learning* by Alice Zheng and Amanda Casari (O'Reilly).

The entry barrier to supervised learning is generally low. You can start with small datasets in many algorithms and train and use models without the need for an extensive compute infrastructure. That is not to say that all supervised learning is compute humble. Many use cases using algorithm ensembles and extensive neural networks can warrant specialized compute infrastructure. In contrast, unsupervised learning usually deals with massive amounts of unlabeled data, which can require significant computing hardware resources for processing.

When trying to choose between supervised and unsupervised learning, ask the following questions:

- Are we trying to understand an existing problem?
- Are we trying to discover previously unknown patterns in data?
- Are we working with labeled data or unlabeled data?
- Is human intervention feasible when working with this data?

There is another category of experience-based learning systems. These systems do not depend on any preexisting data; rather, they generate this data based on experiments. The goal of experience-based learning is to maximize long-term output. This learning pattern is known as *reinforcement learning*.

There are use cases of reinforcement learning in robotics, self-driving cars, and evaluating trading strategies, among other areas. Reinforcement learning can be policy based, model based, or value based. Some algorithms used in reinforcement learning include Deep Q-Networks (DQN), State-Action-Reward-State-Action (SARSA), Asynchronous Advantage Actor-Critic Algorithm (A3C), and Deep Deterministic Policy Gradient (DDPG). You can read more about DQN and SARSA in *Foundations of Deep Reinforcement Learning: Theory and Practice in Python* by Laura Graesser and Wah Loon Keng (Addison-Wesley).

 In enterprises, deploying reinforcement learning encounters hurdles due to intricate algorithms, substantial data needs, and the necessity for precise environment modeling. Training these models demands significant computational resources and time, prompting concerns regarding safety, reliability, and interpretability. Integrating reinforcement learning into existing systems and ensuring compliance with regulations adds further complexity to deployment. Nonetheless, ongoing advancements aim to mitigate these challenges and facilitate the effective adoption of reinforcement learning in enterprise contexts.

Conclusion

In this chapter, we discussed the fundamental concepts behind ML algorithms commonly used in predictive analytics. While we covered some of these in more detail than others, the idea was to establish the building blocks that will allow you to build a strong foundation. As the book progresses, we will cover implementation of more than one of these algorithms. When we are dealing with the implementation of ML models, more often than not the model itself is treated as a service that performs its function, without really getting into the details of how it actually achieves it. It is my intention to connect these foundations to the implementation of the corresponding models so that you can fully appreciate how ML models help achieve predictive analytics. With this in mind, hopefully we can move past the parameter tuning approach, establish a sounder understanding, and ideally be in a position to expand on the discussed use cases.

## CHAPTER 4

Working with Data

Frequently, we are eager to build, train, and use machine learning (ML) models, finding it exciting to deploy them to determine what works and what doesn't. The result is immediate, and the reward is satisfying. What is often ignored or not discussed enough is data preprocessing. In this chapter, we will explore various datatypes, delving into the significance of data preprocessing and feature engineering as well as their associated techniques and best practices. We will also discuss the concept of bias in data. The chapter will conclude with an explanation of the predictive analytics pipeline and some best practices around selecting and working with ML models.

Understanding Data

Enterprises traditionally store data in databases and flat files, so we'll start the chapter by exploring the basics of a traditional relational database.

A relational database stores data in one or more tables. Tables have rows that represent data records and columns that represent individual features. With a customer database, for example, each row could represent a different customer, and you might have columns for customer_ID, name, and phone number.

When determining what columns to include in a table, there are certain things to keep in mind. For instance, if one million customers in your database reside in Pakistan and you store country data as part of the customer record, you will be storing Pakistan one million times. As another example, if you store your customers' social media information and some of your customers aren't active on social media, some of your records will have empty fields. Table 4-1 shows an example of both scenarios.

Table 4-1. Relational database table with data duplication and empty fields

ID	Name	Phone	City	Country	Instagram	Twitter
1	John Doe	+111222333	Los Angeles	USA	@Doe1	<Empty>
2	Kareem K	+923334445	Karachi	Pakistan	<Empty>	@Kareem
3	A Ali	+9211111111	Lahore	Pakistan	@AAli	@Aali
...		...	...	...	...	...
1000000	Master Yoda	+6611122211	Pattaya	Thailand	@TheYoda	<Empty>

Empty fields and data duplication result in storage and performance issues. To avoid this situation, a relational database would split, or *normalize*, this data into two tables: one for country and one for social media, as shown in Figure 4-1.

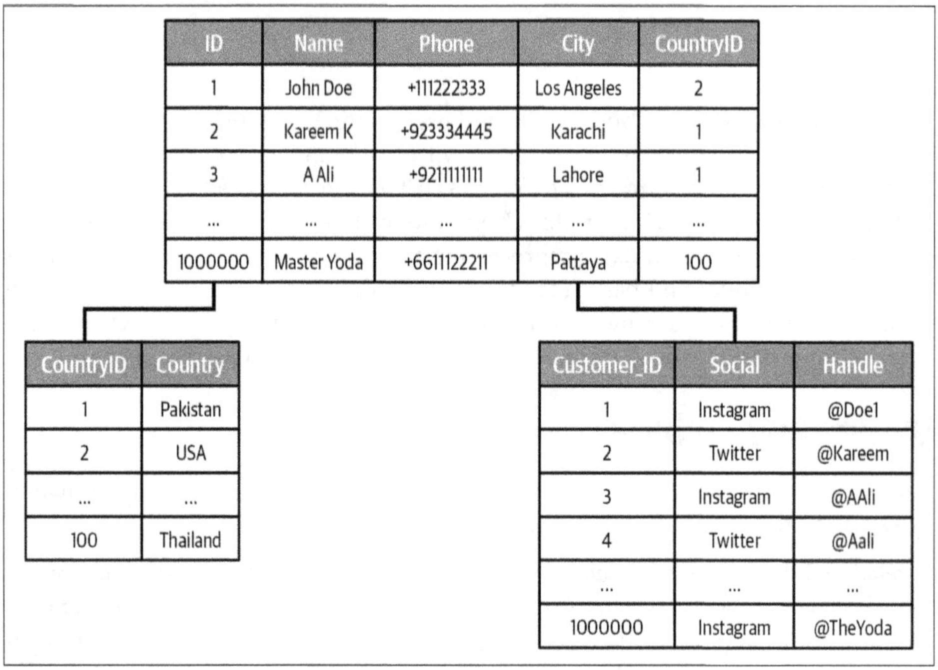

Figure 4-1. Database normalization example

Figure 4-1 represents just one of many possible ways we can normalize data. Tables that have been normalized are joined to each other by relationships that allow us to write data to and fetch data from them. Often when dealing with relational database sources, we will be working with normalized data with tens, hundreds, or even thousands of tables. Another family of database management systems, known as NoSQL, are optimal in these cases because they can handle and store large volumes of data and can be scaled to accommodate growing volumes of data.

There are hundreds of types of relational databases, and you can learn more about them on the DB-Engines website (*https://oreil.ly/JyQEP*). In this chapter, we will cover a few of the more prevalent ones.

We'll start with *key-value stores*, which store data in a simple key-value format. In a key-value store, the preceding customer data can be stored as follows:

```
Customer_ID - 1
Name - John Doe
Phone - +111222333
City - Los Angeles
Country - USA
Instagram - @Doe
Twitter - NA
```

Redis and Memcached are among the many examples of key-value databases available today. Cloud providers also provide their own key-value database services using multimodel services such as AWS DynamoDB.

Another interesting database is known as a *document store*. Some common examples include MongoDB, CouchDB, Couchbase, and Firestore. The structure of a document store is much richer than that of a key-value store in terms of how it stores and represents data. The following code is an example of a document store of a customer record:

```
{
Customer_ID: 1
Name:
    {
        First: John,
        Last: Doe
    },
Phone: +111222333,
Address:
{
City:    Los Angeles,
Country: USA
}
Social:
[
Instagram : @Doe
]
}
```

There are many other NoSQL databases, such as wide column, search engine, and time series. Data within databases will come in all sorts of shapes and sizes, and we need to bring this data into a format that can be used to feed and train our models.

Data can also be stored in flat files; for example, IoT sensor data sitting on an object store. This data could be in many formats, including CSV, Parquet, JSON, or XML. Or it could be unstructured data, such as PDF files, audio and video recordings, and other binary data. In most cases, we are less interested in the files themselves and more interested in the metadata they contain, such as the content of a PDF, the topic and views of a video file, and so on. While this data is often sitting in a database from which it can be fed to an ML model, machine learning can also be used to interpret and classify unstructured data, which means you can use one model to preprocess unstructured data and use another model to draw conclusions from the data.

In short, real-world data comes in all shapes and sizes and is often riddled with errors. We may encounter missing data and duplicate data, or perhaps data formats that our ML libraries don't support. Data preprocessing and feature engineering allow us to ensure that we are feeding high-quality data to our predictive analytics models, and they help us identify and, in some cases, create data points that can help us understand the relationship between the data we have and the values we are trying to predict.

Data Preprocessing and Feature Engineering

Data preprocessing enables us to bring in data in a form that is supported by our predictive analytics models and that can be processed efficiently. *Feature engineering* is the process of creating, transforming, and selecting features to improve the performance of ML models. Let's dive into some data problems and see how to address them.

Handling Missing Data

Missing data can be addressed in several ways:

Drop the records that are missing values.
> This is the simplest way to deal with missing data. However, we must understand whether dropping records will create a bias in our data. Even though values for one feature might be missing, another feature might be contributing significantly to the model train.

Replace empty values with zero(s).
> In most cases, this will remove the programmatic error caused by missing values during training. Consider the data for an IoT sensor that sends a 0 when it does not detect light and a 1 when it does detect light. In this case, 0 signifies an event, and putting a dummy 0 in the record can alter the interpretation of the data.

Replace the data with the mean value from the set.
> Let's say we are dealing with a feature representing the scores of students in a particular subject across a particular country. Replacing empty scores with mean values would be a good estimation in such a case. Other statistical measures, such as median and mode, can also be used in certain cases.

Predict the missing values.

We can use another model to predict the missing values by making the attribute with the missing values the label, provided that there are other attributes that can be used to come up with such a prediction.

Categorical Data Encoding

Certain ML models work with specific types of data. Consider the following data in a training dataset:

```
Property_type: ( apartment, townhouse, villa )
```

In this case, a numerical model is unable to interpret the "apartment", "townhouse", and "villa" strings. However, if we are building a model to predict the rental prices for a properties database, Property_type would be an important feature to consider while training the model. As such, we can replace these categorical string values with numerical figures.

There are several ways to encode features. *One-hot encoding* is one of the most common ways to encode features in machine learning. One-hot encoding creates a separate column for each category of the feature. It marks the column with a 1 when the category exists in a record and a 0 when it does not. Table 4-2 is an example of one-hot encoding on the properties database.

Table 4-2. One-hot encoding

Apartment	Townhouse	Villa
1	0	0
0	0	1
0	1	0

Another simple way to encode a categorical feature is to use *label encoding*, in which each label is replaced by a number. Continuing with the properties database example, if we used the numbers 1, 2, and 3 to represent apartments, townhouses, and villas, respectively, the model might infer that there is some order (of magnitude or otherwise) when it comes to these categories. So it is better to use label encoding when we understand that the categories are unordered or when we are dealing with a binary category with "yes" and "no" values.

In addition to these two types of encoding, we could apply other mathematical techniques, such as converting each category to its binary representation and then having a separate column for each digit of the binary, or using a random hash function to convert the category strings into numbers.

Data Transformation

When dealing with multiple features, we want to ensure that one feature does not overshadow the others. Say our properties dataset includes features for the square footage and price of different properties. While the square footage could be in the hundreds or thousands, the price could be in the millions. When training a model in this case, the price would overshadow the square footage simply because it is represented by a larger numerical scale.

To address this problem, we can use scalers, which would help bring the features to a similar scale. Some commonly used scalers include the following:

Z-score normalization
> This scaler subtracts the mean of the feature from the value and then divides the result by the standard deviation. This helps scale the feature to a normal distribution, with a mean of 0 and a standard deviation of 1.

Min-max scaler
> A min-max scaler brings the scales of multiple features within a common range. For example, we can select a range of 0 to 1 and then use a min-max scaler to scale all the respective features to this range.

Max-abs scaler
> A max-abs scaler scales a feature to its maximum absolute value. As a result, the transformation range for the transformed feature is between –1 and 1. If there are no negative values, the range is from 0 to 1; in this way, the max-abs scaler would act similarly to a min-max scaler with a range of 0 to 1.

Outlier Management

Outliers are data points that do not conform to the overall pattern of the feature's value distribution. Outliers can adversely impact the training and consequently the predictive capability of the model, as the model would be working on a deviated predictive range. To understand outlier detection, let's discuss a few related terms:

Interquartile range (IQR)
> This is where the middle 50% in a dataset lives, or the difference between the 75th percentile and the 25th percentile in the data.

Outliers
> These are data points that are outside the following range:
>
> Minimum = Q1 - IQR*1.5 $\longleftrightarrow$ Maximum = Q3 + IQR*1.5

Figure 4-2 shows an example of interquartile range and outliers. In the figure, Q1 represents the 25th percentile and Q3 represents the 75th percentile.

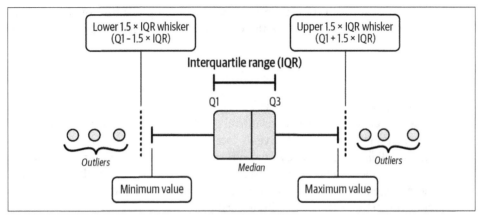

Figure 4-2. Interquartile range and outliers

When managing the impact of outliers, consider the following:

- Outliers can be filtered out using the maximum and minimum ranges. When filtering outliers, it is important to understand the information loss that would occur as a result of the filtering. The goal should be to filter out only outliers that are the result of erroneous data.

- You can replace outliers with maximum or minimum values to reduce their impact on model training.

- Other transformations, such as logging and binning, can be used to minimize the impact of outliers.

- Outliers can also be treated as a separate category of data and then used as part of a layered modeling approach to ensure that the model does not lose the information contained in the outliers.

Handling Imbalanced Data

Imbalanced data can occur when the number of samples of one category far outnumber the number of samples of another category. Using such a dataset as is for training would result in severely biased prediction models. An example of unbalanced data can be seen with fraudulent credit card transactions, where legitimate transactions far outnumber fraudulent ones. You can handle such an imbalance in the following ways:

- Apply a larger weight to the minority class sample. This would increase the impact of the individual sample within the minority class to offset the ratio imbalance in the number of samples.

- Oversample the minority class by synthetically generating additional minority class samples until the desired class ratio is achieved.

- Undersample the majority class by randomly selecting a subset of the majority class from the dataset to achieve the desired ratio of samples with the minority class.

Combining Data

Data in a predictive analytics model can be consumed from one or more data sources. For example, the data from a single relational database could be sitting across multiple tables, which means we would have to combine the data before we can use it for model training. Relational databases provide joins as a way to combine data sitting across multiple tables. Depending on the database technology and the size of the tables, a join can be an expensive operation. Some technologies also allow us to perform joins across tables sitting in multiple databases.

Taking this a step further, we might need to combine data from different types of data sources, such as IoT databases, relational databases, object storage, and other NoSQL databases. Such a data pipeline would consist of the source systems, the target ML platform, and an intermediary that can expose the data to the ML platform the way it needs it. This process of moving data is often known as *ETL* (short for Extract, Transform, and Load) or *ELT* (short for Extract, Load, and Transform). Figure 4-3 shows an example of such a pipeline.

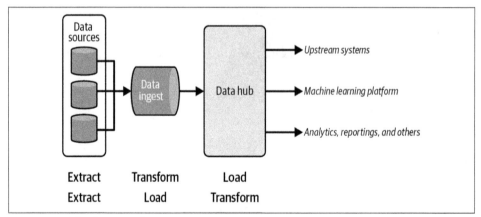

Figure 4-3. The data pipeline

In a typical data pipeline, data is extracted from the data sources and transformed from the source into a format that can be used at the destination. Then the data is loaded into a central repository that is capable of exposing this data to several upstream systems, including ML platforms, to help with predictive analytics. Several commercial ETL tools are available that support numerous data sources, including both commercial and open source options. Several of these are also available as cloud services. Most cloud providers also supply their own variations of ETL services. These tools allow you to capture small data changes in the source systems and then reflect the changes in the target data hub.

Another category of data movement tools are systems that constantly move data from the source to the target using data streams. While the data can be exposed directly to ML platforms, most mature organizations build some sort of data hub to consume the data for several use cases, including use in other upstream systems and reporting scenarios. They also serve as the foundation for ML pipelines.

Feature Selection

As we look at our dataset, we need to ensure that we are selecting the correct features for model training. For example, using too many features can make the training and processing inefficient and can negatively impact its accuracy. In addition, certain features can be redundant, and dropping them would not impact the predictive power of the model, while others can be irrelevant, in that there really isn't much correlation between the feature and the label that needs to be predicted. A few techniques can help us perform feature selection.

A common technique is *correlation analysis*. This process looks at the correlation between each feature and the label to determine which features should be selected. Note that correlation analysis works well for linear relationships but can underestimate the importance of nonlinear relationships. Nonlinear relationships can take various forms, such as quadratic, exponential, logarithmic, or sinusoidal patterns, among others. In these cases, the relationship between variables changes at varying rates, leading to more complex patterns when visualized on a graph. Also, as correlation analysis considers each feature in isolation, it is unable to gauge the impact of a third variable that might be impacting both the feature and the label. Therefore, while correlation analysis is a valuable tool for exploring relationships between variables, it is essential to recognize its limitations, particularly in contexts where nonlinear relationships may be prevalent. For nonlinear relationships, a better measure is mutual information represented by the mi_score, which would enable us to understand how much variation of one variable is predictable by the other.

A second technique worthy of mention is *principal component analysis* (PCA). This technique converts the original features into a set of uncorrelated variables known as *principal components*. By selecting a subset of the principal components that are most apt in terms of data variance, we can perform dimensionality reduction on the training dataset without losing important predictive information.

A third technique, known as *forward selection*, starts with a minimal set of features and then measures the model's performance in terms of prediction. At each iteration, it adds a feature and measures the performance again. In the end, it selects the set of features with the highest prediction scores.

Finally, *backward selection* is similar to forward selection, but it starts with all possible features and eliminates a feature at each iteration until it gets to an optimal prediction score.

Splitting Preprocessed Data

Once the data is ready for training, it is a best practice to split it into the following sets:

Training set
> This is usually the largest chunk of the data (70% or more) used for training the predictive analytics model.

Validation set
> This is a smaller set of data used during training to perform model selection and to fine-tune the model and its hyperparameters.

Testing set
> This data is used to independently gauge the model's performance on unseen data. It is imperative that the testing set be used once the model is trained and fine-tuned as an independent test. It should not be used during the model selection and training cycles.

Understanding Bias

We touched on bias earlier in the chapter. Here, we will discuss what it is and how it impacts our predictive analytics models.

Bias can be explained as the deviation of our model's predictions from actual values in the real world. A model that has a high bias would generally perform poorly for both training and test sets. So ideally we would want to reduce bias. But to do that we should understand some of the common reasons we see bias in the first place. Consider the following scenarios:

An unbalanced training dataset for fraudulent bank transactions, where 1% of the data represents fraudulent transactions and 99% of the data represents legitimate transactions
> With this data, the model has very little information on the fraudulent transactions and can learn to optimize the cost function by marking all transactions as legitimate. Note that the imbalance in the data is not a mistake, as a normal dataset would ideally have very few fraudulent transactions.

A dataset that is not representative of the real world
> Consider a model trained on a dataset of an all-girls school to identify top performers. The model might learn that all top performers are girls and therefore would not generalize well to other unseen datasets.

A dataset whose data is historically biased
> The model would learn and perpetuate this bias. Imagine an organization that is striving to improve diversity among its workforce. If the model were trained on successful candidates from the organization's own historical data, it is likely that the model predictions would inherit the very diversity issue the organization is trying to resolve.

Incorrect assumptions during model selection
> Selecting a linear model to predict a relationship that is nonlinear would result in higher deviation between the predicted and real values, resulting in an underfitted model. Similarly, overly complex or overly trained models would perform well on training data but poorly on test and other previously unseen data. Such models would be suffering from overfitting.

The particular time frame of the training data and whether the same underlying assumptions apply in the period for which we want to perform our predictive analysis
> This can occur when dealing with time series data such as IoT information or stock prices.

While it might not be possible to completely rid your models of bias, there are certain steps you can take to reduce bias and get robust model performance and predictions:

- Technical factors:
  - When dealing with unbalanced data, you can preprocess the data to generate synthetic samples of the underrepresented class, resulting in a more balanced training dataset.
  - You can attach larger weights to the underrepresented class in the model during the training process.
  - Model selection can be a technical process where we select the models that are apt for a certain problem set. Data analysis is of utmost importance to understand the relationship between the features and the labels and to select the appropriate model. A regular regression model would fit well for a linear relationship, while it might be better to use a polynomial regression model or a neural network for a nonlinear relationship.
  - If a model is overfitting, then using cross validation can help evaluate the model across multiple splits of training and testing data to ensure better generalization.

- Nontechnical factors:

  — Understand the data collection process to ensure that any early collection bias is identified and, if possible, reduced at collection time.

  — Get domain experts involved to study the data before it is used to train the models. We want to identify any inherent bias that is historically present in the data. A discussion ought to be had between technical teams and domain experts to not only identify the bias but also understand whether it is logical to use the data as is and, if not, to discuss different strategies to reduce the bias without impacting the correctness of the model.

The Predictive Analytics Pipeline

An ML (or predictive analytics) pipeline represents the end-to-end process that allows us to create and offer trained models for consumption by other services. So far in this book we have talked about and in many cases implemented several stages of this pipeline (see Figure 4-4).

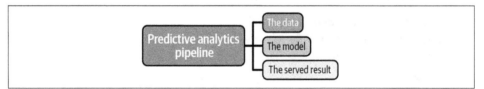

Figure 4-4. The predictive analytics pipeline

The combination of the data and the model contributes to generating actionable predictions for our business. As we expand each stage of the pipeline, we will see a more detailed set of stages that feed into each other.

The Data Stage

Figure 4-5 depicts a data stage that starts at the data source and concludes when the data is in a state where it can be used to train the ML model.

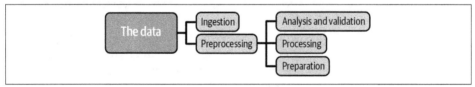

Figure 4-5. The data stage of the predictive analytics pipeline

The data stage begins with ingesting the data from relevant sources using ETL, change data capture (CDC), or other streaming techniques that we discussed earlier in the chapter. As the data is ingested, irrelevant data is discarded and preliminary transformations such as deduplication or denormalization are applied to the data.

Next, the data is analyzed to validate its integrity; that is, to make sure the data is accurate, complete, and consistent. For example, say you were ingesting sales data from a customer relationship management system. You would want to ensure that the data, once ingested, is not corrupted. You would also want to ensure that the data pertains to the time duration you are aiming for with the model, and if you're pulling data from various sources, you'd want to ensure that these sources maintain consistency in terms of time frame and the entities for which the data is being imported. Data can also be studied at this stage to understand any bias that might exist in the data and decide how to cater to it at later stages of the pipeline.

The processing stage then performs any further transformations that are needed on the data, such as categorical data encoding, outlier management, or removing bias for imbalanced data. (We talked about a number of these processes in "Data Preprocessing and Feature Engineering" on page 114.) When the data is ready, you can perform feature selection for the model and split the data into training, validation, and test sets.

The Model Stage

Now that we've prepared the data, we can use the features and labels to train the model. Training the model simply means finding the best fit of the model for the data provided to it. The training process does this by identifying different weights and biases (depending on the type of the ML model). Additionally, there are certain hyperparameters of the model that can be controlled by the user. We already discussed several of these earlier in this book, among them the learning rate, the number of trees in a random forest, n_estimators in a random forest, and the number of hidden layers in a neural network. These hyperparameters can be adjusted during the model validation stage to achieve better performance. The model's performance can be evaluated using the validation set or techniques such as k-folds cross validation, discussed earlier.

Once we are happy with the model and its evaluation metrics for the training and validation data, we can perform model evaluation on test data that is set aside during the data preparation stage. This tells us how well our model generalizes on previously unseen data and is a measure of how well the model might perform in a production environment.

Figure 4-6 depicts the stage of our model at this point. If we are happy with the model evaluation, we can push the model to production. Otherwise, we can go back to the beginning of the model stage for further introspection and optimization.

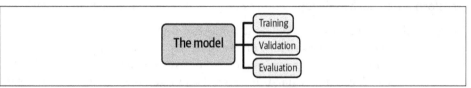

Figure 4-6. The model stage of the predictive analytics pipeline

The Serving Stage

The end result of the model stage is a trained model that can be used to perform predictions on production data. Called the serving stage, this stage consists of two components, as shown in Figure 4-7.

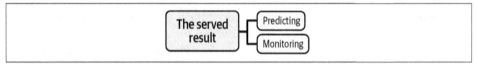

Figure 4-7. The serving stage of the predictive analytics pipeline

An application or a service can consume a model immediately. This means it can query the model directly with a set of features to obtain a prediction. While this method provides the greatest number of real-time predictions, it can have performance implications, especially if the prediction services need to scale to cater to high-volume workloads.

An alternative that is often used when serving predictions is to perform pre-predictions using a range of feature combinations, and then storing the prediction results in a database. Third-party services that need to access these predictions can query the database for predictions rather than going to the model. Modern databases support distributed horizontal scaling, which allows them to serve high-volume workloads at speed. Note that the use case should be such that it can be handled using a finite number of feature combinations for predictions. In the case of continuous data, ranges can be used if needed. Also, there needs to be a mechanism to regularly refresh the predictions in the database from the predictive analytics model.

A predictive analytics model should not be static. To achieve a model that evolves over time, as part of the serving stage we need to perform model monitoring. There are several aspects to consider when it comes to monitoring. The most important of these is the performance of the predictions versus the actual data. There needs to be a way to understand how accurate the model predictions are over time. This would give us a sense of the accuracy of the model and help identify issues earlier in the business cycle.

It is also important to monitor the delivery performance of the serving platform. If predictions are being served directly, we need to ensure that the infrastructure (CPU, memory, disk, IOPS, etc.) of the underlying systems is sufficient and the query response times are acceptable. The same needs to be done when the predictions are being served via an intermediary, such as a database. In this case, however, we would be looking at a different set of matrices to ensure database performance. We can monitor prediction performance at a much deeper level, such as monitoring the performance for each market segment or demographic. This would allow us to better understand the performance and help identify any bias that might exist in the training data.

Model monitoring should also be able to identify how the data distribution in production compares to the distribution used for training the model. If the distribution differs significantly, it is likely that model performance is degraded. Understanding changes in data distribution can help retrain models so that they are a better fit for the business's current data situation.

Finally, for monitoring to have an impact on the model, there needs to be a feedback loop from the monitoring substage back to the data stage so that the observations can be used to fine-tune and train the next version of the model (see Figure 4-8).

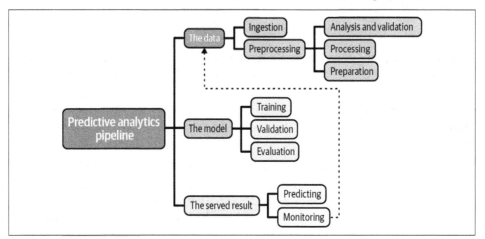

Figure 4-8. Feedback loop of the predictive analytics pipeline

Other Components

A couple of additional components worth mentioning include the feature store and model registry.

Feature store

Predictive analytics pipelines will often use a *feature store*. While the capabilities of the feature store will vary across implementations, the main purpose of a feature store is to provide a central repository where features can be stored and managed.

Different stages of the pipeline can access a feature store for different purposes. For example, you can use the feature store to combine and serve features from multiple sources to a predictive analytics model for training. You can also use a feature store to store historical features and offer them to data scientists and engineers for analysis and comparison. These historical features can sometimes be used to augment existing data for model training and evaluation.

Having a feature store makes it easy to catalog and version features and make them available to models at different times. Once the features are commoditized, they can be mixed and matched and used by multiple models, thus significantly reducing the effort involved in feature engineering for each model. The feature store also allows applications that do not explicitly compute features to make predictions based on features provided by other sources.

Model registry

Much like the feature store, the *model registry* is also a catalog, but for predictive analytics models. It helps store multiple versions of models in a central repository. From the registry, specific versions of the model can be checked out to serve to production, copied, updated, and compared with other versions. Some registries also allow recording of different model metrics with regard to performance and associated metadata.

The model registry becomes a significant part of a predictive analytics pipeline where models can be promoted across different stages, such as development, quality assurance (QA), user acceptance testing (UAT), and production. Much like with software versioning and release, updates to a model can be used to trigger automated workflows for model deployment and serving.

Selecting the Right Model

In the realm of machine learning, the allure of opting for the most intricate or cutting-edge models may be strong. However, it's important to note that this isn't always the most advisable path forward. A guiding principle commonly used in machine learning is Occam's Razor, attributed to the philosopher William of Ockham. It suggests that among competing hypotheses, the one with the fewest assumptions should be selected. In the context of ML models, Occam's Razor translates to the idea that simpler models are preferred over complex ones when both achieve similar levels of performance.

Let's go through some considerations regarding model selection:

Complexity versus performance
Increasing the complexity of a model may not always lead to better performance. While complex models might capture intricate patterns in the data, they can also suffer from overfitting, where the model learns noise in the training data rather than the underlying patterns, making it difficult to generalize the patterns on previously unseen data.

Ability to interpret how the model works
Simpler models are often more interpretable, making it easier for the user to understand how the models come up with predictions. Industries such as finance and healthcare put stringent requirements on transparency and interpretability of the prediction process, which is difficult to achieve with complex models.

Generalization
Simple models are more likely to generalize well to unseen data, compared to complex models. They are less prone to overfitting the training data and can capture the underlying patterns that are consistent across different datasets.

Computational efficiency
Simpler models tend to be computationally more efficient, requiring less time and fewer resources for training and inference. This can be advantageous in scenarios where resources are limited or the use case requires real-time decision making.

In essence, Occam's Razor urges practitioners to prioritize simple, interpretable models that effectively generalize to new data. This approach promotes transparency, efficiency, and improved decision making in ML applications.

Conclusion

When working with predictive analytics, it is imperative to understand the importance of data. Too often we see a focus on model building and execution, and a lack of focus on data analysis and processing. In this chapter, we covered various aspects of working with data for predictive analytics. While we already covered most of these topics in earlier chapters, I wanted to bring all of them together from a theoretical standpoint so that you can refer back to them, relate the seemingly disparate steps, and understand their sequence and usage throughout the predictive analytics pipeline. We also talked about the operationalization of predictive analytics using pipelines and the core components that enable this delivery. I kept the chapter technology agnostic to allow you to map this to whatever set of frameworks and tools you are using in your organization.

## CHAPTER 5

Python and scikit-learn for Predictive Analytics

We started our journey with a brief history of data analytics. We discussed the importance of predictive analytics in the modern enterprise, and we covered some industry use cases to appreciate the real-world implications of its implementation. We then took a slightly deep dive into the statistics and mathematics behind different predictive analytics algorithms (if you are a diver, you can think of that as a 10-meter dive rather than a 100-meter deep sea exploration). I am a big proponent of strong foundations. I believe that once you have a strong grasp of the foundation, you can learn and understand the details much more easily, even though they can evolve over time. Now that we have the analytics foundation established, in this chapter we will get our hands dirty with some actual predictions.

Anaconda and Jupyter Notebooks

This is a hands-on chapter. If you are a data science professional or student, the content should be familiar to you. However, even if you are new to data science, the material and sample code should be clear enough for you to understand, so long as you have a basic grasp of computer programming.

We'll need a few prerequisites in place before we begin. These are shown in Table 5-1.

Table 5-1. Prerequisites

Serial #	Name	Description	Version used in this chapter	URL
1	Python	Python is a high-level programming language used heavily in data science.	V3.9.13	*https://www.python.org*
2	Anaconda Navigator	Anaconda provides an environment for working with Python and R for the purpose of machine learning on a single machine.	Anaconda 3 for Python 3.9	*https://www.anaconda.com*
3	Jupyter Notebook	Jupyter Notebook provides a development environment that allows for the creation and sharing of computational documents. Consider computational documents as a way to share step-by-step documentation with code that can be executed in-line. You will get a Jupyter Notebook as part of the Anaconda installation.	V6.4.12	*https://jupyter.org*
4	Desktop computer	Mac, Windows, or Linux	macOS Ventura V13.1	macOS command line: *https://support. apple.com/en-ae/guide/terminal/apdb 66b5242-0d18-49fc-9c47-a2498b7c91 d5/mac*

We will begin by installing Python and Anaconda Navigator. The Jupyter Notebook will be installed as part of the Anaconda installation. Make sure you have a computer that can run Python code and Anaconda Navigator reasonably well. To make sure everything is up and running, run the following command on your command line for your operating system:

```
python --version
Python 3.9.13
```

You should see "version 3.9+." If you can't find Python, it's probably because either it's not installed or you have not sourced the path for Python in your command line. A quick search for your operating system should help you resolve the path issue.

Now make sure Anaconda is working. On your computer, locate the Anaconda Navigator program and launch it. On your GUI, the icon should look similar to the one shown in Figure 5-1.

Figure 5-1. Anaconda Navigator icon

Once you launch Anaconda Navigator, you should land on a screen similar to the one shown in Figure 5-2.

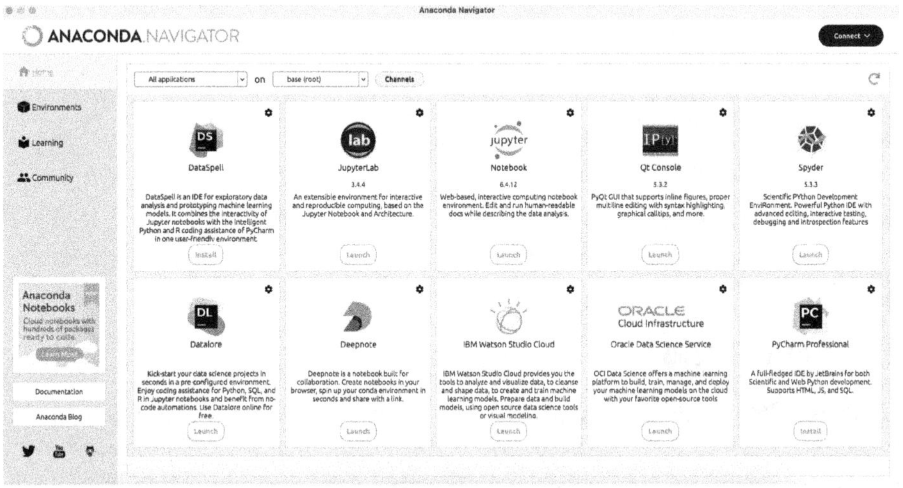

Figure 5-2. Anaconda Navigator home page

Click the Launch button on the Jupyter Notebook tile. You will see a command-line pop-up that will launch a web server. Once the web server has launched successfully, the command line should provide an HTML file that you can open to access the local web server for the notebook, or you can copy the URL, also shown in the command-line pop-up, for the notebook interface (see Figure 5-3).

Once you access the notebook, you should see the interface that lets you create and access computational notebooks.

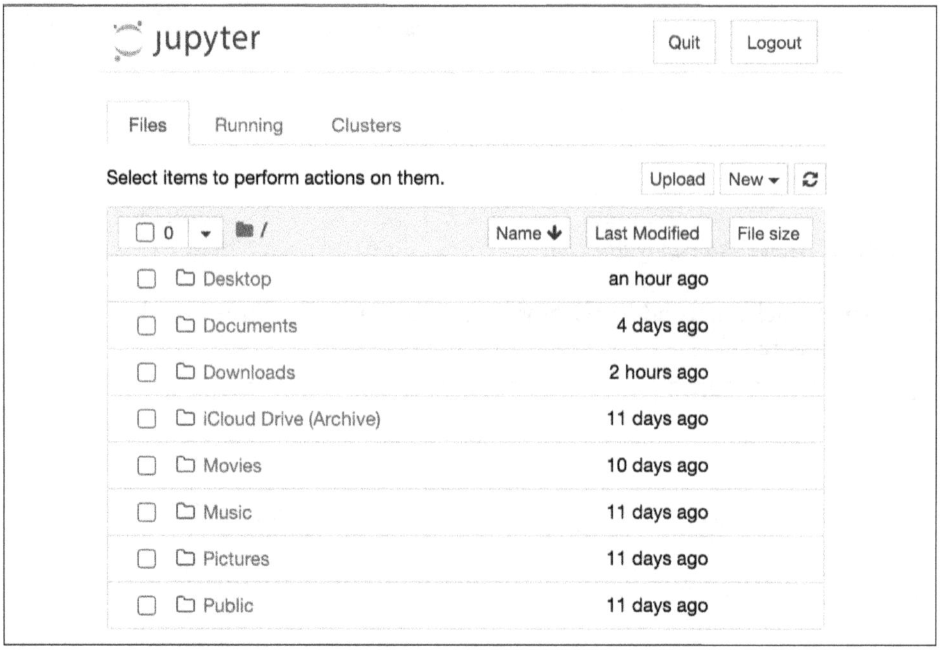

Figure 5-3. Jupyter Notebook interface

NumPy in Python

NumPy is a Python library that provides an *n*-dimensional array object and different functions that can be used on these array objects, including (but not limited to) mathematical, logical, shape manipulation, sorting, selecting, and I/O functions, as well as discrete Fourier transforms, basic linear algebra, basic statistical operations, and random simulation.

In "Statistics and Linear Algebra" on page 46, we discussed how relationships between variables can be represented using equations, and we covered the use of matrices in linear algebra to solve multiple equations. We also discussed how this relates to data science and predictive analytics. It should come as no surprise that NumPy is one of the key packages you will come across when working on data science projects. NumPy brings with it a number of performance optimizations. It only allows for homogeneous datatypes and performs many functions in compiled code to achieve better performance than similar packages, such as the default Python lists.

Introduction to NumPy

In this section, we will go through a few code examples to learn how to use NumPy when working with arrays (matrices). Arrays can be used to represent data. Table 5-2 depicts a dataset that represents the sale of tickets at a cinema across different price categories over the course of a year.

Table 5-2. Cinema ticket sales

Month	Regular	Premium	Gallery
Jan	1000	300	30
Feb	987	400	10
Mar	1003	290	40
...	...	...	...
Dec	1101	400	80

This data can be represented using the following format:

[Jan, Regular] = 1000
[Jan, Premium] = 300
...
[Dec, Gallery] = 80

Therefore, we can consider Table 5-2 to be a two-dimensional array representing ticket sales, where we can use the month and the ticket type as the index to get to the value stored in the block. We can simplify things by representing the ticket types using numbers:

Regular = 0
Premium = 1
Gallery = 2

We can simplify further by representing the months using numbers:

Jan–Dec = 0–11

Now we can get to any value using a coordinate system, as shown in Table 5-3.

Table 5-3. Two-dimensional array

	0	1	2
0	1000	300	30
1	987	400	10
2	1003	290	40
...	...	...	...
11	1101	400	80

If we wanted to know the number of regular tickets sold in March, we could go to the coordinates (2,0), which would give us the value 1003.

Our data is now represented as a two-dimensional matrix. Now let's assume we want to look at data across all the cinemas in a city. If there were 10 cinemas, this data could be represented by 10 two-dimensional arrays, as shown in Figure 5-4.

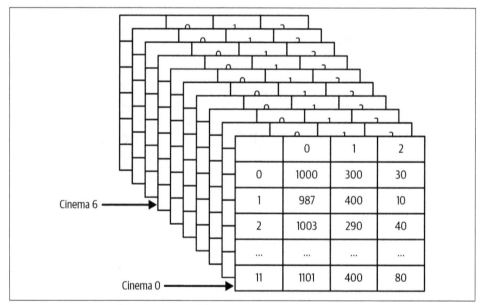

Figure 5-4. Cinema data represented by 10 two-dimensional arrays

These 10 two-dimensional arrays can then be merged into a single three-dimensional array, as shown in Figure 5-5.

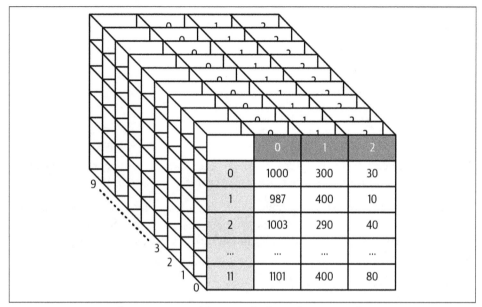

Figure 5-5. Cinema data represented by a single three-dimensional array

If we wanted to know the sales of gallery tickets in cinema 5 in the month of April, we could go to the coordinates (3,2,5) where 3 represents April, 2 represents gallery tickets, and 5 represents cinema 5. Since all the data is now sitting in a single matrix, we can perform fast matrix operations to answer questions such as the following:

- What is the total number of tickets sold across all cinemas in one month?

- How do the sales of regular tickets for cinema 1 compare to those for cinema 7 in the month of June?

- Can I use this data to train a model to predict the sale of tickets for a month in my cinemas?

For the remainder of this section, you can either create your own Jupyter Notebook, use any other Python environment, or download the *Chapter5-Numpy-PAFME.ipynb* notebook from the book's GitHub repository (*https://oreil.ly/VwRwC*) to follow along. If you are new to Python and want to learn more about packages and virtual environments, you can refer to the Python documentation (*https://oreil.ly/m0SJr*). Before you begin, select Kernel > Restart and Clear Output in the menu to make sure you are starting from scratch.

We begin by installing and importing the NumPy library (if it is not already installed):

```
pip install numpy
import numpy as np
```

Note that here we have imported the library and given it an alias, np. We can now use this alias to perform array operations using NumPy.

Next, we create a simple array:

```
np.array([0,1,2,3]) #Code to be executed

array([0, 1, 2, 3]) #Code output
```

For all code blocks in this chapter, the text in the boldface font represents what we need to execute and the text in the regular font represents the output.

The preceding code creates a simple array with four elements. This is a one-dimensional array. That basically means you need a single coordinate to get to an element in the array. We can create multidimensional arrays using the following code blocks:

```
np.array([[1,2,3,4], [4,3,2,1]]) #2D array

array([[1, 2, 3, 4],
       [4, 3, 2, 1]])
threeD = np.array([[[1,2,3], [4,2,1]], [[5,6,7], [4,2,1]]]) #3D array
threeD

array([[[1, 2, 3],
        [4, 2, 1]],

       [[5, 6, 7],
        [4, 2, 3]]])
```

To read the third element of the second element of the first element, we can use the following code:

```
threeD[0,1,2] #Coordinate 0,1,2 or Index 0,1,2

1
```

Figure 5-6 shows the resulting three-dimensional array index.

```
array([[[1, 2, 3],
        [4, 2, (1)],

       [[5, 6, 7],
        [4, 2, 3]]])
```

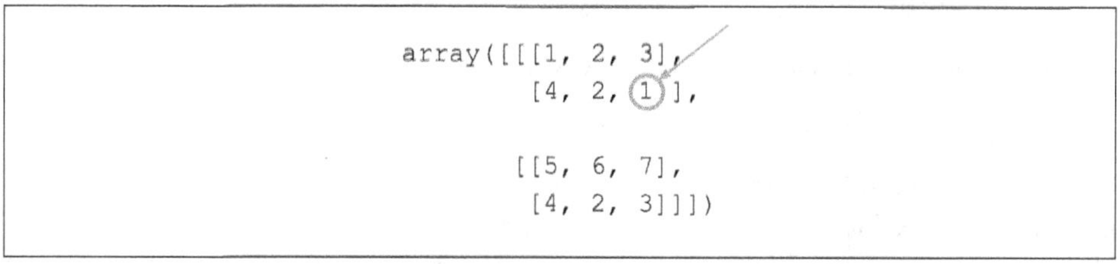

Figure 5-6. Three-dimensional array index

To create an array of floating-point numbers, use the following code:

```
a = np.array([1,2,3,4,5], dtype=np.float32) #Floating-point array
a
```

```
array([1., 2., 3., 4., 5.], dtype=float32)
```

Generating Arrays

In this section, we will look at some operations to generate arrays with different categories. We begin by generating a two-dimensional array of zeros:

```
np.zeros((2,3)) #2D array of 0s
```

```
array([[0., 0., 0.],
       [0., 0., 0.]])
```

Now let's create a three-dimensional array of ones:

```
np.ones((3,2,4)) #3D array of 1s
```

```
array([[[1., 1., 1., 1.],
        [1., 1., 1., 1.]],

       [[1., 1., 1., 1.],
        [1., 1., 1., 1.]],

       [[1., 1., 1., 1.],
        [1., 1., 1., 1.]]])
```

We can do the same with random numbers. This is particularly useful if we want to generate some random data for testing:

```
np.random.rand(2,2,3) #3D array of random numbers
```

```
array([[[0.42577929, 0.14957169, 0.4139802 ],
        [0.27451052, 0.68386878, 0.74906119]],

       [[0.91974295, 0.23597201, 0.05938353],
        [0.48170007, 0.40681348, 0.75663832]]])
```

You will probably get a different set of random numbers in the generated array. We can use the `arrange` method to generate arrays with specific sequences:

```
np.arrange(1,10,2) #Generate an array with specific sequence
```

```
array([1, 3, 5, 7, 9])
```

The `arrange` method generates an array that starts with 1 (included in the sequence), goes up to 10 (excluded from the sequence), and takes a step of 2. So we end up with all odd numbers. We can also use the `eye` function to generate a two-dimensional array with 1 as its diagonal:

```
np.eye(4) #Generate a 2D array with 1 as the diagonal
array([[1., 0., 0., 0.],
       [0., 1., 0., 0.],
       [0., 0., 1., 0.],
       [0., 0., 0., 1.]])
```

The diagonal can be moved up or down as needed:

```
a = np.eye(4,k=-2) #Move the diagonal up or down
a

array([[0., 0., 0., 0.],
       [0., 0., 0., 0.],
       [1., 0., 0., 0.],
       [0., 1., 0., 0.]])
```

The following functions can be used to understand the dimensions, shape, and size of the array:

```
print('Dimensions: ', a.ndim) #Print array dimensions
```

```
Dimensions: 2
```

```
print('Shape: ', a.shape) #axis/axes
```

```
Shape: (4, 4)
```

```
print('Size: ', a.size) #Total number of elements
```

```
Size: 16
```

Array Slicing

We can slice and dice the data in our arrays to get specific subsets from the data. The following code can be used to get the fourth index across all elements in a two-dimensional array:

```
#Starting at element 0 return the 4th index item of each element
a = np.array([[1, 2, 3, 4, 5], [6, 7, 8, 9, 10]])
print(a[0:, 4])

[ 5 10]
```

Similarly, we can slice higher-dimensional arrays. Take a look at the following code:

```
# For all subsets, look at each of the sub-elements
# from 0-2 (2 excluded) and return element 4
a = np.array([[[1, 2, 3, 4, 5], [6, 7, 8, 9, 10]],
              [[4, 7, 2, 3, 1], [2, 5, 6, 1, 6]]])
print('Array:\n', a)
print('Element:\n', a[0:,0:2,3])

Array:
 [[[ 1 2 3 4 5]
  [ 6 7 8 9 10]]

 [[ 4 7 2 3 1]
  [ 2 5 6 1 6]]]
Element:
 [[4 9]
 [3 1]]
```

The code slices a three-dimensional array. Let's break it down further:

- Our three-dimensional array is represented by [[[ ] , [ ]] , [[ ] , [ ]]].

- 0: represents all elements on this dimension starting at index 0. This dimension has two elements represented by [[ ] , [ ]] and [[ ] , [ ]].

- 0:2 represents elements from 0 to 1 (2 is excluded) in each element selected in the preceding step. These elements are represented by [ ], [ ], [ ], and [ ].

- 3 represents the 3 index (the fourth entry in each element selected in the previous step). This ends up being a two-dimensional array:

  ```
  [[4 9]
  [3 1]]
  ```

I would highly recommend that you play around with this to get a good grasp on effective slicing.

We can take this back to the cinema ticket sales dataset we discussed earlier. For example, we could slice the data to know the sales of a specific type of ticket, during a specific month, across a selected set of cinemas.

Array Transformation

We can transform arrays in NumPy to change their shape. The function used for this is called reshape. Let's go through some examples:

```
a = a = np.eye(4,k=-2)
b = np.reshape(a,(8,-1)) #-1 allows NumPyto figure out the dimension
print(a)
print(b)

a:
 [[0. 0. 0. 0.]
 [0. 0. 0. 0.]
 [1. 0. 0. 0.]
 [0. 1. 0. 0.]]
b:
 [[0. 0.]
 [0. 0.]
 [0. 0.]
 [0. 0.]
 [1. 0.]
 [0. 0.]
 [0. 1.]
 [0. 0.]]
```

In the preceding example, a 4×4 array is transformed into an 8×2 array. Note that the dimensions of the array remain the same. The -1 is a useful shorthand for allowing NumPy to determine the missing dimension based on the given dimension and the existing shape of the array. Let's look at another example:

```
a = np.array([1, 2, 3, 4, 5, 6, 7, 8, 9, 10, 11, 12]) #1D array
b = a.reshape(2, 3, 2) #Reshape to 3D array
print('a:\n', a)
print('b:\n', b)

a:
 [ 1 2 3 4 5 6 7 8 9 10 11 12]
b:
 [[[ 1 2]
  [ 3 4]
  [ 5 6]]

 [[ 7 8]
  [ 9 10]
  [11 12]]]
```

In the preceding example, we are transforming a one-dimensional array into a three-dimensional array. Here, both the shape and the dimensions of the array are changing. We can also do a transpose of the array matrix:

```
a = np.array([[1,2,3],[4,5,6]])
b = np.transpose(a) # Transpose the array matrix
print('Original','\n','Shape',a.shape,'\n',a)
print('Transposed:','\n','Shape',b.shape,'\n',b)

Original
 Shape (2, 3)
 [[1 2 3]
 [4 5 6]]
Transposed:
 Shape (3, 2)
 [[1 4]
 [2 5]
 [3 6]]
```

The transpose function on a two-dimensional array flips the columns and the rows.

Other Array Operations

Let's look at a sorting example. A sort operation can be very useful when processing and analyzing data:

```
a = np.array([[5,6,7,4],
              [9,2,3,7]])
print('a:\n', a)
print('Sort along column :','\n',np.sort(a, axis=1)) # Sort on column
print('Sort along row :','\n',np.sort(a, axis=0)) # Sort on row

a:
 [[5 6 7 4]
 [9 2 3 7]]
Sort along column :
 [[4 5 6 7]
 [2 3 7 9]]
Sort along row :
 [[5 2 3 4]
 [9 6 7 7]]
```

To find the element by its value, we can use the where method:

```
a = np.array([1, 2, 3, 4, 5, 4])
x = np.where(a == 5) #Find an element by value
print(x)

(array([4]),)
```

The result is the index of the element where the value is matched. Additional code samples are available in the *Chapter5-Numpy-PAFME* notebook, located on the book's GitHub repository (*https://oreil.ly/wy3Ds*). You can work with the examples to familiarize yourself with the NumPy library in Python. Next, we will explore a business example using the Pandas library for tabular data.

Exploring a Business Example Using Pandas

Let's look at the cinema ticket sales example for this use case. We want to answer a couple of questions with regard to sales of tickets across cinemas, months, and ticket categories. We define these as the following:

Cinemas: 0–8
Months (Jan–Dec): 0–11
Categories (Regular, Premium, Gallery): 0–2

We will start with a one-dimensional array assuming that we have only one cinema and one category. As a result, the only axis we have is for months:

```
# Define dimensions
months = 12

# Create a 1D array with dimensions (months)
# We have just 1 cinema and 1 category
# We are using a random function to generate ticket sales values
# between 80 - 1200
ticket_sales = np.random.randint(80, 1201, size=(months))

print("1D Array Shape:", ticket_sales.shape)
print("Sample Data:")
ticket_sales

1D Array Shape: (12,)
Sample Data:
array([ 233, 725, 356, 501, 412, 125, 1062, 106, 1067, 103, 119,
        1070])
```

The preceding array represents the monthly ticket sales for a single category for a single cinema across 12 months. Next, we will extend our array to represent our three categories:

```
# Define dimensions
months = 12
categories = 3

# Create a 2D array with dimensions (months, categories)
# We just have 1 cinema
# We are using a random function to generate ticket sales values
# between 80 - 1200
ticket_sales = np.random.randint(80, 1201, size=(months, categories))
```

```
print("2D Array Shape:", ticket_sales.shape)
print("Sample Data:")
ticket_sales

2D Array Shape: (12, 3)
Sample Data:
array([[  81,  344,  869],
       [ 448,  546,  726],
       [ 598,  545,  797],
       [ 443,  966, 1040],
       [ 645,  293,  569],
       [ 253,  672,  911],
       [ 719,  629, 1193],
       [ 967,  839, 1131],
       [ 892, 1101,  340],
       [ 854,  491,  552],
       [ 536,  207,  210],
       [ 174, 1081,  404]])
```

Now we have extended our dataset to a two-dimensional array that represents the monthly sales for tickets across 12 months and three categories for a single cinema. We will continue to expand this for a growing business so that we can represent the data across eight different cinemas:

```
# Define dimensions
months = 12
categories = 3
cinemas = 9

# Create a 3D array with dimensions (months, categories, cinemas)
# We are using a random function to generate ticket sales values
# between 80 - 1200
ticket_sales = np.random.randint(80, 1201, size=(cinemas, months, categories))

print("3D Array Shape:", ticket_sales.shape)
print("Sample Data:")
ticket_sales

3D Array Shape: (9, 12, 3)
Sample Data:
array([[[ 838, 1039,  611],
        [1022,  492,  504],
        [ 256,  645,  706],
        [ 759,  681,  612],
        [ 887, 1159,  483],
        [ 724,  243,  666],
        [ 778, 1005,  783],
        [ 675,  941,  772],
        [ 481,  198,  932],
        [ 233,  935,  905],
        [ 365,  233,  385],
```

```
    [ 244,  386,  409]],

   [[ 995,  111,  978],
    [ 511,  650,  582],
    [ 972,  378,  168],
    [ 425,  319,  873],
    [ 984,  183, 1144],
    [ 805,  345,   81],
    [ 210,  950,  161],
    [ 177,  191,  590],
    [ 708,  449,  766],
    [ 257, 1138,  139],
    [1037,  241,  770],
    [ 609,  213,  439]],

      .
      .
      .

   [[ 590,  384,  852],
    [ 329,  832,  605],
    [ 833, 1108,  361],
    [ 691,  444,  866],
    [ 710,  860, 1147],
    [1158,  409,  786],
    [ 865,  864,  289],
    [ 555,  785, 1065],
    [ 422,  162,  823],
    [ 988, 1169,  288],
    [ 787,  624, 1035],
    [1111,  612,  608]]]])
```

You should see nine sets, representing each cinema from cinema0 to cinema8. Also note that the numbers represent the sale of tickets for that cinema, in that month, for a particular ticket category. The numbers you might see in your output are likely to be different as they are generated randomly, but this will not affect your work.

Now that we have generated our data, let's try to answer the two business questions we asked earlier.

Question 1: What is the total number of tickets sold across all cinemas in one month?

We can answer that question by creating a sum of the values across two axes—cinemas and categories—using the knowledge we gained earlier:

```python
# Sum the ticket sales across all cinemas for each month
total_tickets_per_month = np.sum(ticket_sales, axis=(0, 2))
# Print the total number of tickets sold across all cinemas in each month
for month, total_tickets in enumerate(total_tickets_per_month):
    print(f"Month {month}: Total tickets sold = {total_tickets}")

Month 0: Total tickets sold = 17958
```

```
Month 1: Total tickets sold = 14514
Month 2: Total tickets sold = 14355
Month 3: Total tickets sold = 16345
Month 4: Total tickets sold = 18627
Month 5: Total tickets sold = 17443
Month 6: Total tickets sold = 14885
Month 7: Total tickets sold = 17202
Month 8: Total tickets sold = 14455
Month 9: Total tickets sold = 18962
Month 10: Total tickets sold = 15764
Month 11: Total tickets sold = 18636
```

NumPy has made it easy for us to look at total ticket sales across all cinemas for each month. Each line in the output represents total sales of tickets across all cinemas and across all categories for that month.

Now let's answer the second business question:

Question 2: How do the sales of regular tickets for cinema 1 compare to those for cinema 7 in the month of June?

We can answer that question by accessing the correct cell in our three-dimensional array. To compare the two, we need to look at how we defined our array. Our array contains the following axes in the given order:

[cinemas, months, categories]

Recall that **regular tickets** are represented by category 0, **cinemas** are numbered from 0 to 8, and **months** are numbered from 0 to 11. Therefore:

[Cinema1, June, Regular] translates to [1,5,0]

and:

[Cinema7, June, Regular] translates to [7,5,0].

Consider the following code:

```
#(Cinema 1, June = 5 (as January = 0), Regular Category = 0)
june_sales_cinema1_regular = ticket_sales[1, 5, 0]
#(Cinema 7, June = 5 (as January = 0), Regular Category = 0)
june_sales_cinema7_regular = ticket_sales[7, 5, 0]
print("June Sales for Regular Tickets")
print("Cinema 1: ", june_sales_cinema1_regular)
print("Cinema 7: ", june_sales_cinema7_regular)

June Sales for Regular Tickets
Cinema 1: 805
Cinema 7: 908
```

Once again we are able to easily answer the question about comparing regular ticket sales for the month of June between cinema 1 and cinema 7. According to the preceding output, cinema 7 performed better than cinema 1 by 103 regular tickets in the month of June.

Pandas in Python

Pandas is an open source Python package that makes it easy to perform data wrangling in Python. It is built on top of the NumPy library that we discussed in the previous section. Pandas makes it easy to work with data for the purpose of data science and data analytics. The package boasts a number of functionalities:

- Reading data into memory from various formats and writing data back to disk
- Cleaning dirty data (including handling missing data)
- Reshaping datasets
- Indexing and slicing the data
- Supporting joins and merges on data
- Performing data analytics and visualization
- Supporting time series data
- And many others

Just as for NumPy the main object provided by the library was an n-dimensional array, for Pandas the main object is a Pandas DataFrame. A Pandas DataFrame is a two-dimensional data structure. You can think of it as a table with rows and columns, or a two-dimensional array.

In this section, we will cover a subset of the functionality provided by the Pandas package. To follow along, you can either create your own Jupyter Notebook, use any other Python environment, or download the *Chapter5-Pandas-PAFME.ipynb* notebook from the book's GitHub repository (*https://oreil.ly/kXXnb*). Before you begin, go to Kernel > Restart and Clear Output in the menu to make sure you are starting from scratch.

We begin by importing the library:

```
import pandas as pd
```

Like we did with NumPy, we have given Pandas an alias of pd. From this point on, we can call all the Pandas functions using pd.

Import and View Data

The next step is to import and view the data. For the purposes of this chapter, we have sourced sample data about penguins from three islands, referenced by the bokeh.sampledata (*https://oreil.ly/FQi5Q*) package. We read the data in memory using the raw data URL for a copy in our repository:

```
url = "https://raw.githubusercontent.com/paforme/predictiveanalytics\
/main/Chapter5/Datasets/penguins.csv"
penguins = pd.read_csv(url) #Read the data from the URL in a Pandas dataframe
```

We can view the data by simply calling the DataFrame (see Figure 5-7):

```
penguins
```

	species	island	bill_length_mm	bill_depth_mm	flipper_length_mm	body_mass_g	sex
0	Adelie	Torgersen	39.1	18.7	181.0	3750.0	MALE
1	Adelie	Torgersen	39.5	17.4	186.0	3800.0	FEMALE
2	Adelie	Torgersen	40.3	18.0	195.0	3250.0	FEMALE
3	Adelie	Torgersen	NaN	NaN	NaN	NaN	NaN
4	Adelie	Torgersen	36.7	19.3	193.0	3450.0	FEMALE
...	...	...	...	...	...	...	...
339	Gentoo	Biscoe	NaN	NaN	NaN	NaN	NaN
340	Gentoo	Biscoe	46.8	14.3	215.0	4850.0	FEMALE
341	Gentoo	Biscoe	50.4	15.7	222.0	5750.0	MALE
342	Gentoo	Biscoe	45.2	14.8	212.0	5200.0	FEMALE
343	Gentoo	Biscoe	49.9	16.1	213.0	5400.0	MALE

344 rows × 7 columns

Figure 5-7. Penguin data in a Pandas DataFrame

The Use of Public Datasets

You might be wondering why we are using publicly available nonbusiness datasets in this chapter. The idea is to use data that is universally understandable so that the reader can focus on the functions and the techniques without worrying about the nuances of the data itself.

Having said that, let me reiterate that analyzing analysis and understanding data is a very important part of the predictive analytics life cycle. Therefore, as we proceed further in the book, we will build toward business-related use cases along with business-relevant datasets.

The data we are using is about three species of penguins taken across three islands in Antarctica. It provides measurements for the penguins' different body parts and mass. The data contains the following fields:

- species: Species of the penguin
- island: Island where the data was recorded
- bill_length_mm: Length of the bill (beak)
- bill_depth_mm: Depth of the bill
- flipper_length_mm: Length of the flipper
- body_mass: Mass of the penguin
- sex: Gender of the penguin

We can get further information about the DataFrame using the info function:

```
penguins.info() #DF summary

<class 'pandas.core.frame.DataFrame'>
RangeIndex: 344 entries, 0 to 343
Data columns (total 7 columns):
 #   Column             Non-Null Count  Dtype
---  ------             --------------  -----
 0   species            344 non-null    object
 1   island             344 non-null    object
 2   bill_length_mm     342 non-null    float64
 3   bill_depth_mm      342 non-null    float64
 4   flipper_length_mm  342 non-null    float64
 5   body_mass_g        342 non-null    float64
 6   sex                333 non-null    object
dtypes: float64(4), object(3)
memory usage: 18.9+ KB
```

From the info function, we can quickly look at all the fields and their respective data-types, how many records we have in the DataFrame, and its memory usage. This is a great tool to start understanding the dataset.

We can also use the `describe` function to perform a quick statistical analysis on the DataFrame (see Figure 5-8):

```
penguins.describe() #Quick analysis
```

Out[37]:		bill_length_mm	bill_depth_mm	flipper_length_mm	body_mass_g
	count	342.000000	342.000000	342.000000	342.000000
	mean	43.921930	17.151170	200.915205	4201.754386
	std	5.459584	1.974793	14.061714	801.954536
	min	32.100000	13.100000	172.000000	2700.000000
	25%	39.225000	15.600000	190.000000	3550.000000
	50%	44.450000	17.300000	197.000000	4050.000000
	75%	48.500000	18.700000	213.000000	4750.000000
	max	59.600000	21.500000	231.000000	6300.000000

Figure 5-8. The `describe()` output for the Pandas DataFrame

Note that the analysis only covers numerical columns and excludes the `Dtype: object` fields. The function provides useful information such as mean, standard deviation, max and min values, and different percentiles.

Visualize the Data

Data visualization is a big part of data analysis. It helps us look at the big picture, understand trends, and look at large datasets as a whole. The first thing we do is import the *matplotlib* library that helps us plot (visualize) the data:

```
import matplotlib as mpl
```

Let's begin by observing the correlation between body mass and flipper length. A simple way to do this is to plot these two items as a scatterplot. The following code uses the `plot.scatter` function in Pandas to provide a visual representation of our data in the two columns `fillper_length_mm` and `body_mass`. Each filled dot represents a data point pair from these columns. The function uses a basic format:

<dataset>.plot.<chart-type>(<x-coordinate>, <y-coordinate>,<style>,<color>)

```
#Flipper Length vs Body Mass scatter plot
penguins.plot.scatter(x='flipper_length_mm', y='body_mass_g', style='o',
                      c = 'blue')
```

We use the preceding function to plot a scatterplot with flipper length on the *x*-axis and body mass on the *y*-axis. This should yield a result similar to the one shown in Figure 5-9.

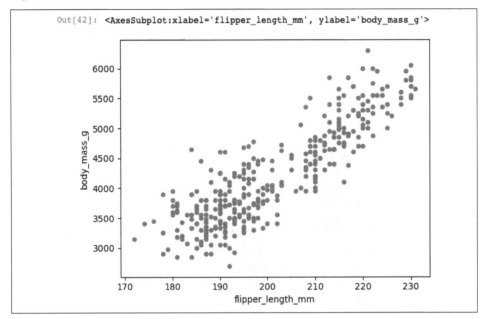

Figure 5-9. Scatterplot of `flipper_length` *versus* `body_mass`

Looking at the plot in Figure 5-9, it is immediately visible that flipper length and body mass are positively correlated. This makes sense, as bigger penguins would probably have bigger feet. Remember that we cannot establish causation, but only a sense of correlation. The question you need to ask yourself is, can we fit a regression line on this data and use it to predict body mass based on flipper length? We will get to the prediction in the following section.

For now, let's look at a few other visualizations. Next, we will create a box plot to compare the body mass ranges across the three species of penguins (see Figure 5-10):

```
penguins.plot.box(column="body_mass_g", by="species")
```

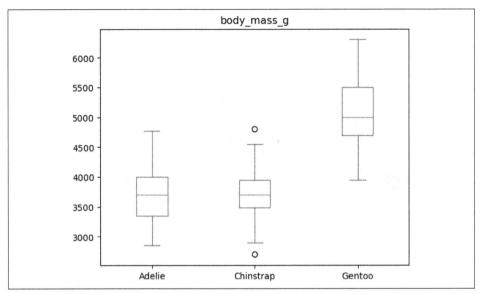

Figure 5-10. Box plot for body_mass ranges across species

The `column` parameter in the command is what we want to plot on the *y*-axis and the `by` parameter is what we want to group on the *x*-axis.

As per our data, we can see that the Gentoo species is generally heavier than the Adelie and Chinstrap species. We can also see that Adelie has a larger variance in terms of `body_mass` when compared to Chinstrap. Let's look at one more plot (see Figure 5-11):

```
penguins.plot.hist(by='sex', column='bill_length_mm')
```

The two histograms plot the `bill_length` for the respective gender using histogram buckets. The by parameter determines the index we want to use for the selection, and the `column` parameter is the field we want to bucket and plot. There is a large frequency of female penguins with bill lengths between 45 and 47.5 mm, while the highest frequency in males is between 50 and 52.5 mm. At this point, we have a decent idea of how to use plots for DataFrames. You can find further details about this in the Pandas DataFrame.plot documentation (*https://oreil.ly/7riUS*).

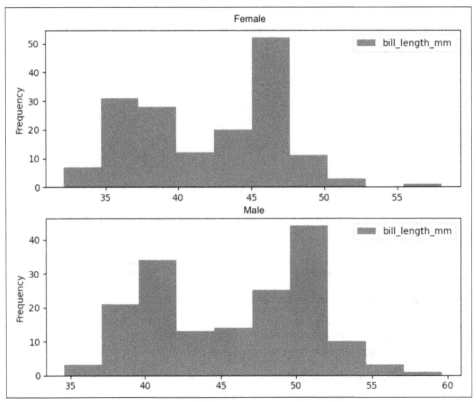

Figure 5-11. Histogram to compare bill length across male and female penguins

Finally, let's look at a slight improvement on the plot shown in Figure 5-9. We create the same plot to analyze the correlation between flipper_length and body_mass, but this time we want to see where each species lies on the scatterplot.

We start with a plot that filters only the Adelie species. We define the *x* and *y* variables. The style defines the color (yellow) and the dot type. We also define a label for the series. We save this in an AxesSubplot object ax. We define subplots for all three species with different colors. In each subsequent definition, we use ax=ax to superimpose these subplots on top of each other. Finally, we define a legend and a *y*-axis label.

If the following code feels complex, don't fret. Just use it as a template and play around with the graph to see what happens. If you are interested in syntax details, review the plot documentation referenced earlier:

```
ax = penguins[penguins.species == 'Adelie'].plot(
    x='flipper_length_mm', y='body_mass_g',
    style='yx', label='Adelie', alpha=0.35)
ax = penguins[penguins.species == 'Gentoo'].plot(
    x='flipper_length_mm', y='body_mass_g',
```

```
        style='ro', label='Gentoo', alpha=0.35, ax=ax)
ax = penguins[penguins.species == 'Chinstrap'].plot(
    x='flipper_length_mm', y='body_mass_g',
    style='b*', label='Chinstrap'   , alpha=0.35, ax=ax)
ax.legend('Adelie Gentoo Chinstrap'.split(), numpoints=5, loc='lower right')
_ = ax.set_ylabel('body_mass_g') # Stacked Visualization
```

This should give us an improved version of the `flipper_length` versus `body_mass` scatterplot. If all goes well, you should see something similar to Figure 5-12, where we can clearly differentiate how the three species compare in terms of body mass and flipper length.

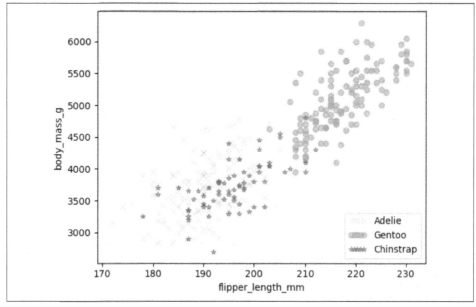

Figure 5-12. Scatterplot showing `flipper_length` versus `body_mass` categorized by species

Data Cleaning and Modification

In the real world, it is unlikely that we will get perfect data every time. Pandas provides us with tools to manipulate data in terms of values and structure to bring it to a form that is usable. In this section, we will look at a few techniques to modify and clean data to fit our requirements. We will continue to work with our penguins DataFrame. To begin, let's ensure that the DataFrame is loaded (see Figure 5-13):

```
penguins
```

	species	island	bill_length_mm	bill_depth_mm	flipper_length_mm	body_mass_g	sex
0	Adelie	Torgersen	39.1	18.7	181.0	3750.0	MALE
1	Adelie	Torgersen	39.5	17.4	186.0	3800.0	FEMALE
2	Adelie	Torgersen	40.3	18.0	195.0	3250.0	FEMALE
3	Adelie	Torgersen	NaN	NaN	NaN	NaN	NaN
4	Adelie	Torgersen	36.7	19.3	193.0	3450.0	FEMALE
...	...	...	...	...	...	...	...
339	Gentoo	Biscoe	NaN	NaN	NaN	NaN	NaN
340	Gentoo	Biscoe	46.8	14.3	215.0	4850.0	FEMALE
341	Gentoo	Biscoe	50.4	15.7	222.0	5750.0	MALE
342	Gentoo	Biscoe	45.2	14.8	212.0	5200.0	FEMALE
343	Gentoo	Biscoe	49.9	16.1	213.0	5400.0	MALE

344 rows × 7 columns

Figure 5-13. Penguins data in a Pandas DataFrame

Now let's look at all the unique values for the sex column of our data. We can use the Pandas unique() function for this purpose:

```
penguins.sex.unique()
```

```
array(['MALE', 'FEMALE', nan], dtype=object)
```

The output tells us some entries are marked as nan. This is a NumPy representation of a null object. While this is good for developers and scientists, we want to make it more user friendly, something like Unknown. For this, we can use the replace() function:

```
#Replace all empty 'sex' entries by 'Unknown'
penguins.sex.replace([np.nan], ['Unknown'], inplace=True)
```

The replace() function looks for all null values (matched using np.nan) in the sex column in our DataFrame and replaces it with Unknown. Calling the unique() function again confirms the replace operation:

```
penguins.sex.unique()
```

```
array(['MALE', 'FEMALE', 'Unknown'], dtype=object)
```

Another way to look for null values in our DataFrame is to use the isnull() function:

```
penguins.isnull().any()      #Look for null values
```

```
species         False
island          False
bill_length_mm   True
bill_depth_mm    True
```

```
flipper_length_mm    True
body_mass_g          True
sex                  False
dtype: bool
```

As we can see in the preceding code, four of our columns have null values. Since body_mass is something we are particularly interested in, for this DataFrame we do not want any entries where body_mass is not recorded (null), as this can skew our conclusions. We can use the dropna() function to remove the subset of the data where body_mass is null. Note that any modifications that happen here are on the data that is loaded in Pandas. We are not making any changes to the original underlying dataset:

```
penguins.dropna(subset=['body_mass_g'], inplace=True) #Drop null bm
penguins.isnull().any()
```

```
species              False
island               False
bill_length_mm       False
bill_depth_mm        False
flipper_length_mm    False
body_mass_g          False
sex                  False
dtype: bool
```

It appears that we have no null values in the data. It looks like every record that had a null field for bill_length, bill_depth, and/or flipper_length also had a null value for body_mass. Since we dropped the entire record and not just the specific field, we ended up cleaning our entire dataset. You can review the penguins DataFrame to ensure that there are no null entries. Also try to figure out how many records were dropped in total by the dropna() function.

Reading from Different Data Sources

Pandas allows you to import data from many different data sources. When we started working with the penguins dataset we used the read_csv function to import data directly from a URL. Let's look at it again:

```
url = "https://raw.githubusercontent.com/mwaskom/seaborn-data/master/penguins.csv"
penguins = pd.read_csv(url) #Read the data from the URL
```

We can use the same function to read from a local datafile, such as a CSV or a space-delimited file. For this exercise, we will look at an abalone dataset (*https://oreil.ly/ K_cgb*) sourced from the University of Toronto's Computer Science department website. Download a copy of the dataset from the book's GitHub repository (*https:// oreil.ly/jQ6oh*) and place it in a location accessible by your Python environment. We will use the following code to load the dataset in a Pandas DataFrame (see Figure 5-14):

```
#Replace this with the location of your dataset file
local_ds = './Datasets/Abalone/Dataset.data'
#This is a space-delimited file
abalone = read_csv(local_ds, delim_whitespace=True)
```

	sex	length	diameter	height	whole_weight	shucked_weight	viscera_weight	shell_weight	rings
0	M	0.455	0.365	0.095	0.5140	0.2245	0.1010	0.1500	15
1	M	0.350	0.265	0.090	0.2255	0.0995	0.0485	0.0700	7
2	F	0.530	0.420	0.135	0.6770	0.2565	0.1415	0.2100	9
3	M	0.440	0.365	0.125	0.5160	0.2155	0.1140	0.1550	10
...	...	...	...	...	...	...	...	...	...
4173	M	0.590	0.440	0.135	0.9660	0.4390	0.2145	0.2605	10
4174	M	0.600	0.475	0.205	1.1760	0.5255	0.2875	0.3080	9
4175	F	0.625	0.485	0.150	1.0945	0.5310	0.2610	0.2960	10
4176	M	0.710	0.555	0.195	1.9485	0.9455	0.3765	0.4950	12

4177 rows × 9 columns

Figure 5-14. Abalone data in a Pandas DataFrame read from a local file

 Once the data is loaded into a Pandas DataFrame, it does not matter whether it came from a URL or a local file. The Pandas DataFrame operations that we have been discussing so far (and will continue to discuss in this section) can be performed on any loaded dataset.

For enterprise applications, it is likely that the data you want to process is sitting in a database. With the growing influence of NoSQL databases in the enterprise market, it would be worth our while to take an example from that spectrum of databases. With that in mind, we will use a dataset of CO_2 emissions by country (*https://oreil.ly/m0_lX*) for this exercise.

You will need a working MongoDB server and a MongoDB Compass client for this exercise. Setting up MongoDB is beyond the scope of this book, but if you are interested you can set up a free cloud-based MongoDB server from the MongoDB website (*https://oreil.ly/lAlL7*). Once the environment is created, you can connect to it using MongoDB Compass. To import the emissions dataset, follow these steps:

1. Download the dataset from the book's GitHub repository (*https://oreil.ly/L2tgr*).

2. Connect to your MongoDB cluster using Compass (*https://oreil.ly/WHyHh*).

3. Click Databases and then "Create database."

4. For the database name enter **pandas**, and for the collection name enter **emissions**.

5. Go to the collection in Compass and select Add Data > Import JSON or CSV File.

6. Select the *GCB2022v27_MtCO2_flat.csv* file from the downloaded dataset, and for "Input file type" select CSV. Ensure that the delimiter is set to "comma." Click Import.

 You can use your own dataset from a compatible MongoDB server as well. If you do, remember to modify the connection, field names, and filters in the upcoming code samples.

Once the data is successfully imported into the MongoDB database, we can start playing with it using Pandas. We will start by installing PyMongo in our environment. This is a Python distribution with tools to work with MongoDB. In your Python environment, use the following command to install PyMongo:

```
pip3 install pymongo
```

Next, we will import the MongoDB client, connect to the MongoDB database, and load our Pandas DataFrame with data from the emissions collection in MongoDB. Ensure that you change the parameter passed to MongoClient to the connection string of your MongoDB server:

```
# The code is used to connect to a MongoDB Atlas database
dbcon = "mongodb+srv://user:pass@url/?retryWrites=true&w=majority"
connection = MongoClient(dbcon)
database = connection.pandas
collection = database.emissions
emissions = pd.DataFrame(list(collection.find()))
# Load the data in a Pandas dataframe.
#'collection.find()' does a query on the MongoDB collection
#to return all records. An SQL equivalent would be
#SELECT * from emissions.
```

If all goes well, the data should be loaded successfully in our emissions DataFrame (see Figure 5-15):

emissions

	_id	Country	ISO 3166-1 alpha-3	Year	Total	Coal	Oil
0	63dfb05da828231151050f75	Afghanistan	AFG	1750	0.000000	NaN	NaN
1	63dfb05da828231151050f76	Afghanistan	AFG	1751	0.000000	NaN	NaN
2	63dfb05da828231151050f77	Afghanistan	AFG	1752	0.000000	NaN	NaN
3	63dfb05da828231151050f78	Afghanistan	AFG	1753	0.000000	NaN	NaN
...	...	...	...	...	...	...	...
63100	63dfb092a828231151060605f1	Global	WLD	2018	36826.506600	14746.830688	12266.016285
63101	63dfb092a828231151060605f2	Global	WLD	2019	37082.558969	14725.978025	12345.653374
63102	63dfb092a828231151060605f3	Global	WLD	2020	35264.085734	14174.564010	11191.808551
63103	63dfb092a828231151060605f4	Global	WLD	2021	37123.850352	14979.598083	11837.159116

63104 rows × 12 columns

Figure 5-15. Emissions data in a Pandas DataFrame read from a MongoDB database

If we want to list all the columns in our dataset, we can use the `columns` attribute:

```
emissions.columns

Index(['_id', 'Country', 'ISO 3166-1 alpha-3', 'Year', 'Total', 'Coal',
'Oil', 'Gas',
       'Cement', 'Flaring', 'Per Capita', 'Other'],
      dtype='object')
```

Let's say we are only interested in the total CO_2 emissions (see Figure 5-16). We can filter the DataFrame accordingly:

```
emissions_filter = ['_id', 'Country', 'ISO 3166-1 alpha-3', 'Year', 'Total']
emissions[emissions_filter]
```

	_id	Country	ISO 3166-1 alpha-3	Year	Total
0	63dfb05da828231151050f75	Afghanistan	AFG	1750	0.000000
1	63dfb05da828231151050f76	Afghanistan	AFG	1751	0.000000
2	63dfb05da828231151050f77	Afghanistan	AFG	1752	0.000000
3	63dfb05da828231151050f78	Afghanistan	AFG	1753	0.000000
...	...	...	...	...	...
63100	63dfb092a828231151060f51	Global	WLD	2018	36826.506600
63101	63dfb092a828231151060f52	Global	WLD	2019	37082.558969
63102	63dfb092a828231151060f53	Global	WLD	2020	35264.085734
63103	63dfb092a828231151060f54	Global	WLD	2021	37123.850352

63104 rows × 5 columns

Figure 5-16. Filtered view of emissions data

Figure 5-17 shows a filtered view of the same data as that shown in Figure 5-16. If we want to create a new DataFrame from the subset of the data, we can use the `.loc` attribute:

```
# Create a new dataframe with the subset of the data
new_emissions = emissions.loc[:,emissions_filter]
```

	_id	Country	ISO 3166-1 alpha-3	Year	Total
0	63dfb05da828231151050f75	Afghanistan	AFG	1750	0.000000
1	63dfb05da828231151050f76	Afghanistan	AFG	1751	0.000000
2	63dfb05da828231151050f77	Afghanistan	AFG	1752	0.000000
3	63dfb05da828231151050f78	Afghanistan	AFG	1753	0.000000
...	...	...	...	...	...
63100	63dfb092a828231151060f51	Global	WLD	2018	36826.506600
63101	63dfb092a828231151060f52	Global	WLD	2019	37082.558969
63102	63dfb092a828231151060f53	Global	WLD	2020	35264.085734
63103	63dfb092a828231151060f54	Global	WLD	2021	37123.850352

63104 rows × 5 columns

Figure 5-17. Filtered copy of emissions data

In this dataset, we can see that the country name is repeated several times across rows. Some of the country names are quite long and take up memory. Memory constraints are common when working with large, real-world datasets. One memory-saving technique is to convert such a field into a category. Let's look at the memory usage of the current DataFrame:

```
new_emissions.info() # Notice the memory usage

<class 'pandas.core.frame.DataFrame'>
RangeIndex: 63104 entries, 0 to 63103
Data columns (total 5 columns):
 #   Column             Non-Null Count  Dtype
---  ------             --------------  -----
 0   _id                63104 non-null  object
 1   Country            63104 non-null  object
 2   ISO 3166-1 alpha-3 61472 non-null  object
 3   Year               63104 non-null  int64
 4   Total              62904 non-null  float64
dtypes: float64(1), int64(1), object(3)
memory usage: 2.4+ MB
```

The current DataFrame is using 2.4+ MB of memory. Next, we will convert the Country and Year field datatypes to `category` and observe the impact on memory usage of the same dataset:

```
for cat in 'Country Year'.split():
    new_emissions[cat] = new_emissions[cat].astype('category')
    #Convert Country and Year to categories to save memory
new_emissions.info() # Notice the memory usage

<class 'pandas.core.frame.DataFrame'>
RangeIndex: 63104 entries, 0 to 63103
Data columns (total 5 columns):
 #   Column             Non-Null Count  Dtype
---  ------             --------------  -----
 0   _id                63104 non-null  object
 1   Country            63104 non-null  category
 2   ISO 3166-1 alpha-3 61472 non-null  object
 3   Year               63104 non-null  category
 4   Total              62904 non-null  float64
dtypes: category(2), float64(1), object(2)
memory usage: 1.7+ MB
```

The memory usage of the same dataset is reduced to 1.7+ MB. Memory optimization is crucial when operationalizing predictive analytics in the enterprise space. Since the datatype is now a category, we can list all unique categories in the field:

```
sorted(new_emissions.Country.cat.categories)

['Afghanistan',
 'Albania',
 'Algeria',
 'Andorra',
 'Angola',
 'Anguilla',
 'Antarctica',
 'Antigua and Barbuda',
 'Argentina',
 'Armenia',
```

```
    'Aruba',
    'Australia',
    'Austria',
    'Azerbaijan',
    'Bahamas',
    'Bahrain',
    'Bangladesh',
    …]
```

Notice how we did not have to use the `unique()` function on the field to list all the unique values. There is another example using the penguins dataset in the Jupyter Notebook for further reference.

Data Filtering and Grouping

Earlier we saw an example of creating subsets of the data using column filters. Now let's see more filtering using the field values. We begin by converting a few datatypes from `object` to `int` and `float` so that we can process them accordingly:

```
convert_dictert_dict = {'Year': int,
                'Total': float,
                } #Define a conversion dictionary
emissions = emissions.astype(convert_dict) #Apply the dictionary
emissions.info()

<class 'pandas.core.frame.DataFrame'>
RangeIndex: 63104 entries, 0 to 63103
Data columns (total 12 columns):
 #   Column             Non-Null Count Dtype
---  ------             -------------- -----
 0   _id                63104 non-null object
 1   Country            63104 non-null object
 2   ISO 3166-1 alpha-3 61472 non-null object
 3   Year               63104 non-null int64
 4   Total              62904 non-null float64
 5   Per Capita         63104 non-null object
 6   Coal               21744 non-null float64
 7   Oil                21717 non-null float64
 8   Gas                21618 non-null float64
 9   Cement             20814 non-null float64
 10  Flaring            21550 non-null object
 11  Other              1620 non-null  object
dtypes: float64(5), int64(1), object(6)
memory usage: 5.8+ MB
```

Let's visualize the following line of code (see Figure 5-18):

```
emissions[emissions.Year == 2020] #Returns the actual records
```

	_id	Country	ISO 3166-1 alpha-3	Year	Total	Per Capita	Coal
270	65b36cee9cf222b8c3f7efa5	Afghanistan	AFG	2020	11.681766	0.299746\r	4.150072
542	65b36cee9cf222b8c3f7f0b5	Albania	ALB	2020	4.728559	1.649392\r	0.331439
814	65b36cee9cf222b8c3f7f1c5	Algeria	DZA	2020	172.504477	3.970031\r	1.098537
1086	65b36cef9cf222b8c3f7f2d5	Andorra	AND	2020	0.448884	5.777148\r	0.000000
...	...	...	...	...	...	...	...
62286	65b36d189cf222b8c3f8e1e5	Zambia	ZMB	2020	7.280663	0.384656\r	2.291770
62558	65b36d189cf222b8c3f8e2f5	Zimbabwe	ZWE	2020	10.607897	0.676970\r	6.721571
62830	65b36d189cf222b8c3f8e405	International Transport	XIT	2020	938.508679	\r	NaN
63102	65b36d199cf222b8c3f8e515	Global	WLD	2020	35264.085734	4.497423\r	14174.564010

Figure 5-18. All records in the emissions dataset where the Year field is 2020

The preceding code returns all records where the Year field in the emissions dataset is equal to 2020. We can also use other numerical operators (see Figure 5-19):

```
#Returns actual records where total emissions are above 300
emissions[emissions.Total > 300]
```

	_id	Country	ISO 3166-1 alpha-3	Year	Total	Per Capita	Coal	Oil
3237	65b36cf19cf222b8c3f7fb3c	Australia	AUS	1995	305.002996	16.941788\r	155.718942	96.126544
3238	65b36cf19cf222b8c3f7fb3d	Australia	AUS	1996	311.886129	17.125455\r	160.375191	98.697016
3239	65b36cf19cf222b8c3f7fb3e	Australia	AUS	1997	320.282630	17.396973\r	167.670194	98.388038
3240	65b36cf19cf222b8c3f7fb3f	Australia	AUS	1998	334.075978	17.959464\r	177.596365	99.146315
...	...	...	...	...	...	...	...	...
63100	65b36d199cf222b8c3f8e513	Global	WLD	2018	36826.506600	4.792753\r	14746.830688	12266.016285
63101	65b36d199cf222b8c3f8e514	Global	WLD	2019	37082.558969	4.775633\r	14725.978025	12345.653374
63102	65b36d199cf222b8c3f8e515	Global	WLD	2020	35264.085734	4.497423\r	14174.564010	11191.808551
63103	65b36d199cf222b8c3f8e516	Global	WLD	2021	37123.850352	4.693699\r	14979.598083	11837.159116

Figure 5-19. Filtered DataFrame using a numerical condition on a column field

We can use the same pattern to get the sum of emissions where the `Total` emissions value is greater than 300:

```
emissions[emissions.Total > 300].sum(numeric_only=True).Total
```

```
3037082.235283
```

Pandas also allows for combining multiple filters (see Figure 5-20). Following is an example of an AND operation that combines an array filter and a numeric match filter:

```
emissions[(emissions.Country.isin(
    ['Afghanistan', 'Pakistan', 'Albania']))
        & (emissions.Year == '2020')] #AND condition
```

	_id	Country	ISO 3166-1 alpha-3	Year	Total	Coal	Oil
270	63dfb05da828231151051083	Afghanistan		AFG	2020	11.681766	4.150072	7.219776
542	63dfb05da828231151051193	Albania		ALB	2020	4.728559	0.331439	3.217576
42158	63dfb081a828231151050423	Pakistan		PAK	2020	210.383928	57.210218	65.651413

Figure 5-20. Pandas filter with AND condition

The preceding filter matches the three mentioned country names within the given array for records from the year 2020.

To ensure that we are working with datatypes that can be grouped, we run a datatype conversion on the fields:

```
convert_dict = {'Year': int,
                'Coal': float,
                'Oil': float,
                'Gas': float,
                'Cement': float
                } #Define a conversion dictionary
emissions = emissions.astype(convert_dict) #Apply the dictionary
```

An important operation in Pandas is the `groupby` operation (see Figure 5-21). It returns a `DataFrameGroupBy` object based on the group condition. We can test this on the emissions data using the `Country` field:

```
grouped = emissions.groupby('Country')
grouped.count()
```

	_id	ISO 3166-1 alpha-3	Year	Total	Coal	Oil	Gas	Cement	Flaring	Per Capita	Other
Country											
Afghanistan	272		272	272	272	73	73	73	73	73	72	0
Albania	272		272	272	272	89	89	89	89	89	72	0
Algeria	272		272	272	272	106	106	106	94	106	72	0
Andorra	272		272	272	272	32	32	32	272	32	72	0
...	...		...	...	...	...	...	...	...	...	...	...
Wallis and Futuna Islands	272		272	272	272	32	32	32	21	32	72	0
Yemen	272		272	272	272	72	72	72	72	72	72	0
Zambia	272		272	272	272	72	72	72	72	72	72	0
Zimbabwe	272		272	272	272	119	119	119	119	119	72	0

232 rows × 11 columns

Figure 5-21. Count of elements when grouped by country in the emissions dataset

Following are a few additional helper functions for grouping:

`.last()`
> To get the last element in each group

`.first()`
> To get the first element in each group

`.getGroup(<Value>)`
> To get the group of elements for the filter defined in *<Value>*

To conclude this chapter, let's look at one final grouping (see Figure 5-22):

```
#Define a filter to get only the needed fields
grouped_filter = ['Coal', 'Oil', 'Gas', 'Cement']
#Get the filtered group results in a new data frame
grouped_new = grouped[grouped_filter]
#Sum all the values by Country
grouped_new = grouped_new.sum()
```

	Coal	Oil	Gas	Cement
Country				
Afghanistan	57.676473	131.577257	20.266629	2.516676
Albania	66.781780	185.838389	16.707287	24.375176
Algeria	117.541470	1653.701878	2154.349422	243.216837
Andorra	0.000000	15.484492	0.000000	0.000000
Angola	1.600747	346.826407	46.112038	26.090758
...	...	...	...	...
Viet Nam	2266.975955	1408.498211	310.350739	620.706079
Wallis and Futuna Islands	0.000000	0.773031	0.000000	0.000000
Yemen	4.977337	595.083134	13.635112	23.039070
Zambia	119.898169	120.614571	0.000000	17.148887
Zimbabwe	626.538130	150.933536	0.000000	20.745471

232 rows × 4 columns

Figure 5-22. Sum of categorized CO$_2$ emissions by country over the years

The preceding code provides us a way to get specific CO$_2$ categories summed up over the year for each country. The result is the DataFrame shown in Figure 5-22. We can use our previous knowledge of data filtering to get CO$_2$ emission totals for specific countries. To take it one step further, we will plot these values in a bar chart (see Figure 5-23):

```
#Filter the dataframe for specific countries
grouped_plot = grouped_new[
    grouped_new.index.isin(
        ['Angola','United Arab Emirates','Viet Nam'])]
```

To conclude, we can sort the data in the new DataFrame to answer the question: Which countries have had the highest total oil CO$_2$ emissions when looking at total emissions from 1750 to 2021?

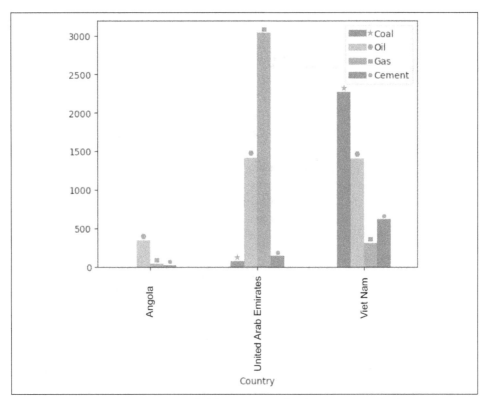

Figure 5-23. Comparing categorized CO_2 emissions for three countries from 1750 to 2021

Here is the code:

```
grouped_new.sort_values(by=['Oil'], ascending=False) #Ascending sort by Oil
```

Figure 5-24 shows the resulting DataFrame.

This gives us the filtered emissions total DataFrame sorted by countries that have oil CO_2 emissions, from highest to lowest.

In this section, we went through several examples to understand how to work with data using Pandas DataFrames. In the next section, we will talk about training and using predictive models using the scikit-learn library in Python.

	Coal	Oil	Gas	Cement
Country				
Global	804190.053522	605476.736614	254057.821146	45066.925255
USA	175444.989793	161275.027109	78542.543572	2795.830555
International Transport	0.000000	43062.671846	0.000000	0.000000
China	187073.411887	34491.543227	7162.011417	15657.812105
...	...	...	...	...
Tuvalu	0.000000	0.286818	0.000000	0.000000
Puerto Rico	0.000000	0.208848	0.000000	0.000000
Antarctica	0.000000	0.153888	0.000000	0.000000
Leeward Islands	0.035070	0.144466	0.000000	0.000000

232 rows × 4 columns

Figure 5-24. DataFrame sorted by oil CO_2 emission totals

Scikit-learn

So far, we spent some time setting up our data science environment and getting our hands dirty with NumPy and Pandas. Now it is time to jump deeper into machine learning and start making some predictions. We'll start our predictions using scikit-learn, an ML library in Python that is widely used in the industry. If you are already in this field as a student or professional, it is very likely that you already have some familiarity with the scikit-learn library.

Note that we spent a significant amount of time covering NumPy and Pandas. The foundations that we built here will be used throughout your predictive analytics journey in this book.

Scikit-learn provides us with the tools to perform machine learning on our data. It supports a large number of ML models and has great documentation (*https://oreil.ly/ JTtoH*) on how to make use of each of them. We will go through some examples to take you through the following workflow:

1. Load the data.
2. Clean the data (as needed).
3. Split the data into training data and testing data. Train (fit) the model with the training data.
4. Use the trained model to make predictions for the testing data.

5. Score the trained model for the testing data (and, optionally, for the training data).

6. Cross-validate the model using multiple metrics.

7. Optimize the model to improve the performance metric.

What you learn in this chapter can be repurposed (with some modification) for other ML models as well. Items that we'll implement in this chapter were discussed at length in Chapter 3. Review that chapter if you need a refresher.

To follow along, you can download the *Chapter5-ScikitLearn-PAFME.ipynb* notebook from the book's GitHub repository (*https://oreil.ly/2lD1x*). Before you begin, select Kernel > Restart and Clear Output in the menu to make sure you are starting from scratch.

To get started, we need to install the scikit-learn Python library in our environment. You can use one of the following two bash commands (depending on the Python environment you are running):

```
conda install -c conda-forge scikit-learn
```

or:

```
pip install -U scikit-learn
```

We'll begin by importing all the libraries and classes needed for this section:

```
import matplotlib.pyplot as plt
import numpy as np
import pandas as pd

#To perform model cross validation and scoring
from sklearn import model_selection, metrics
# To use Linear Regression Models
from sklearn.linear_model    import LinearRegression
# To split data in to training and testing sets
from sklearn.model_selection  import train_test_split
```

Training and Predicting with a Linear Regression Model

Since we are familiar with the penguins data from the Pandas section, we will continue using the same data (see Figure 5-25). Just as a quick refresher, this data is about different physical features of three species of penguins from three different islands in Antarctica:

```
url = "https://raw.githubusercontent.com/paforme/\
predictiveanalytics/main/Chapter5/Datasets/penguins.csv"
penguins = pd.read_csv(url) #Read the data from the URL in a Pandas DataFrame
```

From this code, we end up with a Pandas DataFrame called penguins. We will use this DataFrame throughout this section.

Next, we need to clean the dataset. We know from our previous exploration that there are a few records with empty fields in the dataset. We also learned how to drop records with empty fields:

```
url = "https://raw.githubusercontent.com/paforme/\
predictiveanalytics/main/Chapter5/Datasets/penguins.csv"
penguins = pd.read_csv(url) #Read the data from the URL in a Pandas dataframe
penguins.dropna(
    subset=['body_mass_g'], inplace=True)
    #Clean empty fields before training
penguins.dropna(
    subset=['sex'], inplace=True)
    #Clean empty fields before training
penguins
```

Figure 5-25 depicts the clean penguins DataFrame.

	species	island	bill_length_mm	bill_depth_mm	flipper_length_mm	body_mass_g	sex
0	Adelie	Torgersen	39.1	18.7	181.0	3750.0	MALE
1	Adelie	Torgersen	39.5	17.4	186.0	3800.0	FEMALE
2	Adelie	Torgersen	40.3	18.0	195.0	3250.0	FEMALE
4	Adelie	Torgersen	36.7	19.3	193.0	3450.0	FEMALE
5	Adelie	Torgersen	39.3	20.6	190.0	3650.0	MALE
...	...	...	...	...	...	...	...
338	Gentoo	Biscoe	47.2	13.7	214.0	4925.0	FEMALE
340	Gentoo	Biscoe	46.8	14.3	215.0	4850.0	FEMALE
341	Gentoo	Biscoe	50.4	15.7	222.0	5750.0	MALE
342	Gentoo	Biscoe	45.2	14.8	212.0	5200.0	FEMALE
343	Gentoo	Biscoe	49.9	16.1	213.0	5400.0	MALE

333 rows × 7 columns

Figure 5-25. Clean penguins DataFrame

With the clean dataset, it is now time to start training and predicting. We first split the data into a training set and a testing set. Recall from Chapter 3 that we can break our data into sets so that we can train the model using one set and then check the performance using the other set:

```
penguins_training_data, penguins_testing_data = train_test_split(
    penguins, train_size=0.75, random_state=110) #Split the data
```

The function `train_test_split` helps us do this split. It takes three parameters:

- The DataFrame with all the data.

- The size of the training set. In our case, we will have 75% of our data in the training set and 25% of our data in the testing set.

- A `random_state` number that allows us to create a repeatable data split on the same data, so long as we don't change the `random_state`.

Note that this creates references to the original data. For cleaner results, we create a separate copy of the training and testing data (see Figure 5-26):

```
#Create a copy of the data instead of referencing
penguins_training_data = penguins_training_data.copy()
#Create a copy of the data instead of referencing
penguins_testing_data = penguins_testing_data.copy()
```

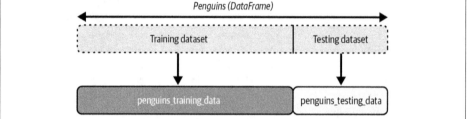

Figure 5-26. Splitting a DataFrame into testing and training datasets

```
l_regression = LinearRegression() # Initialize the model
predictors = ['flipper_length_mm'] # Independent variable(s)
predicted = 'body_mass_g' # Dependent variable
```

We initialize the linear regression model using the `LinearRegression()` constructor (from the `LinearRegression` class). When we initially looked at this dataset we realized there is some sort of positive correlation between a penguin's flipper length and body mass. With that hypothesis, we will try to fit a simple linear regression model to this data and use it to predict the `body_mass` of a penguin using its flipper length. With this in mind, we train the model:

```
# Training the model
l_regression.fit(penguins_training_data[predictors],
                 penguins_training_data[predicted])

> LinearRegression()
```

We use the training dataset to train the model. The function expects the values of `predictors` (which is `flipper_length_mm`) as the first attribute and the values of `predicted` (which is `body_mass_g`) as the second attribute (Figure 5-27).

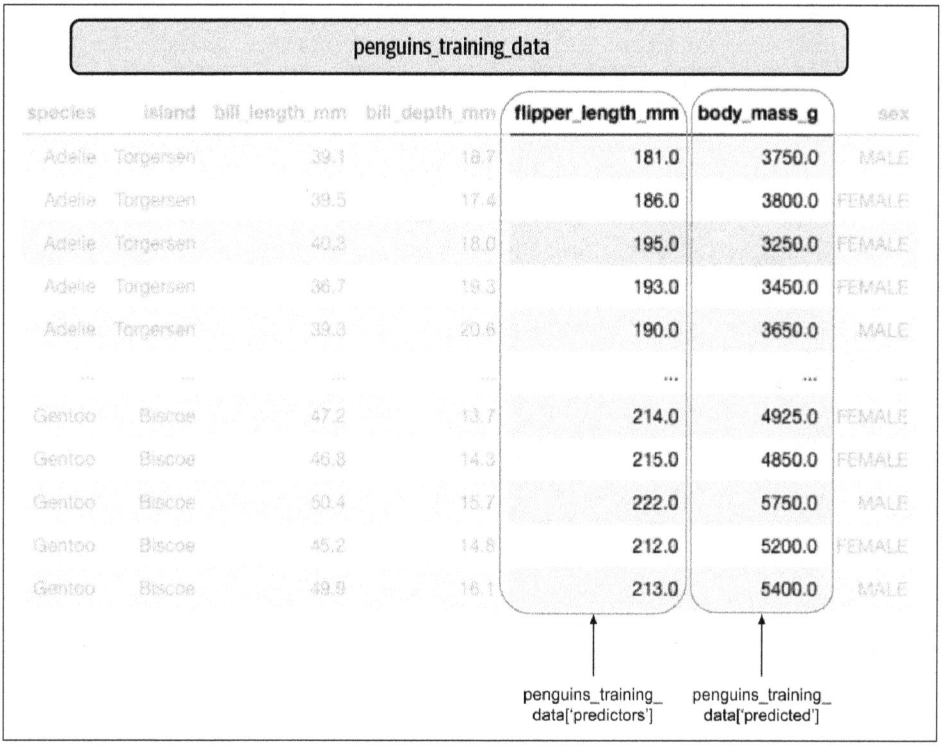

Figure 5-27. Training dataset (predictors and predicted)

We now have a trained linear regression model. Next, we will use this model to make predictions for our `penguins_testing_data`. The idea is to use a different set of data than what the model was trained on. This will give us an idea of how well our model performs on data that it has not seen previously:

```
#predictions on the test data
predictions_bm = l_regression.predict(penguins_testing_data[predictors])
print(predictions_bm)

[3398.48233545 3905.21622455 4665.31705819 4209.256558   4817.33722492
 3145.11539091 3550.50250218 5678.78483638 4057.23639128 4766.66383601
 3753.19605782 5121.37755837 4006.56300237 3347.80894655 3499.82911327
 3702.52266891 4969.35739164 4614.64366928 5577.43805856 3499.82911327
 3854.54283564 5374.74450292 4563.97028037 3398.48233545 3803.86944673
 3145.11539091 3651.84928   5222.72433619 3905.21622455 3195.78877982
 4969.35739164 3803.86944673 3601.17589109 4868.01061383 5020.03078055
 5020.03078055 4259.92994691 3702.52266891 5172.05094728 3955.88961346
 4918.68400274 3347.80894655 3651.84928   4918.68400274 3651.84928
 4563.97028037 5172.05094728 4817.33722492 5020.03078055 4006.56300237
 2942.42183527 4107.90978019 4006.56300237 3601.17589109 4259.92994691
 3449.15572436 3753.19605782 3803.86944673 3854.54283564 3702.52266891
 3651.84928   3753.19605782 2739.72827963 4918.68400274 4107.90978019
```

```
3955.88961346 3702.52266891 3955.88961346 3550.50250218 4868.01061383
4057.23639128 3651.84928   3499.82911327 4665.31705819 5729.45822528
4563.97028037 3905.21622455 4057.23639128 4665.31705819 3702.52266891
5476.09128074 5273.3977251 3246.46216873 3601.17589109]
```

The preceding output represents the `body_mass_mm` values predicted by the model for the testing data using the trained linear regression model and the `flipper_length_mm` values from the testing dataset. Since we have the original values of the body mass for the testing data, we can print those and get a feel for how close the predicted values are:

```
#Actual Body Mass values from the test data
actual_bm = penguins_testing_data['body_mass_g']
print(actual_bm)

164   3700.0
61    4400.0
326   4700.0
183   4300.0
268   5100.0
       ...
111   4600.0
315   5200.0
264   5550.0
46    3425.0
119   3325.0
Name: body_mass_g, Length: 84, dtype: float64
```

While this gives us a vague idea, there are more scientific ways to gauge the efficacy of a trained model. We can start by plotting the testing data and then plotting our linear regression line on top of that data to get an overall picture (see Figure 5-28):

```
plt.scatter(penguins_testing_data[predictors],
            penguins_testing_data[predicted], color="blue")
            # Plot the testing data (body mass vs flipper length)
plt.plot(penguins_testing_data[predictors],
         predictions_bm, color="red", linewidth=1)
         # Plot the predicted values using the predictions as the fitted line

plt.xlabel("flipper_length_mm") #Label the X axis
plt.ylabel("body_mass_g") #Label the Y axis

plt.show()
```

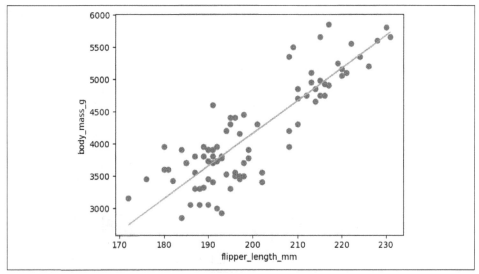

Figure 5-28. Simple linear regression line fitted over the testing data

We can now score our model on the testing data:

```
l_regression.score(penguins_testing_data[predictors],
                   penguins_testing_data[[predicted]])
                   #Scoring the model on Testing Data
```

```
0.7328658873549915
```

In the linear regression model, the `score()` function provides the R-squared (coefficient of determination). If what we are trying to predict is not a constant, and a model predicts an average value while ignoring the inputs, then such a model would have an R-squared equal to 0. A value of 1 can be considered the best value, but note that R-squared can be negative for models that are worse than a model predicting the average value.

We can score the model on our training data as well:

```
l_regression.score(penguins_training_data[predictors],
                   penguins_training_data[[predicted]])
                   #Scoring the model on Training Data
```

```
0.7709020371312678
```

As expected, the model scores higher on the training data than on the testing data.

Next, we do cross-validation on our model (see Figure 5-29). The idea is to check the evaluation metrics for different iterations of data splits and see how they score across those iterations. We do this by splitting the data n-ways. We then take $n-1$ as the training data and the nth block as the testing data. We repeat this n times by moving the testing block each time (with or without shuffling) and scoring the model at each iteration:

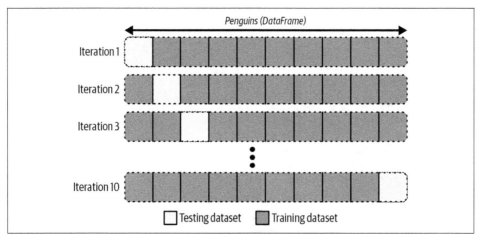

Figure 5-29. Model cross-validation

```
el_regression = LinearRegression() #Empty linear regression model
splits = model_selection.KFold(n_splits=10) #We want to split the data 10 ways

cross_validate = model_selection.cross_val_score(
    el_regression, penguins[predictors],
    penguins[predicted],
    cv=splits,
    scoring='neg_root_mean_squared_error',
    n_jobs=-1)

print(cross_validate) # Neg mean squared error for each train / test split

[-487.26692248 -440.25298463 -395.66019633 -437.66690956 -325.38121202
 -421.35199215 -478.6979478  -358.50691586 -286.60244958 -345.84454605]
```

In the preceding scoring, we look at the negative root mean squared error (RMSE). This is one of the metrics we can use to evaluate our model. The idea is to minimize the RMSE:

```
cross_validate = model_selection.cross_val_score(
    el_regression, penguins[predictors],
    penguins[predicted],
    cv=splits,
    scoring='r2',
    n_jobs=-1)

print(cross_validate) # R-squared for each train / test split

[-0.63451635 0.26538173 0.2523206   0.17600106 -0.11513909 0.20677232
  0.66326511 0.44046001 0.67041167 0.33949315]
```

Here, we look at the R-squared scoring for cross-validating our model. There are a few important observations that we should understand:

- Metrics that should be minimized (such as errors) are negated, as seen in the negative RMSE calculation.

- Metrics that should be maximized (such as R-squared) are not negated. However, we see a few negative values in the R-squared calculation. This is because R-squared can arbitrarily take on negative values at times, as discussed earlier.

- The idea of cross-validation is to check the efficacy of the model across different iterations, not to select which iteration is the best fit. For example, if you were debating between using a linear regression model and a regression tree, cross-validation could help you decide which one performs better under similar training conditions.

Using a Random Forest Classifier

For the random forest exercise, we will look at a classification example. We'll continue to use the penguins dataset. Recall that classification is the process of predicting a discrete class rather than predicting a continuous value. We begin by importing the class for the random forest classifier:

```
from sklearn.ensemble import RandomForestClassifier
```

Next, we will do some data manipulation. To train the model, we will transform our data so that the enumerations in our data are represented by numbers instead of strings.

We learned about this sort of transformation in the Pandas section of this chapter. If we look at our data, there are two fields that we are interested in which are represented by strings—namely, sex and species:

```
#Make sex numeric
penguins.sex.replace(['MALE', 'FEMALE'], [0,1], inplace=True)
#Make species numeric
penguins.species.replace(['Adelie', 'Chinstrap', 'Gentoo'], [1,2,3],
                         inplace=True)
```

The preceding lines of code replace the classification with numeric values, so MALE=0, FEMALE=1, and the three species are now represented by 1, 2, and 3. The next steps are similar to what we did in the linear regression example (see Figure 5-30):

```
#Split data
penguins_training_data, penguins_testing_data = train_test_split(
    penguins, train_size=0.75, random_state=120)
#Make a copy of the training data
penguins_training_data = penguins_training_data.copy()
#Make a copy of the testing data
penguins_testing_data = penguins_testing_data.copy()
```

```
#Independent variables(s)
predictors = ['bill_length_mm', 'bill_depth_mm', 'flipper_length_mm', 'sex']
predicted = 'species' #Dependent variable
penguins
```

	species		island	bill_length_mm	bill_depth_mm	flipper_length_mm	body_mass_g	sex
0	1	Torgersen		39.1	18.7	181.0	3750.0	0
1	1	Torgersen		39.5	17.4	186.0	3800.0	1
2	1	Torgersen		40.3	18.0	195.0	3250.0	1
4	1	Torgersen		36.7	19.3	193.0	3450.0	1
5	1	Torgersen		39.3	20.6	190.0	3650.0	0
...	...	...		...	...	...	...	...
338	3	Biscoe		47.2	13.7	214.0	4925.0	1
340	3	Biscoe		46.8	14.3	215.0	4850.0	1
341	3	Biscoe		50.4	15.7	222.0	5750.0	0
342	3	Biscoe		45.2	14.8	212.0	5200.0	1
343	3	Biscoe		49.9	16.1	213.0	5400.0	0

Figure 5-30. Transformed penguins DataFrame with numeric representation of enumerations (categories)

Our hypothesis here is that we should be able to use the body measurements and gender of the penguin to predict the species. Note how we have not taken the island into account. If you explore the data, you will realize that there is a 1-to-1 mapping between the island and the species, which would make sense. However, if we knew the island, we really would not need an ML model to predict the species. Using the island as an independent variable would create a significant correlation among the independent variables (which, as we know from Chapter 3, is not a good thing) and would render most of them redundant. We could also argue that body_mass has a direct correlation with flipper_length, as we saw in the previous example. So we removed that as being redundant, as well.

We initialize the random forest classifier model. We then pass a parameter n_estima tors=50 to the classifier. We know from Chapter 3 that a random forest is an ensemble of multiple decision trees. The n_estimators defines how many decision trees will be used by the random forest:

```
rf_classifier = RandomForestClassifier(n_estimators=50) #n_estimators
```

We train the model and then use it to predict values for the testing dataset:

```
rf_classifier.fit(penguins_training_data[predictors],
                  penguins_training_data[predicted]) #Training the RF_classifier
> RandomForestClassifier(n_estimators=50)

predictions_sp = rf_classifier.predict(
    penguins_testing_data[predictors]) #Prediction Stage. Test data set
print(predictions_sp)

[2 1 2 1 3 1 2 1 1 3 1 1 3 1 1 1 2 2 1 2 1 1 2 1 1 3 3 3 2 1 1 1 1 2 1 3 3
 3 2 3 3 3 2 1 3 2 3 1 3 1 1 3 3 3 1 2 3 2 1 3 2 3 3 1 3 3 2 1 3 3 1 3 2
 1 3 2 1 3 1 1 3 1 1]
```

Note that these are classifications for the data. A simple way to check how many of them actually match the data in the testing dataset is to run an equality comparison and then sum the counts of all that match:

```
#Number of Accurate results
sum(penguins_testing_data['species'] == predictions_sp)
83

#Number of Inaccurate Results
sum(penguins_testing_data['species'] != predictions_sp)
1
```

As we can see from the preceding code, the random forest is able to predict species correctly for 83 out of 84 records.

We now score the model on the test data:

```
rf_classifier.score(penguins_training_data[predictors],
                    penguins_training_data[[predicted]]) #Scoring on Training Data

0.9880952380952381
```

The classifier has a score of 0.988. This is evident from the fact that it only had one incorrect classification. You can try out a couple of things to explore this more:

- Add body_mass_g to the predictors, train the model, and then score it on the test dataset. See if there is any improvement in the score.
- Score the model on the training data and evaluate the result. Is this higher than the score you got for the test dataset?

Training a Decision Tree

To conclude this section on scikit-learn, we will train a decision tree to allow us to predict the **sex** of a penguin. We continue with the same dataset:

```
import pandas as pd
from sklearn import metrics
from sklearn.tree import DecisionTreeClassifier #Decision tree classifier
from sklearn.model_selection import train_test_split
```

We begin by importing the libraries and classes needed for this section. Next, we import the penguins dataset and clean it:

```
url = "https://raw.githubusercontent.com/paforme/\
predictiveanalytics/main/Chapter5/Datasets/penguins.csv"
penguins = pd.read_csv(url) #Read the data from the URL in a Pandas dataframe
penguins.dropna(subset=['body_mass_g'], inplace=True) #Clean the data
penguins.dropna(subset=['sex'], inplace=True) #Clean the data

penguins = penguins.reset_index(drop=True)
penguins
```

If you need further explanation on importing and cleaning data, you can refer to "Training and Predicting with a Linear Regression Model" on page 168. In the following code, we are converting all the string enumerations (categories) in the data to numeric values. This is needed for training the model for classification:

```
from sklearn.preprocessing import OneHotEncoder

# Select only the columns to be encoded
columns_to_encode = ['species', 'island']

# Initialize OneHotEncoder
one_hot_encoder = OneHotEncoder(sparse=False)

# Fit and transform the categorical columns
encoded_features = one_hot_encoder.fit_transform(penguins[columns_to_encode])

# Convert the encoded features into a DataFrame
encoded_df = pd.DataFrame(
    encoded_features,columns=one_hot_encoder.get_feature_names_out(
        input_features=columns_to_encode))

# Concatenate the encoded features with the original DataFrame
penguins_encoded_df = pd.concat([penguins, encoded_df], axis=1)

# Drop the original categorical columns
penguins_encoded_df.drop(columns=columns_to_encode, inplace=True)

penguins_encoded_df
```

In the preceding code, we are using one-hot encoding. As a reminder, this allows us to convert a category into a numerical representation by creating a column for each category separately and then using a binary value of 1 when the category is true for that record and 0 when it is false. Consider the original data row:

species	bill_length_mm	bill_depth_mm	flipper_length_mm	body_mass_g	sex
Adelie	39.1	18.7	181.0	3750.0	MALE

The preceding data after encoding is represented as follows:

species_ Adelie	species_ Chinstrap	species_ Gentoo	bill_ length_mm	bill_ depth_mm	flipper_ length_mm	body_ mass_g	sex
1.0	0.0	0.0	39.1	18.7	181.0	3750.0	MALE

Note how the species column is now represented by three individual columns, and that since the species value was Adelie the new column, species_Adelie, has a value of 1 while the others have a value of 0.

Next, we define the predictors and the predicted:

```
predictors = ['species_Adelie','species_Chinstrap','species_Gentoo',
              'bill_length_mm', 'bill_depth_mm', 'body_mass_g']
predicted = 'sex'
```

We split the penguins data with a training set size of 80%:

```
penguins_training_data, penguins_testing_data = train_test_split(
    penguins_encoded_df, train_size=0.80, random_state=112)
```

For the decision tree exercise, our hypothesis is that we can predict the gender of the penguins using species_Adelie, species_Chinstrap, species_Gentoo, bill_ length_mm, bill_depth_mm, and body_mass_g. We have removed islands because it has a 1-to-1 mapping with the species. We can experiment with body_mass_g and flipper_length_mm to see whether either of them is redundant.

We start without flipper_length_mm:

```
dt_classifier = DecisionTreeClassifier() #Initialize the model
dt_classifier = dt_classifier.fit(
    penguins_training_data[predictors],
    penguins_training_data[predicted]) #Train the model
```

Next, we initialize the decision tree classifier model and train it using the training dataset:

```
#Start predicting
predictions = dt_classifier.predict(penguins_testing_data[predictors])
print(predictions)

['FEMALE' 'MALE' 'FEMALE' 'FEMALE' 'MALE' 'MALE' 'MALE' 'FEMALE' 'MALE'
 'MALE' 'MALE' 'FEMALE' 'MALE' 'FEMALE' 'MALE' 'MALE' 'MALE' 'MALE' 'MALE'
 'MALE' 'FEMALE' 'MALE' 'MALE' 'MALE' 'FEMALE' 'FEMALE' 'FEMALE' 'FEMALE'
 'MALE' 'FEMALE' 'FEMALE' 'FEMALE' 'FEMALE' 'MALE' 'FEMALE' 'MALE'
 'FEMALE' 'MALE' 'MALE' 'FEMALE' 'FEMALE' 'MALE' 'MALE' 'MALE' 'FEMALE'
 'MALE' 'FEMALE' 'MALE' 'FEMALE' 'MALE' 'MALE' 'MALE' 'FEMALE' 'FEMALE'
 'FEMALE' 'FEMALE' 'MALE' 'MALE' 'MALE' 'FEMALE' 'MALE' 'FEMALE' 'FEMALE'
 'FEMALE' 'FEMALE' 'MALE' 'FEMALE']
```

We can quickly check how many of these predictions were incorrect by doing a comparison with the actual values in the testing dataset:

```
sum(predictions!=penguins_testing_data[predicted])
7
```

The decision tree misses eight predictions in the testing dataset. Note that you might get a different number here.

We can also score the model on the testing data to get a much better understanding of the model's score performance:

```
print(dt_classifier.score(penguins_testing_data[predictors],
                    penguins_testing_data[predicted])) #Scoring on test data

0.8955223880597015
```

The model scores 0.896 against the testing data. We can graph the decision tree to better understand how the tree is structured and what the node splits look like. We begin by importing the necessary libraries and classes:

```
import pydotplus
from six import StringIO
from IPython.display import Image
from sklearn.tree import export_graphviz
dot_data = StringIO()
export_graphviz(dt_classifier, out_file=dot_data,
                filled=True, rounded=True,
                special_characters=True,
                feature_names = predictors,
                class_names=['MALE','FEMALE'])
                #Define the node characteristics
tree = pydotplus.graph_from_dot_data(dot_data.getvalue())  #Create the Tree
tree.write_png('penguins.png') #Export the tree as a image
Image(tree.create_png()) #Print the image
```

Note that you might need to install Graphviz and PyDotPlus in your environment. Depending on your environment, you might have to use conda or pip for the installation.

We can use the export_graphviz class to plot and display our decision tree. In the constructor, we define the shape and fill for each node, and we pass the predictors (feature_names) and the labels for the predictions (class_names). We then follow this up with creating, exporting, and displaying the tree (see Figure 5-31).

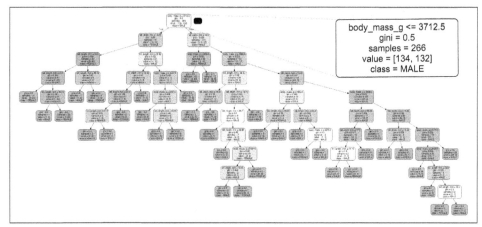

Figure 5-31. Decision tree to predict the gender of the penguins based on multiple features

In each node, notice the following items:

- The first item is the feature being used to decide on the split and the corresponding value (e.g., body_mass_g <= 3712.5).
- The second item is the Gini coefficient. Remember from Chapter 3 that as we move down the tree, the idea is to get to a Gini value of 0.
- The third item is samples, which means the number of samples that are part of the node.
- The fourth item is value, which represents the number of samples in each class in the node. For example, [134, 132] means there are 134 male samples and 132 female samples.
- The fifth item is the dominant class for the node.

The decision tree in Figure 5-31 has a max depth of 9, which can cause overfitting and suboptimal classification performance. From Chapter 3, we know that one of the ways to optimize decision trees is to predefine the maximum depth of the tree:

```
#Initialize the Decision Tree with a maximum depth of 3
dt_classifier = DecisionTreeClassifier(max_depth=3)
dt_classifier = dt_classifier.fit(
    penguins_training_data[predictors],
    penguins_training_data[predicted]) #Train the model

predictions = dt_classifier.predict(
    penguins_testing_data[predictors]) #Predict using testing data

print(dt_classifier.score(
    penguins_testing_data[predictors],
```

```
penguins_testing_data[predicted])) #Score the new model
```

0.9253731343283582

The newly trained decision tree with the reduced depth performs better on our test data compared to the previously trained decision tree. Figure 5-32 shows our new decision tree, with the improved score.

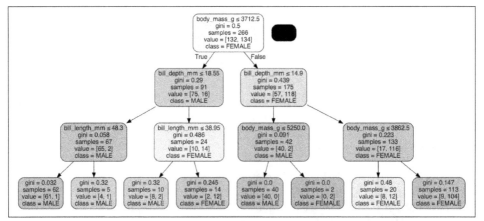

Figure 5-32. Decision tree to predict the gender of the penguins based on multiple features with max depth = 3

We end up with a much simpler decision tree than before. This tree not only scores better on our test data, it is easier to understand and would potentially be much faster to traverse when predicting classes for new data. Try out a few other options on your own:

- Add the `flipper_length_mm` feature to the predictors, then train and score the model on the testing data. Evaluate any change in the score. Does it improve?

- With the `flipper_length_mm` added, remove `body_mass_g` from the predictors and perform the training and scoring cycle again. How does the score change this time? What can you infer about the features `flipper_length_mm` and `body_mass_g` from this experiment?

A Clustering Example (Unsupervised Learning)

As a fun exercise, let's take our penguins data without the species labels and try to create three clusters based on `bill_length` and `body_mass` using the k-means algorithm discussed in Chapter 3. You can see the output of using the k-means algorithm to cluster this data on the left in Figure 5-33. The plot on the right is the actual species label in the original data. The clustering algorithm does a decent job at mapping the clusters, except for a few mismapped instances that can be seen on the cluster boundaries. The centroids are marked with an x in the plot on the left. You can download the *Chapter5-UnsupervisedLearning-PAFME.ipynb* notebook from the book's GitHub repository (*https://oreil.ly/Gcgzi*) if you would like to experiment with this example.

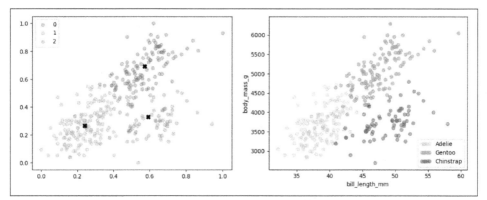

Figure 5-33. Using clustering for classification

Conclusion

In this chapter, we covered the foundations for NumPy and Pandas, the most useful foundational Python libraries for machine learning and predictive analytics. We discussed the theoretical concepts behind NumPy and useful operations and helper functions provided by both libraries. We then used this knowledge to explore scikit-learn, an ML library in Python, to examine the operations of training and using predictive models. We covered data operations, model training and optimization, predictions, and scoring. Though we discussed three specific ML models in this chapter, the concepts discussed can be applied to other models as well. Keeping that in mind, I would highly encourage you to try training and using other ML models and datasets using scikit-learn.

## CHAPTER 6

TensorFlow and Keras for Predictive Analytics

TensorFlow was created and made open source by Google. It is one of the most-used platforms worldwide for machine learning. Tensorflow.org defines TensorFlow (*https://www.tensorflow.org*) as "an end-to-end platform for machine learning."

TensorFlow has wide-ranging applications, including structured data processing, automated image classification, advanced optical character recognition (OCR), video analysis, and sentiment analysis, to name a few. It provides the tools for data ingestion and processing, ML model creation, ML model training, ML model deployment, and ML model life cycle management. Support for graphics processing units (GPUs) and tensor processing units (TPUs) allows users to work on compute-intensive deep neural networks. The fact that models can be deployed on a wide range of devices, including mobile phones, client machines and servers, edge devices, and the cloud, is one of the many reasons for its high rate of adoption among data professionals and enterprises. Figure 6-1 provides a high-level picture of the TensorFlow platform. You can find excellent documentation on the TensorFlow site (*https://www.tensorflow.org*).

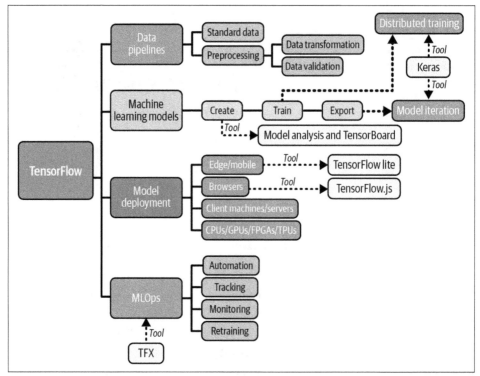

Figure 6-1. TensorFlow platform

Keras is a deep learning API built on top of TensorFlow 2. Keras simplifies the adoption of deep learning for individuals and enterprises by providing an easy-to-use API with extensive documentation. Since it is built on top of TensorFlow 2, it can help users scale by supporting various operations in the ML life cycle, from data engineering and preprocessing to distributed training to model iteration and management. Furthermore, its ability to be run anywhere and its extensive support for different categories of processing units make Keras popular among enterprises trying to use deep learning to solve complex business problems.

In this chapter, we'll discuss how to use TensorFlow and Keras for predictive analytics.

TensorFlow Fundamentals

TensorFlow uses the concept of *tensors*, which are multidimensional arrays that are similar to NumPy arrays in many ways, including the fact that a tensor supports uniform datatypes. When we work with tensors in this chapter we will be using functionality from the NumPy and Pandas libraries, primarily for data preprocessing. We will continue our hands-on approach and use code examples to clarify concepts. You can follow along using the code in *Chapter6-Tensors-PAFME.ipynb*, located on the book's GitHub repository (*https://oreil.ly/IFRcs*). You can use any compatible Python environment. All code examples in this chapter are based on TensorFlow V2.x.

To begin, we need to install TensorFlow. The following is a simple `pip` command in Python:

```
pip3 install tensorflow

import tensorflow as tflow
from tensorflow import keras
import numpy as np
```

We can perform a quick check on the TensorFlow and Keras versions that we installed:

```
tflow.__version__
'2.11.0'

keras.__version__
'2.11.0'
```

Now that we have that out of the way, we can start creating some basic tensors:

```
String_t = tflow.constant("I love coding")
print(String_t)


tf.Tensor(b'I love coding', shape=(), dtype=string)
```

We just created a tensor out of a string. There are a couple of items to notice here:

- `dtype=string` tells us the tensor stores items with a datatype string. Recall that all elements in a tensor have to be of the same datatype.

- `shape=()` tells us what the tensor dimensions look like. Since this is just a single scalar entity, the shape of the tensor is shown as empty.

Now we'll create another tensor, but this one is a one-dimensional array. Notice the `shape=(3,)`:

```
Vector_t = tflow.constant([10,20,20])
print(Vector_t)

tf.Tensor([10 20 20], shape=(3,), dtype=int32)
```

Think of a vector as a row in a table. Since it is just one row, it has only one dimension. This is denoted by the fact that the shape only has one number in it. The value of the number explains the size of the dimension. Since there are three elements in this array, the size of the dimension is 3.

A simple way to create a matrix is to think about it as a table with two rows and two columns. The shape tells us there are two dimensions and that each dimension has two elements. Let's try creating a 3 × 2 matrix:

```
Matrix_t = tflow.constant([[1,10],[2,20]])
print(Matrix_t) #note the shape gives us the 2 x 2 matrix dimensions.

tf.Tensor(
[[ 1 10]
 [ 2 20]], shape=(2, 2), dtype=int32)
```

Tensors support mathematical operations such as addition, subtraction, multiplication, and division. Since we are discussing multidimensional arrays, note that these operations can be scalar or matrix arrays. Let's look at three straightforward examples to understand this better:

```
Matrix_3t = 3 * Matrix_t
print(Matrix_3t)

tf.Tensor(
[[ 3 30]
 [ 6 60]], shape=(2, 2), dtype=int32)
```

In the preceding code, we multiply each element in the matrix by a scalar (3). Similarly, we can multiply two matrices by each other:

```
Matrix_t2 = tflow.constant([[1,10],[2,20]])
scalar_multiply = Matrix_t * Matrix_t2
print(scalar_multiply) #Scalar Multiplication (Element wise)

tf.Tensor(
[[  1 100]
 [  4 400]], shape=(2, 2), dtype=int32)
```

Notice how this is a scalar multiplication where each element in the first matrix is multiplied by its counterpart in the second matrix.

The following operation is a matrix multiplication:

```
matrix_multiply = Matrix_t @ Matrix_t2
print(matrix_multiply) #Matrix Multiplication

tf.Tensor(
[[ 21 210]
 [ 42 420]], shape=(2, 2), dtype=int32)
```

If you need a refresher on matrix multiplication, please refer to Chapter 3. If you are new to TensorFlow, it might be worth your while to try out a few more mathematical operations. You can refer to the TensorFlow documentation for further examples and detailed explanations.

Now let's look at a few other useful functions when it comes to tensors. Consider the following:

```
c = tflow.constant([[4.0, 5.0], [6.0, 8.0], [6.0, 9.0]]) # Some useful functions
print(c)

tf.Tensor(
[[4. 5.]
 [6. 8.]
 [6. 9.]], shape=(3, 2), dtype=float32)
```

We just created a tensor that is a 3 × 2 matrix. If we want to find the largest element in the tensor, we can use the reduce_max function:

```
print(tflow.reduce_max(c)) # Find the largest entry

tf.Tensor(9.0, shape=(), dtype=float32)
```

The preceding operation returns scalar element 9. Since it is a scalar, the shape is empty. What if we wanted to find the index of the largest element? In that case, we can use the argmax function:

```
print(tflow.math.argmax(c)) # Find the index of the largest entry

tf.Tensor([1 2], shape=(2,), dtype=int64)
```

The returned index is [1 2]. The numbers represent the indices of the largest element across the given dimension. A dimension is also known as an axis. Since we have not specified the axis, it defaults to 0. In this case, axis 0 consists of rows, so when we go across the axis the first element in each row is compared. The largest number across the rows for the first element is 6, and its first occurrence is at index 1. Similarly, the largest element across all the rows for the second element is 9, and its index is 2.

Another useful function is softmax, which is used for multiclass predictions (we discussed this briefly in "Neural Networks" on page 86; for more details about this function, you can refer to the TensorFlow documentation):

```
print(tflow.nn.softmax(c)) # Compute the softmax

tf.Tensor(
[[0.26894143 0.7310586 ]
 [0.11920291 0.880797  ]
 [0.04742587 0.95257413]], shape=(3, 2), dtype=float32)
```

In addition to creating tensors using constants, we can also create tensors using arrays or NumPy arrays:

```
#Create Tensors from Numpy Arrays
n_Tensor = tflow.convert_to_tensor(np.array(['AX','BX','ZD']))
#Create Tensor from an Array
a_Tensor = tflow.convert_to_tensor([1.5,2.4,3.9])
```

```
print(n_Tensor)
print(a_Tensor)
print(tflow.nn.softmax(a_Tensor)) #Check the probabilities adding to 1

tf.Tensor([b'AX' b'BX' b'ZD'], shape=(3,), dtype=string)
tf.Tensor([1.5 2.4 3.9], shape=(3,), dtype=float32)
tf.Tensor([0.06904751 0.1698295  0.761123  ], shape=(3,), dtype=float32)
```

Notice how the sum of the output of the softmax function is 1. This is very useful when performing multiclass predictions to understand the corresponding probabilities of each class.

A good understanding of how indices work is imperative in TensorFlow to search and slice data. Let's look at a few examples to understand how this works:

```
v_tensor = tflow.constant([5,7,9,10,20])
print(v_tensor)
print(v_tensor[2]) #Second index
print(v_tensor[2:5]) #Second to 4th index inclusive

tf.Tensor([ 5  7  9 10 20], shape=(5,), dtype=int32)
tf.Tensor(9, shape=(), dtype=int32)
tf.Tensor([ 9 10 20], shape=(3,), dtype=int32)
```

The first print statement simply prints the array. The second print statement prints the element with index 2 in the array. This is the value 9. Remember that indexes start at 0. The third print statement provides a range to print. The range starts at the first number (2) and ends before the second number (5). The starting number is inclusive in the range and the ending number is not inclusive. As a result, in the range from index 2 to index 5 we print index 2 through index 4.

Now let's look at a two-dimensional matrix:

```
m_tensor = tflow.constant([[1,2,3],[4,5,6],[7,8,9]])
print(m_tensor)
print(m_tensor[2,1]) #first index in the second element
print(m_tensor[2,]) #all second index elements

tf.Tensor(
[[1 2 3]
 [4 5 6]
 [7 8 9]], shape=(3, 3), dtype=int32)
tf.Tensor(8, shape=(), dtype=int32)
tf.Tensor([7 8 9], shape=(3,), dtype=int32)
```

The first statement prints a 3 × 3 matrix. There are two dimensions in this array and each dimension has three elements. You can think of it as a table with three rows and three columns.

The second statement provides the location of the value. Since this array has two dimensions, we need to specify the index for each dimension separated by a comma.

Indexes start inward and move outward. With [2,1] we are looking at the second row and first column of our matrix. This number is 8.

The third statement looks for [2,]. When no index is defined for a dimension, all elements will be picked up. This effectively returns all elements in row 2.

To understand the shape of a tensor, we can use the shape() function:

```
s_tensor = tflow.constant([[5,7],[9,10],[20,10]])
print(s_tensor)
print(s_tensor.shape) #Prints the shape of the tensor (3 x 2 matrix)

tf.Tensor(
[[ 5  7]
 [ 9 10]
 [20 10]], shape=(3, 2), dtype=int32)
(3, 2)
```

The preceding output tells us we have three elements for our first axis (axis 0) and two elements for our second axis (axis 1).

We can also reshape a tensor to create another tensor:

```
st_tensor = tflow.reshape(s_tensor, [2, 3]) #Not the same as transpose
print(s_tensor)
print(st_tensor)

tf.Tensor(
[[ 5  7]
 [ 9 10]
 [20 10]], shape=(3, 2), dtype=int32)
tf.Tensor(
[[ 5  7  9]
 [10 20 10]], shape=(2, 3), dtype=int32)
```

Notice how we have linearly picked up elements from the first shape and filled up the second shape. We go across the first row and start filling the first row in the new shape. Then we move to the second and third rows.

Reshaping a tensor is not the same as transposing a tensor. If you want to transpose a tensor, you can use the transpose() function:

```
transpose_tensor = tflow.transpose(s_tensor) #Notice the difference
print(transpose_tensor)


tf.Tensor(
[[ 5  9 20]
 [ 7 10 10]], shape=(2, 3), dtype=int32)
```

This is a matrix transpose. If you want to refresh your memory of what a transpose operation is, you can refer to Chapter 3.

So far we have talked about tensors with regular shapes. However, in real life, data is not always uniform. Missing values and attributes that differ across elements within the same dataset can result in irregularly shaped tensors. Let's look at a couple of examples.

In the following matrix, each row has a variable number of elements:

```
weird_list = [[1],[2,3,4],[2,4],[12,5,4,6,6]]
#Try assigning this to a regular tensor
weird_tensor = tflow.ragged.constant(weird_list)
print(weird_tensor)
# Notice that it ignores the size of each element
# (if it was uniform then this would form the second element in the shape)
print(weird_tensor.shape)

<tf.RaggedTensor [[1], [2, 3, 4], [2, 4], [12, 5, 4, 6, 6]]>
(4, None)
```

A dataset such as the one shown in the preceding example can be represented by ragged tensors. If you print the shape of a ragged tensor, it will give you the size of the regular axis. In this case, it is the rows, and there are four of them. However, for an axis that is variable, it will say None. You can have elements with an unknown number of columns in this tensor.

Here is a tensor with a lot of zeros. It is called a sparse tensor:

```
mostly_empty_list = [1,3,5]
my_indices = [[0,0],[1,1],[2,3]]
full_shape = [3,4]

mostly_empty_tensor = tflow.sparse.SparseTensor(
    indices=my_indices, values=mostly_empty_list,
    dense_shape=full_shape)

print(tflow.sparse.to_dense(mostly_empty_tensor))

tf.Tensor(
[[1 0 0 0]
 [0 3 0 0]
 [0 0 0 5]], shape=(3, 4), dtype=int32)
```

In the preceding example, we provide the values as a list, the indices for each value, and the full shape of the tensor (including the null values). The tensor then places these values at the specified indices and fills the rest of the tensor with zeros. Try printing the mostly_empty_tensor. What do you think the contents of this tensor represent?

Linear Regression Using TensorFlow

The rest of this chapter will delve into predictive analytics using TensorFlow. To understand how TensorFlow can be used for predictive analytics, we will start with linear regression.

We talked extensively about linear regression concepts in Chapter 3 and saw examples of linear regression in Chapter 5 using scikit-learn. Let's look at an example using TensorFlow to get a grasp of the ML process. We will be working with the Keras library, and all code is TensorFlow 2.0 compatible. If you want to follow along, you can use the code in *Chapter6-LinearRegression-PAFME*, located on the book's GitHub repository (*https://oreil.ly/VkZxb*). Before you begin, it might be a good idea to ensure that you are working with a fresh copy of the notebook by selecting Kernel > Restart and Clear Output. You can also use the code in any compatible Python environment.

We'll begin by importing the necessary libraries:

```
import numpy as np #Preprocessing
import pandas as pd #Preprocessing
import seaborn as sns #Visualization
import matplotlib.pyplot as plt #Visualization
import tensorflow as tflow #Predictive Analytics
from tensorflow import keras #Modeling and Predicting
from tensorflow.keras import layers #Model Building
from pandas import options, read_csv #Data import
```

The comments next to each library in the code give a rough classification of its use. We are going to use the dataset from Kaggle (*https://oreil.ly/6ELSf*) for the exercise. You can download a copy of the dataset from the book's GitHub repository (*https://oreil.ly/U6Ycs*). This dataset is built for regression analysis and consists of the fields shown in Table 6-1.

Table 6-1. Attributes of the real estate prices dataset

Serial #	Attribute
1	No
2	X1 transaction date
3	X2 house age (predictor)
4	X3 distance to the nearest MRT station (predictor)
5	X4 number of convenience stores (predictor)
6	X5 latitude
7	X6 longitude
8	Y house price of unit area (predicted)

(MRT in the table stands for Mass Rapid Transit.)

The final attribute, Y house price of unit area, is our predicted attribute. Attributes X1 through X6 are our predictors. Let's now move on to data preparation.

Data Preparation

In this section, we will import and prepare the data before training our model. This will include removing unwanted columns, splitting the data into training and testing sets, and for each set, separating the features from the labels. The following code allows us to import the data and review it, as shown in Figure 6-2. You can refer back to Table 6-1 to understand which of these attributes will be used by our model:

```
#Replace this with where you uncompressed the dataset
local_ds = './Datasets/Real estate.csv'
local_ds = read_csv(local_ds)
local_ds
```

Note that if you're on Windows, you can type a full filepath as long as you escape the backslashes: for example, C:\\Users\\<username>\\Downloads\\Real estate.csv.

	No	X1 transaction date	X2 house age	X3 distance to the nearest MRT station	X4 number of convenience stores
0	1	2012.917	32.0	84.87882	10
1	2	2012.917	19.5	306.59470	9
2	3	2013.583	13.3	561.98450	5
3	4	2013.500	13.3	561.98450	5
4	5	2012.833	5.0	390.56840	5
...	...	...	...	...	...
409	410	2013.000	13.7	4082.01500	0
410	411	2012.667	5.6	90.45606	9
411	412	2013.250	18.8	390.96960	7
412	413	2013.000	8.1	104.81010	5
413	414	2013.500	6.5	90.45606	9

Figure 6-2. Real estate prices dataset

Next, we will create a copy of the dataset and remove the unwanted fields from the data. The processing will mainly depend on Pandas and NumPy, so most of this should look familiar even if you are new to this (see Figure 6-3):

```
k_dataset = local_ds.copy()
k_dataset.pop('No')
k_dataset.pop('X1 transaction date')
k_dataset.pop('X5 latitude')
```

```
k_dataset.pop('X6 longitude')
k_dataset
```

	X2 house age	X3 distance to the nearest MRT station	X4 number of convenience stores	Y house price of unit area
0	32.0	84.87882	10	37.9
1	19.5	306.59470	9	42.2
2	13.3	561.98450	5	47.3
3	13.3	561.98450	5	54.8
4	5.0	390.56840	5	43.1
...	...	...	...	...
409	13.7	4082.01500	0	15.4
410	5.6	90.45606	9	50.0
411	18.8	390.96960	7	40.6
412	8.1	104.81010	5	52.5
413	6.5	90.45606	9	63.9

414 rows × 4 columns

Figure 6-3. Real estate data slice for linear regression

Now we will split the data into the training and testing sets. As a reminder, the training set is what we use to train our model and the testing set is what we use to test the trained model on previously unseen data. We create an 80–20 split between the training and testing datasets:

```
#Create training dataset as 80% of whole dataset
k_training_ds = k_dataset.sample(frac=0.8, random_state=0)
#Create test dataset by dropping training dataset indexes from whole dataset
k_testing_ds = k_dataset.drop(k_training_ds.index)
```

We can look at the distribution of our predictors (Figure 6-4) using the describe() function:

```
k_training_ds.describe()
```

	X2 house age	X3 distance to the nearest MRT station	X4 number of convenience stores	Y house price of unit area
count	331.000000	331.000000	331.000000	331.000000
mean	17.652266	1154.274016	3.996979	37.361329
std	11.305017	1319.156009	2.964945	13.763673
min	0.000000	23.382840	0.000000	7.600000
25%	9.950000	289.324800	1.000000	26.950000
50%	16.100000	515.112200	4.000000	37.900000
75%	27.550000	1604.902500	6.000000	45.500000
max	42.700000	6488.021000	10.000000	117.500000

Figure 6-4. Distribution of predictors

From Figure 6-4, we can see that the three predictors we are using all have quite different scales in terms of data range. For example, X2 house age ranges from 0 to 42.7, while X3 distance to the nearest MRT station ranges from 23 to 6488. We will address this shortly. We can also see that the predictors and the predicted values are sitting in the same dataset. So, let's separate them:

```
k_training_ds = k_training_ds.copy() #Copy of the data
k_testing_ds = k_testing_ds.copy() #Copy of the data

#Separate the features and labels (predictors and predicted)
k_train_predict = k_training_ds.pop('Y house price of unit area')
#Separate the features and labels (predictors and predicted)
k_test_predict = k_testing_ds.pop('Y house price of unit area')
```

In the preceding code, we remove the predicted variable value 'Y house price of unit area' from the training and testing datasets and store these removed values in separate datasets.

Model Creation and Training

Since the columns in our dataset consist of attributes with different ranges, it is advisable to transform this data so that all the columns are at the same scale. In our dataset, the scale of X3 is roughly 150 times greater than that of X2. This is only because they are being expressed in different units. Just because X3 has a bigger scale does not automatically mean it is also a better predictor. But when we do mathematical analysis on this data, larger numbers can influence our findings more. This is not ideal behavior.

As we discussed in Chapter 4, the process of transforming data to bring all data columns to the same scale is known as *normalization*. When it comes to model training, we might be able to get the best fit without normalization, but normalization can help us get there more quickly and with less effort in terms of training speed and performance. Normalization can also help stabilize the training process by keeping the activations within a certain range, making it easier to converge to an optimal solution. In addition, normalization can have a regularization effect by adding noise to the activations during training that can help avoid overfitting and improve generalization.

Keras provides a preprocessing layer for normalizing continuous features (predictors), as shown in the following code:

```
#A preprocessing layer which normalizes continuous features
normalizer = tflow.keras.layers.Normalization(axis=-1)
```

The layer works by scaling inputs in a distribution around 0 with a standard deviation of 1. It does this by precalculating the mean and variance of the data and calling the following function at runtime:

$$\frac{input - mean}{\sqrt{variance}}$$

The normalization function takes the axis of the tensor as input. Our data is a table, which means it has rows and columns. To help you understand this, take a look at the data formats shown in Table 6-2.

Table 6-2. Rows as data dimensions

Feature 1	Value	Value	Value
Feature 2	Value	Value	Value
Feature 3	Value	Value	Value
Feature 4	Value	Value	Value

In the format shown in Table 6-2, the features are represented by the rows. Therefore, when you want to normalize you would use rows for indices. In the case of Table 6-2, the function would track four means and variances, one for each feature. The value of the axis for the normalization function would be 0.

Now consider the data format shown in Table 6-3.

Table 6-3. Columns as the feature dimension

Feature 1	Feature 2	Feature 3
Value	Value	Value
Value	Value	Value
Value	Value	Value

In this format, the features are represented by columns. Therefore, the function would track three means and variances, one for each feature, and the value of the axis for the normalization function would be 1. Note that when axis=-1, it assumes the last axis of the input as the feature dimension. This is the default value and what we will use in this example.

Once the normalizer is created, we need to adapt it for the data. This process involves calculating the mean and variance for each feature:

```
normalizer.adapt(np.array(k_training_ds))
```

We can test out the normalizer layer by checking the mean values calculated when we adapted the layer:

```
print(normalizer.mean)
tf.Tensor([[  17.652266   1154.2739        3.9969788]], shape=(1, 3),
dtype=float32)
```

We can also test the normalization by looking at some test data. In the following code, we take the first 10 records from the training dataset:

```
print('Original: ', np.array(k_training_ds[0:9]))
print('\nNormalized: ', normalizer(np.array(k_training_ds[0:9])).numpy())

Original:  [[1.030000e+01 2.114473e+02 1.000000e+00]
 [2.400000e+01 4.527687e+03 0.000000e+00]
 [3.450000e+01 3.249419e+02 6.000000e+00]
 [2.560000e+01 4.519690e+03 0.000000e+00]
 [1.440000e+01 1.699803e+02 1.000000e+00]
 [3.660000e+01 4.888193e+02 8.000000e+00]
 [3.580000e+01 1.707311e+02 7.000000e+00]
 [3.480000e+01 4.052134e+02 1.000000e+00]
 [1.050000e+01 2.791726e+02 7.000000e+00]]

Normalized:  [[-0.6513389  -0.71580166 -1.0123346 ]
 [ 0.56234723  2.5611227   -1.3501196 ]
 [ 1.4925447  -0.62963563  0.67659056]
 [ 0.70409167  2.5550513   -1.3501196 ]
 [-0.288119   -0.74728376 -1.0123346 ]
 [ 1.678584   -0.50521857  1.3521606 ]
 [ 1.6077119  -0.74671376  1.0143756 ]
 [ 1.5191216  -0.56869286 -1.0123346 ]
 [-0.63362086 -0.66438407  1.0143756 ]]
```

Here, you can see the original data and the normalized data and how the feature scales are matched after they go through normalization.

The next step in TensorFlow is to define the model. We will be using the keras.sequential model for the definition. The sequential API in Keras allows us to define a model as a set of layers where the output for each layer becomes the input for the next layer. For our linear regression, we will be using two layers—a normalization layer, and a linear transformation to produce a dense layer that produces one output:

```
#Define the model
linear_model = tflow.keras.Sequential()
#Add a pre-processing layer
linear_model.add(normalizer)
#Apply linear transformation via a dense layer that produces 1 output
linear_model.add(layers.Dense(1))
linear_model.summary()

Model: "sequential_3"
```

Layer (type)	Output Shape	Param #
normalization (Normalization	(None, 3)	7

```
n)

dense (Dense)                   (None, 1)                    4

=================================================================
Total params: 11
Trainable params: 4
Non-trainable params: 7
```

The next step is to compile the model. For this example, we will be defining two parameters—loss, which is the loss function that needs to be used to achieve model fitting; and optimizer, which is the method used for optimizing the loss:

```
linear_model.compile(
    optimizer=tflow.keras.optimizers.Adam(learning_rate=0.1),
    loss='mean_absolute_error')
```

We are using the Adam optimizer to optimize the mean absolute error. More information on Keras optimizers can be found in the TensorFlow documentation.

The next step is to train the model by calling the fit() method. It would be great if we could visualize the training performance of our model. This is where TensorBoard comes into play. TensorBoard is a visualization toolkit available with TensorFlow to track different metrics, such as loss and accuracy, in ML models. For our purposes, we want to see how long it takes for our model to converge and what is the final error.

We do the initial setup needed to run TensorFlow in our notebook, and then we execute the fit() method:

```
%load_ext tensorboard #TensorBoard extension for notebook

import tensorflow as tf #Import the needed libraries
import datetime
log_dir = "logs/fit/" + datetime.datetime.now().strftime("%Y%m%d-%H%M%S")
tensorboard_callback = tf.keras.callbacks.TensorBoard(
    log_dir=log_dir, histogram_freq=1)
#Fit model
linear_model.fit(
    k_training_ds,
    k_train_predict,
    epochs=100,
    verbose=0,
    validation_split = 0.2, # Validation 20%
    callbacks=[tensorboard_callback])
```

The fit() method uses the following input:

k_training_ds
    The training dataset predictor values

`K_train_predict`
The training dataset predicted Y values

`epochs`
The number of cycles required for the model to be trained

`validation_split`
The fraction of the data used for model validation

`Callbacks`
Used here to log in to TensorBoard

Predictions and Model Evaluation

In this section, we evaluate our model and use it to make predictions.

In the notebook, use the following to launch TensorBoard:

```
%tensorboard --logdir logs/fit
```

We are interested in the `epoch_loss` graph. This tells us how our model converged over the epoch cycles for training and validation. In Figure 6-5, the loss for training converges to a value close to 6, and for the validation data it converges to a value close to 7. Convergence occurs at around 45 epoch cycles, after which our model is no longer learning as the loss values flatline.

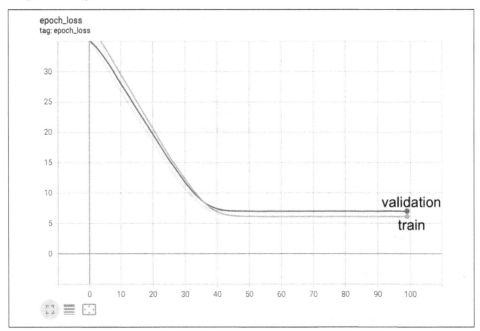

Figure 6-5. TensorBoard `epoch_loss`

We can further evaluate the model on the test data:

```
evaluation = linear_model.evaluate(k_testing_ds, k_test_predict, verbose=1)
print(evaluation)

3/3 [==============================] - 0s 2ms/step - loss: 6.6714
6.6713972091674805
```

For the test data, the loss evaluates to approximately 6.7, which is close to what we saw for our training data. This tells us our model fares well on unseen data and is probably not overfitted.

We can finally do a few predictions and compare them with real values:

```
predictions = linear_model.predict(k_testing_ds[5:8])
print(predictions)

1/1 [==============================] - 0s 18ms/step
[[45.694748]
 [42.129364]
 [35.750698]]
```

We can look at the real values in the testing data to get a feel for how close or far these values are from the real numbers:

```
print(k_test_predict[5:8])

38    47.7
39    46.2
42    34.7
Name: Y house price of unit area, dtype: float64
```

Not bad for a simple model trained over a small dataset. As part of working with TensorFlow, we looked at the steps in the ML life cycle as shown in Figure 6-6.

Now that you understand how to build and execute a simple linear regression model using TensorFlow and Keras, we will expand this knowledge to understand how to work with deep neural networks using the same set of tools and technologies.

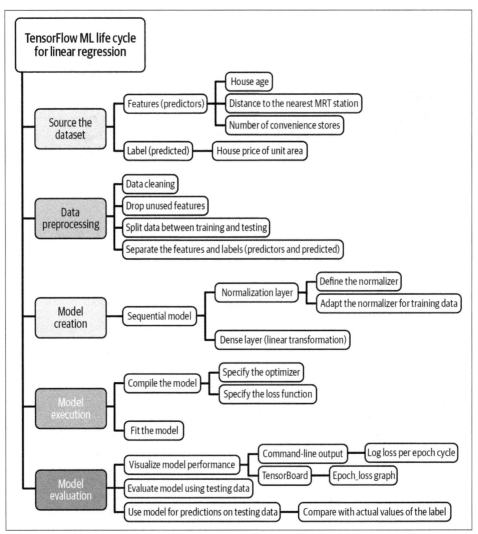

Figure 6-6. TensorFlow ML life cycle for linear regression

Deep Neural Networks in TensorFlow

In this section, we will take things a step further by using a new dataset and building and training a deep neural network (DNN) to perform predictive analytics on the data. We discussed neural networks in some detail in Chapter 3. In the previous section, we built a sequential model with two layers: a normalization layer (mostly used for preprocessing the data) and a linear layer for a single-prediction output. Note that this was a linear model, so our predictions were following a linear or straight line. In this section, we will build a neural network with four layers. Two of the layers are the same as before, and two will be hidden layers. If you would like to follow along, please review the code in *Chapter6-DNN-PAFME.ipynb*, located on the book's GitHub repository (*https://oreil.ly/THrFl*).

Before you begin, ensure that you are working with a fresh copy of the notebook (select Kernel > Restart and Clear Output). You can run the code in the notebook or export the code to any compatible Python environment of your choice.

 Even though the Jupyter Notebook has the complete end-to-end code for what we are discussing, we will only be focusing on the code sections that are unique to building and using the DNN. If you need further explanation of the code, please refer to the corresponding code block in the previous section.

The dataset that we will use in this exercise is sourced from the UC Irvine Machine Learning Repository (*https://oreil.ly/VcrB3*). You can download a copy of the dataset from the book's GitHub repository (*https://oreil.ly/drYZj*). This data is about the physical characteristics of abalones. Abalones are sea snails that are used as a source of food and decoration. With this dataset we will use the physical measurements of the abalone to predict its age.

Normally, predicting the age of an abalone requires cutting through its shell, doing some chemical analysis, and then counting the number of rings using a microscope. According to the UC Irvine Machine Learning Repository, the number of rings plus 1.5 provides the age of the abalone. This process is cumbersome and difficult to scale. With a DNN, we will attempt to predict the age of abalones using physical measurements that don't require cutting and microscopes. Our data consists of the set of attributes shown in Table 6-4.

Table 6-4. Abalone dataset attributes

Serial #	Attribute
1	sex (predictor)
2	length (predictor)
3	diameter (predictor)
4	height (predictor)
5	whole_weight (predictor)
6	shucked_weight (predictor)
7	viscera_weight (predictor)
8	shell_weight (predictor)
9	rings (predicted) (age = rings + 1.5)

Once the data is imported, the dataset should look like Figure 6-7.

	sex	length	diameter	height	whole_weight	shucked_weight	viscera_weight	shell_weight	rings
0	M	0.455	0.365	0.095	0.5140	0.2245	0.1010	0.1500	15
1	M	0.350	0.265	0.090	0.2255	0.0995	0.0485	0.0700	7
2	F	0.530	0.420	0.135	0.6770	0.2565	0.1415	0.2100	9
3	M	0.440	0.365	0.125	0.5160	0.2155	0.1140	0.1550	10
4	I	0.330	0.255	0.080	0.2050	0.0895	0.0395	0.0550	7
...	...	...	...	...	...	...	...	...	...
4172	F	0.565	0.450	0.165	0.8870	0.3700	0.2390	0.2490	11
4173	M	0.590	0.440	0.135	0.9660	0.4390	0.2145	0.2605	10
4174	M	0.600	0.475	0.205	1.1760	0.5255	0.2875	0.3080	9
4175	F	0.625	0.485	0.150	1.0945	0.5310	0.2610	0.2960	10
4176	M	0.710	0.555	0.195	1.9485	0.9455	0.3765	0.4950	12

Figure 6-7. Abalone dataset

All the column values are numeric. However, the sex of the abalone is categorical. While some ML algorithms can work directly with categorical data, others cannot. Table 6-5 is a quick reference showing which models can handle categorical data inherently and which ones might require encoding.

Table 6-5. Algorithm support for categorical data

Can inherently handle categorical data	Need to encode categorical data into numeric values
Logistic regression	Decision trees[a]
Support vector machines (SVMs)	Random forests[a]
k-nearest neighbors	Gradient boosting machines (GBMs)[a]
Neural networks (deep learning)	Naive Bayes algorithm
Principal component analysis (PCA)	Some clustering and rule-based algorithms

[a]While some algorithms can handle categorical data, encoding might be required in certain implementations or to improve performance.

Since we are working with a neural network, we need to transform this data so that the sex is represented numerically, or drop the field from the data altogether. If we want to keep the data, one way to do this is to create one-hot encoding. As we discussed in Chapter 5, one-hot encoding simply means converting a categorical column into an equivalent set of numeric columns.

We use the following code to perform one-hot encoding using Pandas. Thankfully, Pandas has a simple function that can do this for us. When we run this code, we end up with the following dataset:

```
k_dataset = abalone.copy() #Make a copy of the dataset
k_dataset = pd.get_dummies(k_dataset) # Do one hot encoding of categorical fields
k_dataset
```

Next, we split the dataset into testing and training sets, separate the label (rings) from the training and testing data, and create a normalizer. All these steps are very similar to what we covered in the previous section.

As we can see, the sex column has been split into three different columns (Figure 6-8). If the sex was female, the sex_F field for that row in the data is set to 1 and the rest are set to 0. The same applies to the other categories.

whole_weight	shucked_weight	viscera_weight	shell_weight	rings	sex_F	sex_I	sex_M
0.5140	0.2245	0.1010	0.1500	15	0	0	1
0.2255	0.0995	0.0485	0.0700	7	0	0	1
0.6770	0.2565	0.1415	0.2100	9	1	0	0
0.5160	0.2155	0.1140	0.1550	10	0	0	1
0.2050	0.0895	0.0395	0.0550	7	0	1	0
...	...	...	...	...	...	...	...
0.8870	0.3700	0.2390	0.2490	11	1	0	0
0.9660	0.4390	0.2145	0.2605	10	0	0	1
1.1760	0.5255	0.2875	0.3080	9	0	0	1
1.0945	0.5310	0.2610	0.2960	10	1	0	0
1.9485	0.9455	0.3765	0.4950	12	0	0	1

4177 rows × 11 columns

Figure 6-8. Abalone dataset with one-hot encoding

Now our data is ready for some predictive analytics using a DNN:

```
dnn_model = tflow.keras.Sequential() #Define the model
dnn_model.add(normalizer) #Add a preprocessing layer
dnn_model.add(layers.Dense(64, activation='relu')) #nonlinear layer 1
dnn_model.add(layers.Dense(64, activation='relu')) #nonlinear layer 2
dnn_model.add(layers.Dense(1))
#Apply linear transformation via a dense layer that produces 1 output
dnn_model.summary()
```

Model: "sequential_1"

Layer (type)	Output Shape	Param #
normalization_1 (Normalizat ion)	(None, 10)	21
dense_3 (Dense)	(None, 64)	704
dense_4 (Dense)	(None, 64)	4160
dense_5 (Dense)	(None, 1)	65

```
Total params: 4,950
Trainable params: 4,929
Non-trainable params: 21
```

Figure 6-9 shows a crude visualization of the preceding DNN. Note that the figure does not show bias neurons.

We can also build a sequential model using Keras. After the normalizer layer, we add a dense layer with 64 units in each layer. These units define the number of neurons in the layer. The parameters in each layer represent the total possible connections to the next layer. The output shape defines the dimensionality of the output space. Due to the large number of neurons in the hidden layers, we get a much higher number of trainable parameters in this model.

For the hidden layers, we also specified the rectified linear unit (ReLU) activation function. You can refer to the discussion of neural networks in Chapter 3 for further details. Note that the output layer does not have an activation function. This means its output will be the linear combination of the inputs from the layer before.

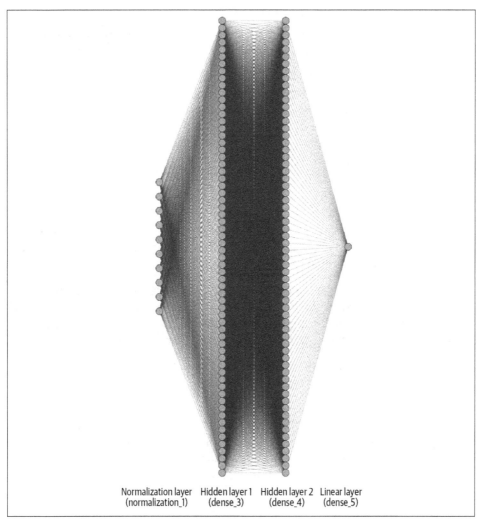

Normalization layer   Hidden layer 1   Hidden layer 2   Linear layer
(normalization_1)   (dense_3)   (dense_4)   (dense_5)

Figure 6-9. Visualizing the deep neural network

There is an important concept that we should discuss here. We talked about normalization and understand the purpose of the normalization layer. We also understand that we need a linear output layer to give us a single prediction in this case. But how do we determine the number of hidden layers and the number of neurons in each layer? Unfortunately, there is no magic formula to calculate these. But there are a number of factors that should be considered while deciding on the architecture of the neural network. Ask yourself the following questions:

Do I have large amounts of data?
> If so, you can experiment with more complex models. Otherwise, stick to simpler models to avoid overfitting the model to the training data.

Am I rich in computational resources?
> When you are working with DNNs with a large number of hidden layers and neurons, you will need a lot more computational power to train your model and use it for predictions.

How complex is the problem I am trying to solve?
> The more complex the problem is, the deeper the neural network requirement might be to solve it.

Am I allowed to experiment?
> See whether you can find a baseline from a similar use case and experiment with varying architectures to evaluate model performance via different metrics (accuracy, precision, recall, etc.).

Is it important for me to understand how my model is coming up with its results?
> If the ability to interpret the model is important to you, simpler architectures are a better choice because it might become increasingly difficult to understand the underlying logic as the number of layers and the number of neurons increase.

What do I know about the business problem that I am solving?
> This can impact decisions such as deciding how many nodes to allocate to which features.

As you can see, there is no one-size-fits-all solution here. Generally, you should start with a simple architecture and work your way up in terms of complexity. Continue to evaluate accuracy and performance while making use of the preceding considerations. You would also want to monitor your model for overfitting and adjust accordingly.

Now that we have discussed the considerations behind the complexity of a neural network architecture, we can compile and fit the model against our training dataset and load the output in TensorBoard. Figure 6-10 depicts the epoch_loss graph.

In Figure 6-10, the loss for training converges to a value slightly below 1.4, and for the validation data it converges to a value close to 1.5. The model learns more quickly initially. However, the learning slows down after 40 epoch cycles. To understand why, we can look at the model against the test data.

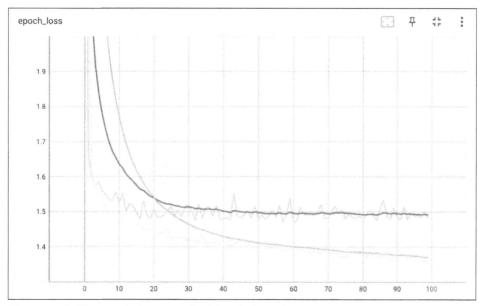

Figure 6-10. The `epoch_loss` *graph of the abalone dataset using DNN*

Evaluation of the test data reveals `oss: 1.5485`. This is close to what we observed with the training data. We can also look at a few predictions:

```
predictions = dnn_model.predict(k_testing_ds[5:8])
print(predictions)

1/1 [==============================] - 0s 95ms/step
[[ 9.567473]
 [11.055283]
 [11.383731]]

[python]
print(k_test_predict[5:8])

24    10
25    11
26    11
Name: rings, dtype: int64
```

As a fun exercise, let's see what happens when we use a DNN to solve the real estate prices problem from earlier in this chapter. The necessary code is a combination of the two exercises we already worked through. However, if you want to test it out, you can review the code in *Chapter6-DNN2-PAFME.ipynb*, located on the book's GitHub repository (*https://oreil.ly/MkC-N*). As a reminder, it might be a good idea to select Kernel > Restart and Clear Output to ensure that you are working with a fresh copy of the notebook. You can run the code in the notebook or export the code to any compatible Python environment of your choice.

Figure 6-11 shows the epoch_loss graph for the real estate prices problem using a DNN versus the earlier linear regression model.

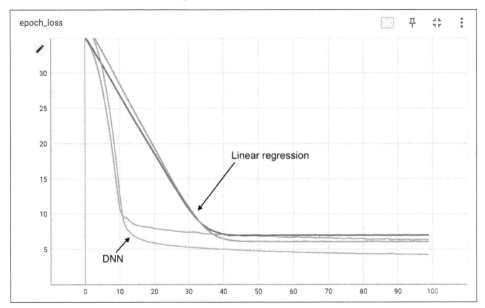

Figure 6-11. Real estate pricing dataset: epoch_loss using DNN versus linear regression

We can make a couple of observations here:

- The DNN converges more quickly in this model than in the linear regression model.

- The loss value for the DNN is lower in this model than in the linear regression model.

We can use these observations and other techniques, such as model cross-validation, to determine which model is the best fit for the problem we are trying to solve. Additionally, we could adjust the number of hidden layers and the number of neurons in the hidden layers and see how it impacts model convergence and other metrics.

Conclusion

In this chapter, we covered the fundamental concepts of TensorFlow, including its setup and its use. We looked at a sequential model using Keras for linear regression and extended this discussion to a deep neural network. We also compared the performance of two models on the same dataset. When working with different models, determining whether the model predictions are accurate enough and whether further tuning is required depends on the business context of what we are trying to achieve with the predictive analysis. The business context would define the corresponding level of acceptable accuracy or loss, which can be used as a guideline for the model. As we discussed before, models are not just built, trained, and then used. They are continuously retrained and tweaked. We will discover more about model life cycle management when we talk about machine learning with hyperscalers in later chapters.

## CHAPTER 7

Predictive Analytics for Business Problem-Solving

So far we have talked about the foundations of predictive analytics. We have talked about algorithms and how they work, libraries and tools that are available for working with predictive analytics, and how to set up these libraries and tools and use them with generic data. In this chapter, we will discuss three use cases, each from a different vertical industry, to see how predictive analytics can be applied in the field. The purpose is to look at scenarios that represent business problems and how predictive analytics can be applied to solve them. As we go through this process, we will cover data preprocessing, specifics of various configurations, and the reasons behind some of the decisions we make as part of building enterprise models for predictive analysis.

Prediction-Based Optimal Retail Price Recommendations

In the retail industry, one of the key metrics for success is revenue. Several techniques are employed across large retail chains to maximize revenue from sales, and the enterprise usually has control over the selling price of a commodity within a particular price range, which can vary by product and region. For example, some cities follow the Manufacturer's Suggested Retail Price (MSRP), while others allow selling above or below that price. In the United Arab Emirates, for instance, gasoline prices are fixed countrywide each month; in the United States, prices can vary from one state to another. Additionally, retail prices for certain items can be higher at airports and hotels than at malls and independent stores. Price variations can also occur due to discounts and promotions; most businesses can offer discounts on their products at different points in time, and a key decision they need to make is how much of a discount should be offered. The idea behind price manipulations is to maximize the sales revenue for the item, which could be a loaf of bread, a gallon of gas, a PC graphics card—basically anything that is being sold and whose price can vary.

Data-driven enterprises will often turn to data analysis to determine the optimal retail price of a commodity. In this section, we will look at how we can help an enterprise build a system that can recommend the optimal retail price for an item based on historical sales data. We will focus on the data analysis piece of such a system. There are two key parts to this data analysis:

- Predicting the number of sales based on different retail prices within a particular range
- Calculating the optimal price within that range that maximizes revenue

We will utilize a sales dataset that represents the daily sales of a particular item, and we will make the following assumptions:

- We have access to historical daily sales data for the item.
- The quantity that the enterprise sells is dependent on the selling price of the item.

Figure 7-1 shows a sample from the dataset we will use for this exercise.

day	price	sales_quantity	item_code
0	1.0	13217.0	52
1	1.0	13132.0	52
2	1.01	12706.0	52
3	1.01	12671.0	52
4	1.02	12748.0	52
5	1.02	13157.0	52
6	1.03	12789.0	52
7	1.03	12824.0	52
8	1.04	12732.0	52
9	1.04	12848.0	52
10	1.05	12707.0	52

Figure 7-1. Dataset sample for retail price recommendation

Our dataset contains the data fields shown in Table 7-1.

Table 7-1. Field description for retail dataset

Serial #	Field name	Description
1	day	Increasing sequence representing one day
2	item_code	Unique code to identify the item (commodity) under discussion
3	price	Price of the item on that day
4	sales_quantity	Number of items sold on that day

We will build the recommendation system in layers. The crucial piece is to get accurate recommendations. If you would like to follow along, you can find the code in *Chapter7-PriceRecommendation-PAFME.ipynb*, located on the book's GitHub repository (*https://oreil.ly/ModqT*).

First we import all the required libraries:

```
import matplotlib.pyplot as plt
import numpy as np
import pandas as pd
import seaborn as sns

#from sklearn import model_selection, metrics
#To perform model cross validation and scoring
# To use Linear Regression Models
from sklearn.linear_model      import LinearRegression
# To split training/testing data
from sklearn.model_selection  import train_test_split
# To check how well our model is performing
from sklearn.metrics import mean_squared_error, mean_absolute_error, r2_score
```

As our dataset source, we are using the *prod.csv* file, which you can download from the book's GitHub repository (*https://oreil.ly/YWndS*).

Let's start by importing the dataset and visualizing the different attributes and their correlations:

```
url = "./Datasets/sale_price/prod.csv" #Replace with where you download the data
sales = pd.read_csv(url) #Read the data from the URL in a Pandas dataframe
sales = sales.copy()
#Take data for itemcode 52
sales = sales[sales['item_code'] == 52]
%matplotlib inline
sns.pairplot(sales, diag_kind='kde') #Plot the dataset
```

We are interested in the correlation between `price` and `sales_quantity`. Figure 7-2 shows the plot for `sales_quantity` versus `price` for our dataset.

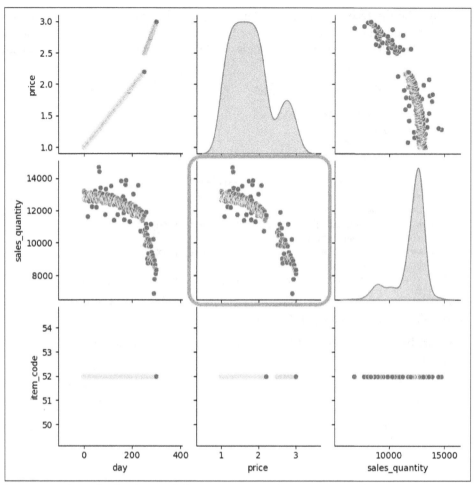

Figure 7-2. Pair plot for the retail dataset

Using a Simple Linear Regression Model

We will start with a simple linear regression model to predict `sales_quantity` based on `price`. This step typically involves feature selection. For our example, we are only considering one feature, price:

```
predictors = ['price'] #Feature
predicted = ['sales_quantity'] #Label
```

At this point, you would want to perform any data preprocessing that might be required. Such preprocessing may include the following, which we discussed in earlier chapters:

- Removing null entities
- Splitting categorical features into numerical fields
- Scaling/normalizing features

Our data has a few null values. We use the following code to identify and remove these rows from our dataset:

```
# Find rows with empty data including NaN
rows_with_empty_data = sales[sales.isna().any(axis=1)]
print("Rows with empty data including NaN:")
print(rows_with_empty_data)

Rows with empty data including NaN:
     day  price  sales_quantity  item_code
300  300    3.0             NaN         52
301  301    3.0             NaN         52
302  302    3.0             NaN         52
303  303    3.0             NaN         52
304  304    3.0             NaN         52

sales = sales.dropna() #Remove rows with empty fields
# Recheck dataset for empty values
rows_with_empty_data = sales[sales.isna().any(axis=1)]
print("Rows with empty data including NaN:")
print(rows_with_empty_data)

Rows with empty data including NaN:
Empty DataFrame
Columns: [day, price, sales_quantity, item_code]
Index: []
```

 We already saw some examples of encoding techniques for converting categorical data into numerical values. We will discuss another technique, scaling features, in "Using Multivariate Regression" on page 233.

We now split the data into testing and training sets, define our linear regression model, and train it using the training dataset:

```
#Split the data
training_data, testing_data = train_test_split(sales,
                                               train_size=0.75,
                                               random_state=110)
#Create a copy of the data instead of referencing
training_data = training_data.copy()
```

```
#Create a copy of the data instead of referencing
testing_data = testing_data.copy()

l_regression = LinearRegression() # Initialize the model

l_regression.fit(training_data[predictors],
                 training_data[predicted]) # Training the model
```

At this point, we have a trained model that we can use to predict sales_quantity. We perform these predictions on the testing dataset. Note that testing data has not been used in training and therefore is previously unseen by our linear model:

```
#predictions on the test data
predictions = l_regression.predict(testing_data[predictors])
print(predictions)

[[12562.21100083]
 [13087.111566  ]
 [11673.91773669]
 [ 9937.70817496]
 [13389.93881514]
 [12319.94920152]
 [11249.95958789]
 [11855.61408617]
 [13066.92308272]
 ...
```

We store the actual values for sales_quantity in another array, called actual:

```
actual = testing_data[predicted] #Actual sales quantities for the testing data
print(actual)

      sales_quantity
111         12467.0
55          12867.0
201         12366.0
282          8909.0
24          12861.0
..              ...
181         12184.0
277          9140.0
94          12933.0
281          9190.0
228         11636.0

[75 rows x 1 columns]
```

Next, we plot the actual testing data versus the predictions to visualize the fit for our regression model (see Figure 7-3):

```
# Plot the testing data
plt.scatter(testing_data[predictors], actual, color="blue", marker=".")
# Plot the predicted values using the predictions as the fitted line
plt.plot(testing_data[predictors], predictions, color="red")

plt.xlabel(predictors) #Label the X axis
plt.ylabel(predicted) #Label the Y axis

plt.show()
```

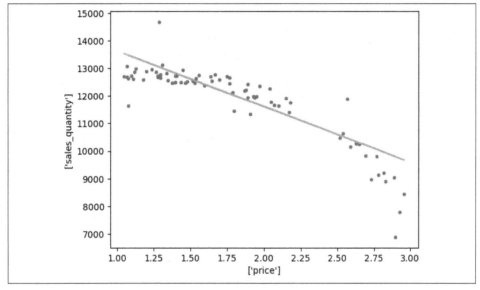

Figure 7-3. Simple linear regression: `sales_quantity` *versus* `price`*, testing data*

We can also visualize the model fitting across the entire dataset for this item (`item_id=52`) by plotting a prediction line from 1 to 3 at regular intervals. We do this using the NumPy function, `linspace()`:

```
print(np.linspace(1, 3))
```

```
[1.         1.04081633 1.08163265 1.12244898 1.16326531 1.20408163
 1.24489796 1.28571429 1.32653061 1.36734694 1.40816327 1.44897959
 1.48979592 1.53061224 1.57142857 1.6122449  1.65306122 1.69387755
 1.73469388 1.7755102  1.81632653 1.85714286 1.89795918 1.93877551
 1.97959184 2.02040816 2.06122449 2.10204082 2.14285714 2.18367347
 2.2244898  2.26530612 2.30612245 2.34693878 2.3877551  2.42857143
 2.46938776 2.51020408 2.55102041 2.59183673 2.63265306 2.67346939
 2.71428571 2.75510204 2.79591837 2.83673469 2.87755102 2.91836735
 2.95918367 3.         ]
```

Next, we capture this feature range and convert it into a Pandas DataFrame so that we can assign a feature name to it, then use this generated feature to plot our predictions on top of the actual sales dataset for the particular item (see Figure 7-4). Refer to Chapter 3 for examples of a best-fit line superimposed on actual data to visualize the model fit. This is precisely what we are doing here; however, it is no longer theoretical, but implemented as functions with real data:

```
#generate points in range at equal intervals
feature_range = np.linspace(1, 3)
#Convert points to a dataframe with price label
feature_range = pd.DataFrame(feature_range,columns=['price'])
plt.plot(sales[predictors], sales[predicted],
         'b.', feature_range[predictors],
         l_regression.predict(feature_range[predictors]), 'r')
         #Plot all sales data for item_id=52 and the
         #prediction line using the generated features

plt.xlabel(predictors) #Label the x axis
plt.ylabel(predicted) #Label the y axis

plt.show()
```

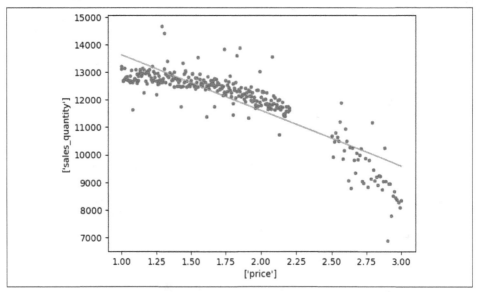

Figure 7-4. Simple linear regression: sales_quantity versus price, all data

From the shape of the fitting, we can see that the line does not fit well, especially around the two extremes. To add to this visual analysis, we can look at some metrics for the trained model. We compute a few metrics to gauge how well our model is performing:

```
#R-squared score
r2 = r2_score(actual, predictions)
#Root Mean Squared Error
rmse = mean_squared_error(actual, predictions, squared=False)
#Mean Absolute Error
mae = mean_absolute_error(actual, predictions)

print("R-Squared: ",r2 )
print("RMSE: ",rmse)
print("MAE: ",mae)

R-Squared:  0.7559499163970946
RMSE:  699.5835213671534
MAE:  496.9973124296419
```

This is our first attempt at modeling the data for our price recommender. Next, we will see whether we can improve the fit for our model using other modeling techniques and then select what is best for our use case. We will keep collecting the scoring metrics in a table (see Table 7-2) so that we can compare them as we go along. Fitting a model is, in most cases, an iterative approach, and machine learning (ML) practitioners would go through several of these iterations to come up with a model that best fits their business requirements.

Table 7-2. Predictive model metric scores

Metric	Simple linear regression
R-squared	0.7559499163970946
Root mean squared error	699.5835213671534
Mean absolute error	496.9973124296419

Using a Polynomial Regression Model

In this section, we will model the same data using a polynomial regression model. Recall that a polynomial regression model helps us when the relationship between the independent and dependent variables is nonlinear (i.e., it cannot be represented with a straight line). In statistics terms, when our dependent variable (y) is represented as a function of our independent variable (x), the power of x is greater than 1. We will be working under the following assumptions:

- Independent variable = price
- Dependent variable = sales_quantity
- Relationship = polynomial

You can download *Chapter7-PriceRecommendation-PAFME-Polynomial-1.ipynb* from the book's GitHub repository (*https://oreil.ly/gvJiv*) to follow along.

We begin by importing the required libraries and classes:

```
import matplotlib.pyplot as plt
import numpy as np
import pandas as pd


#To perform model cross validation and scoring
from sklearn import model_selection, metrics
# The linear regression class in scikit learn supports polynomial regression
from sklearn.linear_model     import LinearRegression
# To create testing and training splits of data
from sklearn.model_selection  import train_test_split
#modeling scoring metrics
from sklearn.metrics import mean_squared_error, mean_absolute_error, r2_score
#Preprocessing class to generate polynomial features
from sklearn.preprocessing import PolynomialFeatures
```

Note that we are still using the `linear_model` class in scikit-learn. This is because you can use the same class to train a polynomial regression model. A simple way to understand this is by analyzing Figure 7-5.

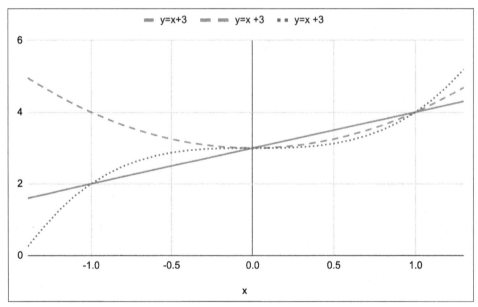

Figure 7-5. Linear, quadratic, and cubic equations

When we plot y as a function of x we get a straight line for y = x and curves for the other two with higher powers. However, if we were to plot $y = x^2+3$ against x^2 (instead of x), this graph would be a straight line, as shown in Figure 7-6.

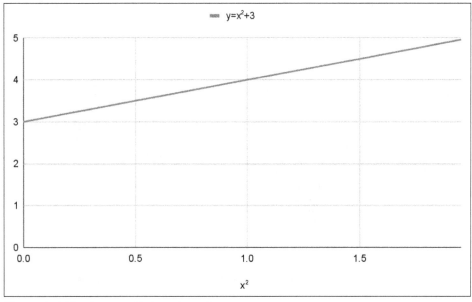

Figure 7-6. Plotting $y = x^2+3$ against x^2

While the relationship between y and x is nonlinear, the relationship between y and x^2 can be represented using a straight line. We can do the same with higher-degree polynomials. As a result, the linear regression library is able to model polynomial relationships.

Additionally, we have imported `PolynomialFeatures` to generate polynomial data features from our independent variables. The dataset used here is the same as in the previous exercise. We continue importing the dataset and defining the features and labels:

```
url = "./Datasets/sale_price/prod.csv"
sales = pd.read_csv(url) #Read the data from the URL in a Pandas DataFrame
predictors = ['price']
predicted = ['sales_quantity']
sales = sales.copy()
sales = sales[sales['item_code'] == 52]
sales = sales.dropna() #Preprocess the data to drop empty values
```

With the data imported, we can now train the polynomial model. We'll start by defining the polynomial degree that we want to consider. We currently do not know what degree of polynomial would be a good fit for our data. Therefore, we will train our model with increasing degrees of polynomials and then compare them to see what fits best:

```
#Polynomial range
degree_min = 1
degree_max = 5
```

Now we define a loop to train and test the models in the resulting range:

```
# Train models with increasing polynomial degree and compare scoring metrics
for poly_d in range(degree_min,degree_max+1):
    #Polynomial generator
    poly_gen = PolynomialFeatures(degree=poly_d, include_bias=False)
    #Generate polynomial features
    poly_features = poly_gen.fit_transform(sales[predictors])
    X_train, X_test, y_train, y_test = train_test_split(
        poly_features, sales[predicted], train_size=0.75,
        random_state=110) #create Test/Train split
```

In the preceding code, we did the following:

- We defined the polynomial feature generator using the PolynomialFeatures class that we imported. Note that the degree passed to the function is a variable based on a specific iteration of the for loop we are in. Also, we do not need to add bias to the data, because we are going to use the linear regression model that automatically takes care of this (fit_intercept in LinearRegression is set to true by default).

- We generated the polynomial features for our sales data.

- We split the data into training and testing subsets. Note that we used poly_features to create the split and not just sales[predictors].

The next section of the for loop defines the polynomial regression model, fits the model on the training dataset, and performs predictions on the test data:

```
poly_reg_model = LinearRegression() #Define the model
poly_reg_model.fit(X_train, y_train) #Fit the model
poly_reg_y_predicted = poly_reg_model.predict(X_test)
#predict based on test data
```

Finally, we print the R-squared score, root mean squared error (RMSE), and mean absolute error (MAE) for each iteration:

```
#R-squared score
    r2 = r2_score(y_test, poly_reg_y_predicted)
    #Root Mean Squared Error
    rmse = mean_squared_error(y_test, poly_reg_y_predicted, squared=False)
    #Mean Absolute Error
    mae = mean_absolute_error(y_test, poly_reg_y_predicted)
    print("Degree: ", poly_d)
    print("R-Squared: ",r2 )
    print("RMSE: ",rmse)
    print("MAE: ",mae, "\n")

Degree:  1
R-Squared:  0.7559499163970946
RMSE:  699.5835213671534
MAE:  496.9973124296419

Degree:  2
R-Squared:  0.8854371932495116
RMSE:  479.3159856299965
MAE:  293.40036676505747

Degree:  3
R-Squared:  0.8880765913904459
RMSE:  473.7623614777194
MAE:  289.5699290080416

Degree:  4
R-Squared:  0.8858440705704365
RMSE:  478.46406746871514
MAE:  290.7304541259328

Degree:  5
R-Squared:  0.8857688900250951
RMSE:  478.62159441099567
MAE:  290.77975855952593
```

These scores are depicted in Figure 7-7.

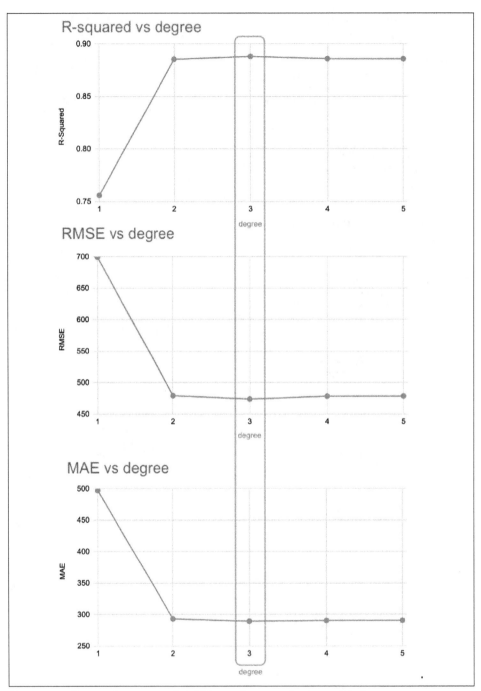

Figure 7-7. Comparing metrics for different degrees of polynomials in a polynomial regression

For our dataset, the maximum R-squared score is achieved at the third-degree polynomial, and both RMSE and MAE have minimum values at the same degree (within the range of 1 to 5). We can visualize the fit of the third-degree polynomial prediction model on the sales data. To do this, we rerun the model training using `degree_max = 3`. Once the model training is complete, the following code helps us visualize our model:

```
#Generate x features in range
feature_range = np.linspace(1, 3)
#Generate polynomial features
poly_features = poly_gen.fit_transform(feature_range.reshape(-1,1))

#Make predictions on polynomial features
y_predicted = poly_reg_model.predict(poly_features)
plt.scatter(sales[predictors], sales[predicted]) #Plot actual data
plt.plot(feature_range,y_predicted, c="red") #Plot predictions

plt.xlabel(predictors)
plt.ylabel(predicted)
```

We generate `price` within the range of 1 to 3, then use it to generate polynomial features. Note that we are applying a `reshape()` operation on `feature_range` because the `fit_transform` function expects a 2D array but `feature_range` by default is a 1D array. Now we can plot the actual data and then the prediction line that shows us the fit of the model (see Figure 7-8).

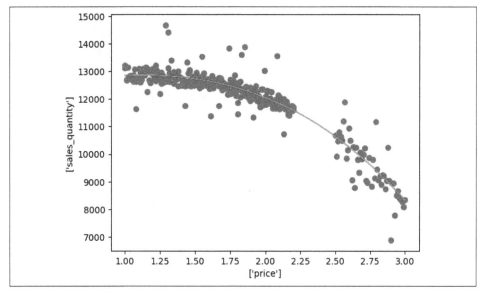

Figure 7-8. Third-degree polynomial regression: `sales_quantity` *versus* `price`, *all data*

Visually, we can see that the prediction line is a better fit compared to the linear model we discussed earlier. We can now compare the scores between both models, as shown in Table 7-3.

Table 7-3. Predictive model metric scores

Metric	Simple linear regression	Third-degree polynomial regression	Fourth-degree polynomial regression
R-squared	0.7559499163970946	0.8880765913904459	0.8858440705704365
Root mean squared error	699.5835213671534	473.7623614777194	478.46406746871514
Mean absolute error	496.9973124296419	289.5699290080416	290.7304541259328

Our third-degree polynomial regression model has a higher R-squared score and produces much lower values for RMSE and MAE. Based on our current investigation, we will go forward with our third-degree polynomial regression model for our dataset.

Now that we have a way to predict the sales quantity of a product based on its price, the next step is to figure out what price is going to maximize our sales revenue for the item. To recap:

- `price` is the unit price of the item.
- `sales_quantity` is the number of items sold in a day.

The total revenue from the item for the day can be defined as:

`price` of the item on that day × number of items sold that day (`sales_quantity`)

It is likely that the optimal price to maximize sales is driven by other external factors, such as the cost of the item to the business or the minimum profit margin expected on the item. Considering this, it would be realistic to assume that each item would have a baseline price and a range above or below that price that could be used to come up with an optimal selling price. The following code helps us calculate the respective sales totals for a day based on the price we set for the item:

```
y_predicted = y_predicted.flatten() #Flatten the predicted values to a 1d array
#Multiply feature_range values with predicted sales_quantity
# (Total Sales = price * sales_quantity)
total = feature_range*y_predicted
total

array([12854.40798534, 13386.91078617, 13917.07135795, 14444.45330157,
       14968.60542649, 15489.06175077, 16005.34150105, 16516.94911255,
       17023.37422911, 17524.09170312, 18018.56159558, 18506.22917607,
       18986.52492277, 19458.86452244, 19922.64887042, 20377.26407065,
       20822.08143566, 21256.45748656, 21679.73395305, 22091.23777343,
       22490.28109457, 22876.16127194, 23248.16086959, 23605.54766017,
```

```
23947.57462492, 24273.47995364, 24582.48704475, 24873.80450525,
25146.62615072, 25400.13100533, 25633.48330186, 25845.83248164,
26036.31319461, 26204.04529931, 26348.13386285, 26467.66916093,
26561.72667785, 26629.36710648, 26669.63634829, 26681.56551334,
26664.17092028, 26616.45409634, 26537.40177734, 26425.98590769,
26281.16364039, 26101.87733703, 25887.05456778, 25635.60811141,
25346.43595526, 25018.42129529]])
```

The preceding array depicts how the total sales revenue for the day is predicted to change as we change the item price from 1 to 3.

Next, we find the maximum value for the total sales in the array and the corresponding price for this value:

```
ymax = max(total) #Maximum value for total sales revenue
xpos = np.where(total == ymax) #Position of x(price) for Maximum value of total
xmax = feature_range[xpos] #Value of x(price) where total is maximized
```

In the preceding code, ymax provides the maximum value for the total sales revenue and xmax provides the corresponding price to achieve the maximum sales revenue. We plot total sales revenue versus price to get a better understanding of how the revenue forecast changes with price:

```
fig = plt.figure()
ax = fig.add_subplot()
line = ax.plot(feature_range, total)#Plot total sales revenue vs item price

ax.annotate(xmax, xy=(xmax, ymax),
            xytext=(xmax, ymax + 2000),
            arrowprops=dict(facecolor='red'),)
            #Label the maximum point with the price value

#Vertical line for price
ax.axvline(xmax, color='red', linestyle='dashed')
#Horizontal line for total sales revenue
ax.axhline(ymax, color='red', linestyle='dashed')

plt.title("Sales revenue variation vs price\nItem_id 52",
          fontdict={'horizontalalignment': 'right'})
plt.xlabel(predictors)
plt.ylabel('Total sales revenue / day')

plt.show()
```

Figure 7-9 shows the total predicted sales revenue versus price.

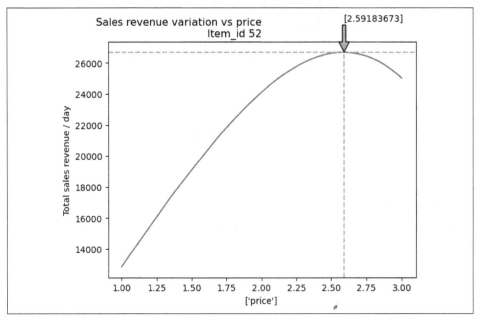

Figure 7-9. Total predicted sales revenue versus price

Finally we print the optimal selling price and the corresponding maximum daily sale that we calculated in the previous steps:

```
print("Optimal selling price: ", xmax[0])
print("Maximum Daily sale: ", ymax)

Optimal selling price:  2.591836734693877
Maximum Daily sale:  26681.56551334295
```

If we analyze Figure 7-9, we can see that the sales revenue increases as the price increases, until it reaches the optimal point, after which it starts to dip again. The xmax value gives us the sweet spot that maximizes the sales revenue for the day. Model training in this case is per item. The relationship between price and sales quantity can vary from item to item. Therefore, we can train a model for each item for which we are trying to predict the optimal selling price.

Let's look at another item, item_id 55, and see how we can use the same approach to get to the optimal selling price. To follow along, you can use the code in *Chapter7-PriceRecommendation-PAFME-Polynomial-2.ipynb*, located on the book's GitHub repository (*https://oreil.ly/UJ4Kd*). The dataset we'll be using is similar to what we used before, only for a different item, so we will not go through the code line by line. The minor changes in this code are as follows:

- The item_id = 55.

- The price range is from 3 to 5.5.

With this code, we produce the following scores for the various polynomial degrees:

```
Degree:  1
R-Squared:  0.8851430150842249
RMSE:  497.8022250113159
MAE:  372.4902877873549

Degree:  2
R-Squared:  0.9011934531197527
RMSE:  461.71181545053577
MAE:  343.9573255538185

Degree:  3
R-Squared:  0.9015868720634368
RMSE:  460.7916975185649
MAE:  349.4669826011889

Degree:  4
R-Squared:  0.8992727128479514
RMSE:  466.1779163321006
MAE:  353.45284680920014

Degree:  5
R-Squared:  0.9002130083498551
RMSE:  463.9969145022886
MAE:  349.50221110759304
```

We do not have a clear winner, like we did in the previous example, but we can see that both the second- and third-degree polynomials are good choices. We could augment the data and play with the data range, but for the sake of simplicity we will go ahead with a second-degree polynomial. Figure 7-10 shows how our prediction model fits the actual values.

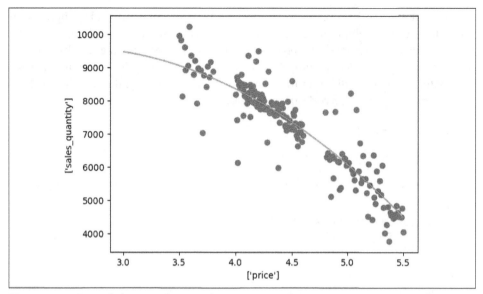

Figure 7-10. Second-degree polynomial regression: `sales_quantity` *versus* `price,`
`item_id 55`

The optimal price calculations based on a second-degree polynomial regression
model are depicted in Figure 7-11.

For `item_id 55`, we can predict an optimal selling price of approximately $4.17 that
will get us to a daily sales revenue of a little over $33,000.

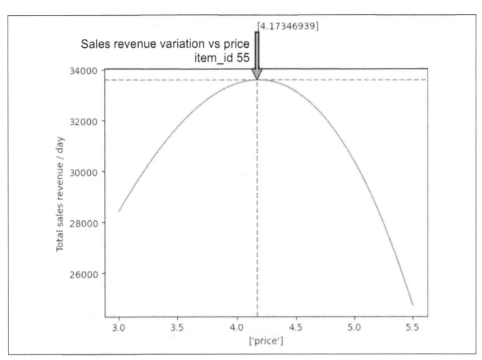

Figure 7-11. Total predicted sales revenue versus price, `item_id 55`

Using Multivariate Regression

So far, we have covered linear and polynomial linear regression for modeling our data. For both of these models, we worked under the assumption that the feature impacting sales quantity for a particular item is the item's unit price. But other factors can also impact sales. In this section, we will see how the temperature on a particular day can impact sales. In predictive analytics terms, we will have two independent features, `price` and `max_temp`, and one dependent variable, `sales_qty`. This form of analysis is known as *multivariate analysis* as it deals with figuring out the impact of multiple variables on our predictions. The code for this analysis can be found in *Chapter7-PriceRecommendation-PAFME-Polynomial-1-MultiVariate.ipynb*, located on the book's GitHub repository (*https://oreil.ly/ryBOo*).

We begin by importing the required libraries, most of which should be familiar to you by now:

```
import matplotlib.pyplot as plt
import numpy as np
import pandas as pd
import pickle #Saving and loading models

# For preprocessing predictors
from sklearn import preprocessing
# To perform model cross validation and scoring
from sklearn import model_selection, metrics
# The linear regression class in scikit learn supports
# polynomial regression
from sklearn.linear_model    import LinearRegression
# To create testing and training splits of data
from sklearn.model_selection  import train_test_split
# Modeling scoring metrics
from sklearn.metrics import mean_squared_error, mean_absolute_error, r2_score
#Preprocessing class to generate polynomial features
from sklearn.preprocessing import PolynomialFeatures
```

Next, we import the sales data. This is a similar dataset to what we saw before; the only difference is that it contains the highest temperature recorded (max_temp) for the day along with the price and sales quantity. The dataset used in this exercise is in the file *prod3.csv*, located on the book's GitHub repository (*https://oreil.ly/s7CzI*):

```
#Import sales data with temperature information
url = "./Datasets/sale_price/prod3.csv"
#Read the data from the URL in a Pandas dataframe
sales = pd.read_csv(url)
predictors = ['price','max_temp']
predicted = ['sales_quantity']

sales = sales.copy()
sales = sales[sales['item_code'] == 52] #We are interested in Item_id=52
sales
```

Figure 7-12 shows the predictive model metric scores.

	day	price	sales_quantity	max_temp	item_code
0	0	1.00	11447.0	8.0	52
1	1	1.00	12478.0	25.0	52
2	2	1.01	11739.0	19.0	52
3	3	1.01	13090.0	23.0	52
4	4	1.02	12951.0	14.0	52
...	...	...	...	...	...
295	295	2.96	8775.0	24.0	52
296	296	2.97	6840.0	35.0	52
297	297	2.98	7175.0	9.0	52
298	298	2.99	7764.0	15.0	52
299	299	3.00	8189.0	22.0	52

300 rows × 5 columns

Figure 7-12. Predictive model metric scores

Note that for our predictors, we have included both price and max_temp. Let's try to visualize this data on a 3D scatterplot:

```
#Get plotting data
x=sales['price']
y=sales['max_temp']
z=sales['sales_quantity']
#Plot the data in 3D
fig = plt.figure(figsize=(10,8))
ax = fig.add_subplot(111, projection='3d')
ax.scatter(x, y, z, c='blue', marker='.')
#Set axis labels and title
ax.set_xlabel('price')
ax.set_ylabel('high temperature')
ax.set_zlabel('sales quantity')
plt.title('Sales_quantity vs price vs max_temp - Item_id 52')
#Plot the graph
plt.show()
```

We are plotting our sales quantity against price and max_temp. The data helps answer the following business question: On a given day, what is the number of items sold for item_id 52, with price set to x and max_temp at location y?

The preceding code should help generate a 3D plot similar to the one shown in Figure 7-13.

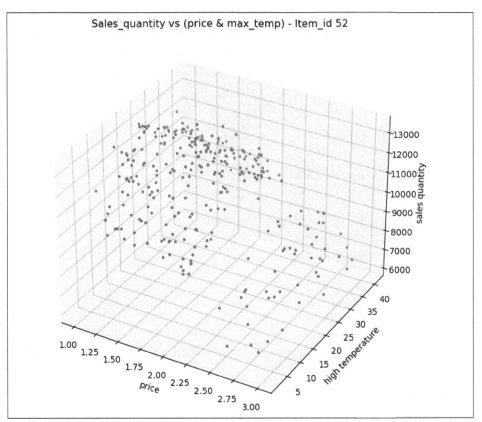

Figure 7-13. Sales quantity versus price at high temperature (multivariate)

Each axis on the plot represents each variable we are working with.

Next, we will scale both of our predictors (independent variables). Scaling is usually required when the range covered by different variables varies significantly. In this case, the item's price varies from 1 to 3 and the temperature varies from 0 to 40. While these scales are not drastically different, we will include scaling regardless so that you can follow along with different variables or a different dataset that might have more variation in the scales:

```
#Preprocessing the predictors to scale them
scaler = preprocessing.MinMaxScaler(feature_range=(0, 1))
scaler = scaler.fit(sales[predictors])
sales[predictors] = scaler.transform(sales[predictors])
sales
```

We scale the data using `MinMaxScaler` so that each variable will fall in the range from 0 to 1, as shown in Figure 7-14.

	day	price	sales_quantity	max_temp	item_code
0	0	0.000	11447.0	0.153846	52
1	1	0.000	12478.0	0.589744	52
2	2	0.005	11739.0	0.435897	52
3	3	0.005	13090.0	0.538462	52
4	4	0.010	12951.0	0.307692	52
...	...	...	...	...	...
295	295	0.980	8775.0	0.564103	52
296	296	0.985	6840.0	0.846154	52
297	297	0.990	7175.0	0.179487	52
298	298	0.995	7764.0	0.333333	52
299	299	1.000	8189.0	0.512821	52

Figure 7-14. Scaled features (`price`, `max_temp`)

Now it is time to define and train the model. Similar to the previous section, we train multiple models with increasing polynomial degrees and compare the scoring metrics for each to figure out which model is the best fit for our data:

```
#Polynomial Range
degree_min = 1
degree_max = 5

# Train models with increasing polynomial degree and compare scoring metrics
for poly_d in range(degree_min,degree_max+1):
    #Polynomial generator
    poly_gen = PolynomialFeatures(degree=poly_d, include_bias=False)
    #Generate polynomial features
    poly_features = poly_gen.fit_transform(sales[predictors])
    X_train, X_test, y_train, y_test = train_test_split(
        poly_features,sales[predicted],
        train_size=0.75, random_state=110) #create Test/Train split

    poly_reg_model = LinearRegression() #Define the model
    poly_reg_model.fit(X_train, y_train) #Fit the model
    poly_reg_y_predicted = poly_reg_model.predict(
        X_test) #predict based on test data

    r2 = r2_score(y_test, poly_reg_y_predicted) #R-squared score
    rmse = mean_squared_error(
        y_test, poly_reg_y_predicted,
        squared=False) #Root Mean Squared Error
    mae = mean_absolute_error(
        y_test, poly_reg_y_predicted) #Mean Absolute Error
```

```
print("Degree: ", poly_d)
print("R-Squared: ",r2 )
print("RMSE: ",rmse)
print("MAE: ",mae, "\n")

file1 = "model" + str(poly_d)
file2 = file1 + "_poly"
#Store the model in a file at each iteration
pickle.dump(poly_reg_model, open(file1, "wb"))
#Store the polynomial feature generator model in a file at each iteration
pickle.dump(poly_gen, open(file2, "wb"))
```

At a high level, we are training polynomial regression models in a loop with increasing polynomial degrees and printing the respective scores for each iteration. If you need to understand this code line by line, you can refer to the explanation in "Using a Polynomial Regression Model" on page 221. The preceding code produces the following results:

```
Degree:  1
R-Squared:  0.7555878925181352
RMSE:  702.5486307222614
MAE:  540.3235750718316

Degree:  2
R-Squared:  0.939814908354835
RMSE:  348.62577831543433
MAE:  266.2397451754418

Degree:  3
R-Squared:  0.9404913067261566
RMSE:  346.66120372505924
MAE:  250.07397854683367

Degree:  4
R-Squared:  0.9289660375763467
RMSE:  378.7459995524183
MAE:  261.7178583469461

Degree:  5
R-Squared:  0.9234899818928994
RMSE:  393.0738804429705
MAE:  270.37503321410856
```

From the preceding output, you can see that the third-degree polynomial regression model has the highest R-squared score and the lowest error scores. Based on this, we will continue with a third-degree polynomial regression model. Note that we are saving the polynomial regression model and the polynomial generator for each iteration in a file. Later, we will load the models from these files rather than making code changes to get to the X-degree polynomial model that we want to use.

Now that our model is trained, it is ready to perform some predictions. We begin by loading the corresponding models from our third iteration:

```
poly_d = 3 #Use third degree polynomial
file1 = "model" + str(poly_d)
file2 = file1 + "_poly"
#Load 3rd degree polynomial model
poly_reg_model = pickle.load(open(file1, "rb"))
poly_gen = pickle.load(open(file2, "rb")) #Load polynomial generator model
```

Now we create simple sample features and analyze the corresponding predictions:

```
predict_test = pd.DataFrame([2,2,2],columns=['price'])
predict_test['max_temp'] = [5,22,45]
predict_test = scaler.transform(predict_test) #Scale features
#Generate polynomial features from sample
predict_poly_features = poly_gen.fit_transform(predict_test)
#Use the model to make predictions
predicted_test = poly_reg_model.predict(predict_poly_features)
predicted_test
array([[10371.62028047],
       [11703.81900753],
       [ 9028.39953932]])
```

For the preceding code, we are keeping `price` constant at 2 and varying `max_temp`. If we were to use our previous model (the one without the temperature data), we would end up with the same prediction irrespective of how the temperature varies. However, our new model considers temperature data. We can see that we are selling more items when the temperature is pleasant (71.6°F [22°C]) and that sales tend to drop when the temperature decreases or increases. When working with data, it is important to look at the output and ensure that it makes sense from a real-world perspective. While this does not guarantee that the model is accurate, it does indicate whether we are on the right track.

To better visualize our predictions, we will generate our feature range. But because we have two features, we cannot just use `linspace` to generate an equally spaced sequence for a single variable. To see what I mean, take a look at the following code:

```
#Generate synthetic feature data
xy = np.mgrid[5:40:0.1,1:3:0.05].reshape(2,-1).T
```

The preceding line of code generates temperature data from 5 to 40 with a step size of 0.1. For each temperature entry, it generates price data from 1 to 3 with a step size of 0.05. It then creates a second array from this generated data. This is depicted in Figure 7-15.

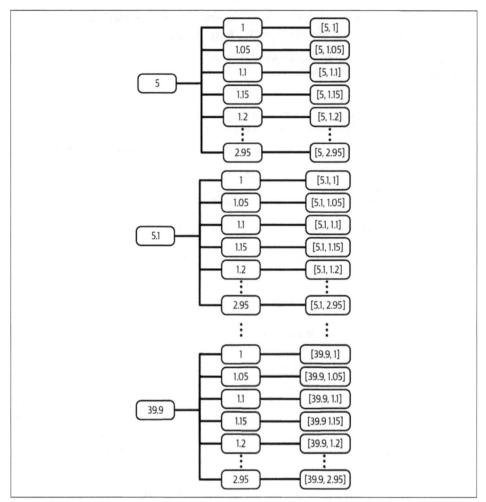

Figure 7-15. Synthetic features

The following code helps us store the generated data in a Pandas DataFrame for ease of use:

```
#Assign generated feature data to a pandas dataframe
syn_data = pd.DataFrame(xy[:,1],columns=['price'])
syn_data['max_temp'] = xy[:,0]
```

Next, we use this synthetic data to make predictions from our trained model:

```
syn_data_scaled = syn_data.copy()
#Scale features
syn_data_scaled[predictors] = scaler.transform(syn_data_scaled[predictors])
predict_poly_features = poly_gen.fit_transform(syn_data_scaled[predictors])
predicted_test = poly_reg_model.predict(predict_poly_features)
```

Then we add these predictions to our existing dataset plot to visualize our model (see Figure 7-16):

```
xp=xy[:,1] #Price axis
yp=xy[:,0] #Temperature axis
zp=predicted_test #Sales axis
fig = plt.figure(figsize=(10,8))
ax = fig.add_subplot(111, projection='3d') #3D plot
ax.scatter(xp, yp, zp, c='red', marker='.') #Plot predictions
ax.scatter(x, y, z, c='blue', marker='.') #Plot actual data
#Set axis labels and title
ax.set_xlabel('price')
ax.set_ylabel('high temperature')
ax.set_zlabel('sales quantity')
plt.title('Prediction of Sales_quantity vs (price & max_temp) - Item_id 52')
#Plot the graph
plt.show()
```

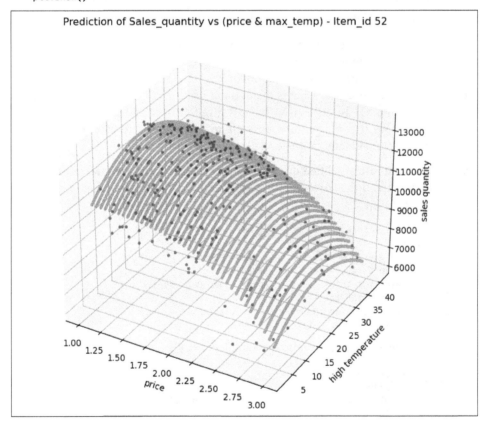

Figure 7-16. Predictions of sales quantity versus price and high temperature (multivariate)

The dots in Figure 7-16 represent the original data. Each curve represents how `sales_quantity` varies with `max_temp` while `price` is kept constant. We can do a quick visual analysis of the plot to come up with the following deductions:

- For a fixed price, sales are highest when the temperature ranges from 68°F to 77°F (20°C to 25°C). As it gets colder or hotter, sales tend to drop.
- Looking at a cross section (slice), on a given day (i.e., `max_temp` is fixed), sales increase (nonlinearly) as the price of the item decreases.

With our predictions ready, we store them in the same Pandas DataFrame as before and calculate the corresponding total sales:

```
syn_data['sales_quantity'] = predicted_test
syn_data['sales_quantity'] = syn_data['sales_quantity'].round(decimals = 0)
syn_data['total'] = syn_data['price'] * syn_data['sales_quantity']
```

As a reminder, total sales revenue = per unit price × quantity of items sold.

It is now time to ask the question: "What is the optimal price that maximizes our total sales revenue for an item?" However, since we are working with multivariate data, we need to qualify this question with additional information: "On a day when the high temperature is recorded as *t*, what is the optimal price that maximizes our total sales revenue for an item?" In other words, for a given temperature, let's figure out the optimal price. (See if you can come up with an example where you would want to figure out the optimal temperature for a given price.)

We continue with our modified question to obtain the maximum total sales revenue from our dataset and the corresponding optimal price for a given value of high temperature (`max_temp`):

```
#Assume high temperature to be 30.
ref_temp = 30
#Obtain all reference data for this temperature
ref_data = syn_data[syn_data['max_temp'] == ref_temp]
#Maximum value for total sales revenue in our data subset
ymax = max(ref_data['total'])
#Optimal item price for the maximum total sales
xmax = ref_data.loc[ref_data.total == ymax,'price'].values[0]
```

Next, we plot the total sales revenue against the price; Figure 7-17 shows this plot:

```
fig = plt.figure()
ax = fig.add_subplot()
line = ax.plot(ref_data['price'], ref_data['total'])
#Plot total sales revenue vs item price

ax.annotate(xmax,
            xy=(xmax, ymax),
            xytext=(xmax, ymax + 2000),
            arrowprops=dict(facecolor='red'),)
```

```
                #Label the maximum point with the price value

ax.axvline(xmax,
           color='red',
           linestyle='dashed') #Vertical line for price
ax.axhline(ymax,
           color='red',
           linestyle='dashed') #Horizontal line for total sales revenue

plt.title("Sales revenue variation vs price\nItem_id=52 max_temp=30",
          fontdict={'horizontalalignment': 'right'})
plt.xlabel(predictors)
plt.ylabel('Total sales revenue / day')

plt.show()
```

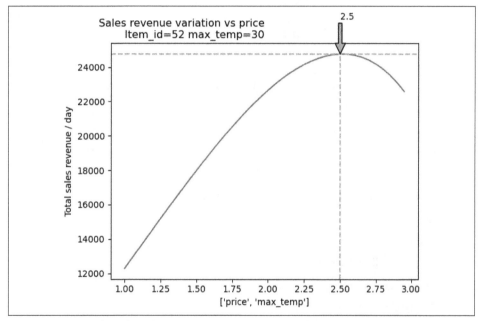

Figure 7-17. Total predicted sales revenue versus price (`item_id 55` / `max_temp 30`)

Now, we print the optimal selling price that allows us to achieve maximum daily sales, and the corresponding sales revenue:

```
print("Optimal selling price: ", xmax)
print("Maximum Daily sale: ", ymax)

Optimal selling price:  2.5
Maximum Daily sale:  24772.5
```

You can vary the `ref_temp` value and generate different graphs to see how the optimal selling price and maximum daily sales vary as the temperature changes.

Let's now summarize everything we have discussed in this section. Our optimal retail price recommendation system consists of two main parts:

- The predictive model for calculating potential sales
- The optimal price calculator that optimizes total revenue

Figure 7-18 summarizes what we discussed so far.

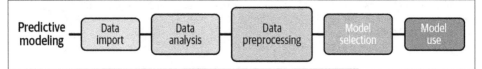

Figure 7-18. Predictive modeling steps

Following is a more detailed summary of the steps we performed:

1. Data import
2. Data analysis to determine the independent variables that impact sales
   a. Single-feature analysis.
   b. Multivariate analysis.
3. Data preprocessing
   a. Scale features.
   b. Generate polynomial features for training.
4. Model selection
   a. Train the models:
      i. Simple linear regression model.
      ii. Polynomial regression model(s).
   b. Visualize model fit.
   c. Test the models and analyze the model scores.
   d. Model a subselection (degree of polynomial).
   e. Save models to disk.
5. Model use
   a. Load models from disk.
   b. Generate synthetic feature ranges.
   c. Scale synthetic features.
   d. Generate polynomial features from scaled synthetic features.

e. Use the loaded model to make predictions over generated feature ranges.

f. Save predictions to a Pandas DataFrame.

g. Visualize the predictions:

   i. Understand the data patterns.

Figure 7-19 summarizes the steps for optimal price calculation.

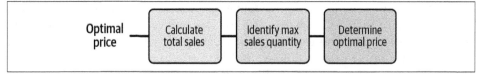

Figure 7-19. Optimal price calculation steps

Following is a more detailed summary of Figure 7-19:

1. Calculate total sales based on price and predicted sales quantity for the day.

2. Identify the maximum sales quantity based on this calculation.

3. Identify the optimal price that predicts the maximum sales quantity.

When implementing this configuration, it is important to consider the following additional factors:

Data ingest, preprocessing, and training
- If working with very large amounts of data, it might not be possible to load the entire dataset in memory for processing and training. In such cases, data can be persisted to various mediums, including (but not limited to) object storage, databases, and big data filesystems.
- Ingest further data changes for model retraining.
- Ingesting further data changes for retraining also allows preprocessing and model training to be done in stages if needed.

Model storage
- Models can be persisted in databases or other cataloged storage systems to avoid file sprawl and support sharing, versioning, and change management.

Predictions storage
- Depending on the number of queries from the application, it might make more sense to run predictions from a selected model and store them to a database.
- These predictions can then be queried by the application from a database rather than going to the prediction engine every time. This can provide tremendous performance benefits, especially for chatty applications, and allow A/B testing using multiple models.

Model reevaluation and retraining

- Cross-validate the model (discussed previously).

- Compare model predictions with real-world output (predicted sales versus actual sales numbers).

- Conduct A/B testing, where half of the application users can use one model and the other half can use another model, and then compare the results.

In this section, we used predictive modeling to arrive at a product's optimal selling price to maximize sales. This is a prevalent use case in the retail industry for assisting and in many cases automating sales price calculations as well as determining optimal discount levels. In the next section, we will look at recommender systems. Recommender systems are used in retail and in many online businesses today to determine what is the best item to recommend to users. The end goal is to increase service consumption, convert user interaction to a new sale, or increase the number of items in the user's cart.

An Introduction to Recommender Systems

Recommendations are a part of our everyday lives. When we want to purchase a car, we go online and read reviews written by people who already purchased the car we're considering; many times these reviews are accompanied by star ratings, usually on a scale of 1 to 5. We also talk to people in our circle who have the same or a similar car and ask them for their advice. Similarly, when we're shopping online we look at reviews and ratings provided by people who already purchased the item, and when we're trying to decide whether a movie is worth watching we refer to IMDb or Rotten Tomatoes ratings. Online media services such as Netflix, Amazon Prime, Disney+, and many more are examples of platforms that engage customers using recommendations for what to watch next.

There is a lot going on when it comes to recommender systems, and not all of it is machine learning or predictive analytics. In this section, we will cover the fundamental components of recommender systems and look at some implementations using scikit-learn, with a focus on model-based systems. We will conclude with some additional reading material to build on what we've discussed.

Recommender systems have evolved like most other technologies, and the past decade has seen increased use of machine learning when it comes to recommender systems. There are several approaches to this, but we will focus on an approach known as *collaborative filtering*. With this approach, we begin by analyzing how our users interact with our products, which could be items purchased from an ecommerce website, movies streamed on Hulu, or songs played on Spotify. This interaction could be implicit or explicit.

Implicit interactions are recorded by applications as the user interacts with the service. Following are some examples of implicit data collected through this form of interaction:

- What movies has the user watched?
- How much time have they spent on a specific drama series?
- Which pages has a user browsed on an ecommerce website?
- What links has the user clicked?
- What items has the user purchased?

Organizations can collect a lot of implicit data as part of the user journey. The reliability of this data varies. For example, a user's purchase history is very reliable, but clicks and page history can be unreliable in terms of both casual browsing (window-shopping) and manipulation from bots and other fraudulent interaction sources.

Explicit data is what businesses collect when they specifically ask the user for their feedback, which is not necessarily an essential part of the user journey. Likes, ratings, and reviews are all examples of explicit user feedback. Since explicit feedback is not essential to purchasing a product or streaming a series, it will often be sparse to begin with. How this data builds up over time depends on the service's total number of active users and how creative it is in terms of extracting feedback from these users.

Another issue with explicit feedback is standardization. For example, although a 3-star rating might imply mediocrity to you, for someone who is sparing with compliments it could imply good or even excellent. It is important to find ways to standardize such feedback across users to keep the outcome as objective as possible—for example, rather than considering the actual value of the rating, consider the ratio of the rating versus the average of all the ratings given by a user.

Implicit and explicit data help us establish the interaction between users and products. Once this is done, the next task is to figure out the missing product score for the user. This score could be based on ratings, popularity, or some other metric. We can then use the score to help us sort all the products in reference to a particular user and recommend the top N items according to the score.

We can use multiple approaches to get to this score. One approach that is commonly used is *product-based content filtering* (aka item-based content filtering). When using this approach, we can determine how similar products are by representing each product as a vector and then figuring out the cosine similarity between the two vectors. Alternatively, we could calculate the Euclidean distance between the vector points. What method we use will vary depending on the use case and what makes sense in terms of its application in the real world.

Let's work through a simple example to understand this better. Table 7-4 represents a movie database that provides the ratings for three movies by three users. We will use the movie rating as our scoring metric.

Table 7-4. User–movie interaction

	Movie 1	Movie 2	Movie 3
User 1	5		3
User 2	7	6	9
User 3		8	6

As we need to calculate the similarity between items, we need to create item pairs. The following item pairs exist in our sample dataset:

Movie 1 – Movie 2
Movie 2 – Movie 3
Movie 1 – Movie 3

The cosine rule can be applied as follows:

$$Similarity\left(\vec{A}, \vec{B}\right) = \frac{\vec{A} \cdot \vec{B}}{\|\vec{A}\| * \|\vec{B}\|}$$

We can represent our three users using the following vectors:

$$M_1 = 5U_1 + 7U_2$$
$$M_2 = 6U_2 + 8U_3$$
$$M_3 = 3U_1 + 9U_2 + 6U_3$$

Hence:

$$Similarity(M_1, M_2) = \frac{(5 \times 0) + (7 \times 6) + (0 \times 8)}{\sqrt{5^2 + 7^2}\sqrt{6^2 + 8^2}} = 0.488$$

We can do similar calculations for:

$$Similarity(M_2, M_3)$$

and:

$$Similarity(I_1, I_3)$$

In our case:

$$Similarity(M_2, M_3) = \frac{(0 \times 3) + (6 \times 9) + (8 \times 6)}{\sqrt{6^2 + 8^2}\sqrt{3^2 + 9^2 + 6^2}} = 0.909$$

and:

$$Similarity(M_1, M_3) = \frac{(5 \times 3) + (7 \times 9) + (0 \times 6)}{\sqrt{5^2 + 7^2}\sqrt{3^2 + 9^2 + 6^2}} = 0.808$$

Now that we have solved the similarity between each movie pair, we can determine the missing ratings (scores) using the following formula:

$$Rating(U_x, M_i) = \frac{\sum_{k=1}^{n} Rating(U_x, M_k) * Similarity(M_i, M_k)}{\sum_{k=1}^{n} Similarity(M_i, M_k)}$$

The missing rating for Movie 1 for User X is calculated by dividing the weighted sum of all ratings provided by User X (weighted by the similarity between Movie 1 and that movie) by the sum of all similarities between Movie 1 and other movies.

In our example, if we were to figure out the $Rating(U_1, M_2)$ it would translate to the following:

$$Rating(U_1, M_2) = \frac{(5 \times 0.488) + (3 \times 0.909)}{0.488 + 0.909} = 3.70$$

What we have effectively done is calculate the predicted rating for Movie 2 when it comes to User 1. We can apply the same logic to calculate all the missing ratings. Once we have all the ratings we can:

1. Sort the movies by ratings for each user.
2. Remove (or not) movies already watched by the user.
3. Present the top N movies to each user as recommendations.

We use the preceding equations to make sure we clearly understand the concept. This is one of many ways to calculate similarities and scoring (rating). What is more important is the process.

The approach we just used is based on similarities between different products, which results in recommendations. Another approach that is commonly implemented in recommender systems is *user-based collaborative filtering*. In this approach, rather than figuring out similarities between products, we establish similarities between users based on their existing interaction with the products. For each user, we discover a group of similar users. This could be based on purchase history of common products, multiple shared product ratings, or other similar user-product interaction. The details can vary from implementation to implementation.

Once we have established this similar group, we will use this group to determine the list of items to be recommended to the user. Note that the group is not a general grouping, but is based on the user's interaction with the products. Therefore, as the interaction changes, so does the group, which in turn changes the derived list of recommendations. This will result in a personalized recommendation for each user.

There are simpler approaches, such as having recommendations based on general popularity ratings, or content-based recommendations that recommend content to a user based on what they have already watched (e.g., movies from the same genre). Each approach has advantages and limitations. General rating recommendations end up recommending the same list of items to all users (or all users in a particular group, such as a country). This does not make them very personalized. Content-based recommendations will only allow users to explore content similar to what they have already interacted with (you can add randomization to help with this limitation).

Meanwhile, collaborative filtering has what is commonly known as a *cold-start problem*, in which we do not have any data about the user when the person starts using a service. Since the approach is dependent on user-product interaction, it becomes difficult to come up with a personalized list of recommendations for such users. Popularity-based recommendations could be used initially to help users get started and then move them to personalized recommendations. Additional parameters can be used to establish similarity in content, and different algorithms can be used to establish user similarity. There is no one-size-fits-all recommender system, and as such, these systems are often used as ensembles (a combination of multiple approaches) to provide the best user experience for a service.

Building Recommender Systems Using surprise scikit in Python

To start working on recommender systems, we will utilize a Python library called *surprise*, which assists in constructing and evaluating recommender systems. I chose to start with this because it is built with inspiration from many modules in scikit-learn. Therefore, many of the concepts we have discussed so far, including data ingestion and preparation, feature selection, testing and training splits, model fitting, cross validation, prediction, and scoring, will be visible throughout our discussion in this section. Also, *surprise* abstracts away a lot of complicated boilerplate code by providing easy-to-use datasets, a choice of prediction algorithms, and tools to evaluate individual algorithms and compare them with others. Go to the book's GitHub repository (*https://oreil.ly/MdR7A*), where you can find all the code in *Chapter7-Surprise-RecommendationEngine-PAFME* .

All the code in this chapter has been tested in the Jupyter Notebook environment. You can, however, take this code and test it in any compatible Python environment.

The dataset used in this code is sourced from the MovieLens 100K Dataset (*https://oreil.ly/CQ_TI*), a dataset of movie ratings compiled by GroupLens, a research lab in the Department of Computer Science and Engineering at the University of Minnesota, Twin Cities. For the exercise, you can download a copy of the dataset from the book's GitHub repository (*https://oreil.ly/yjC4b*).

Once we have ensured our prerequisites for our Python environment, we start importing the required libraries:

```
import pandas as pd
import numpy as np
import itertools as it
from surprise import accuracy, Dataset, SVD, KNNBasic
from surprise import KNNWithMeans, KNNBaseline, Reader
from surprise.model_selection import cross_validate
from surprise.model_selection import train_test_split
from collections import defaultdict
from itertools import chain
```

In the case of *surprise*, we are importing a few algorithms: SVD, KNNBasic, and KNNWithMeans. Additionally, we are importing the *cross_validate* and *train_test_split* libraries, which are very similar to what we have used in scikit-learn so far. No real surprise here (pun intended).

We begin by defining what data we want to import. We will use the MovieLens 100K built-in dataset provided by *surprise*. We then define a simple function to load built-in datasets and load the MovieLens 100K dataset using this function:

```
def data_loader(dataset):
    data = Dataset.load_builtin(dataset)
    return data
dataset = "ml-100k"
data = data_loader(dataset)
```

If you are already working with recommender systems, chances are good that you know this dataset quite well. If not, let me give you a brief overview. The MovieLens dataset contains the explicit movie ratings provided by users. The ratings in the dataset are given in the following format:

```
(0, 0, 3.0)
(0, 528, 4.0)
(0, 377, 4.0)
(0, 522, 3.0)
```

The first number represents the User ID (often referred to in code as uid); the second number is the Movie ID (often referred to in code as rid); and the third number is the rating the user gave to the movie, with a range of 1 to 5. Note that *surprise* was developed to work with recommender systems that deal with explicit user-product interaction, such as explicit movie ratings. Since we will be employing the k-nearest neighbor algorithm in the *surprise* library, it would be beneficial to briefly discuss it now.

K-nearest neighbor algorithm

The k-nearest neighbor (kNN) algorithm can be used as a supervised learning algorithm for classification and regression problems. kNN assumes that data points that are in proximity to each other are similar and therefore can be counted as part of a single group. This proximity is based on distance, which can be calculated using a similarity measure. Take a look at the data points shown in Figure 7-20.

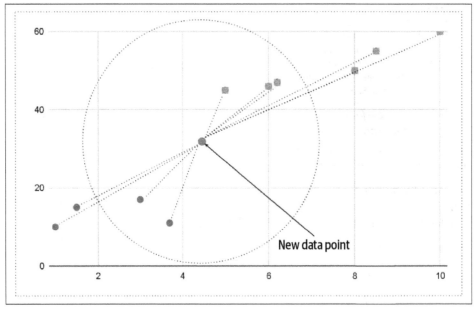

Figure 7-20. kNN representation

The plot in Figure 7-20 provides data that is split into two classes. When a new data point is added, we look at neighbors of this data point. To understand the proximity of the neighbors, we calculate the distance between the new data point and all the other data points. Once the proximity is established, we need to figure out the nearest neighbors. The number of neighbors that are considered is determined by the value of k in the kNN algorithm.

In our example, let's say the value of k was set to 5. For a classification problem, we would look at the five neighbors and then decide on a classification based on the *mode*, the highest occurrence of a class within the neighbors. If this is a regression problem, a value could be determined using an average or a weighted average of the values of the neighbors. For example, the average rating of a movie could be predicted using the average of the ratings of all the movies that are neighbors to it in the algorithm.

These data points can represent anything, from movies plotted across two genres to penguins plotted across bill length and body weight. In our example, we are considering a couple of parameters to plot the data in two dimensions. It becomes important to figure out how to calculate the distance between the data points. kNN can use many different methods to calculate the distance. Here are a few common ones for your reference:

Euclidean distance. Simply put, this is a straight-line distance between the new data point represented by a real valued vector (p) and the neighbor (q) we are trying to calculate the distance from. It is calculated by squaring the differences between the parameters of p and q, summing them, and then calculating the square root of the sum. The calculation can be represented using the following formula:

$$\sqrt{\sum_{i=1}^{n}\left(p_i - q_i\right)^2}$$

Manhattan distance. The Manhattan distance metric calculates the absolute difference between p and q. The mathematical formula that represents the Manhattan distance between p and q is as follows:

$$\sum_{i=1}^{n}\left|p_i - q_i\right|$$

Hamming distance. Hamming distance is often used with categorical values such as booleans or strings, although it can be used with integers as well. The idea here is to identify where two vectors might be different. Mathematically, the hamming distance can be represented as follows:

$$D_H = \sum_{i=1}^{n}\left|p_i - q_i\right|$$

$$p = q \Rightarrow D = 0$$
$$p \neq q \Rightarrow D = 1$$

For example, let's represent two movies by a vector using the genres they belong to: action, comedy, horror, or drama. The two movies can be defined as shown in Table 7-5.

Table 7-5. Hamming distance

	Action	Comedy	Horror	Drama
Movie A	1	0	1	1
Movie B	1	1	0	1

In vector notation, this could look like the following:

> Movie A: $(1,0,1,1)$
> Movie B: $(1,1,0,1)$

Since the two movies differ in the comedy and horror genres, the hamming distance between the two movies is 2.

Cosine similarity. This is a useful metric to determine the similarity between two vectors based on their direction and orientation. The cosine similarity is based on the cosine of the angle between the vectors and is not dependent on their size. The mathematical formula that represents cosine similarity is as follows:

$$\text{Cosine similarity}\left(\vec{p}, \vec{q}\right) = cos(\theta) = \frac{\vec{p} \cdot \vec{q}}{\|\vec{p}\| * \|\vec{q}\|}$$

where:

> θ is the angle between the two vectors.
> $\vec{p} \cdot \vec{q}$ is the dot product between the two vectors.
> $\|\vec{p}\| \|\vec{q}\|$ is the length of vectors p and q.
> $\|\vec{p}\| * \|\vec{q}\|$ is the cross product between vectors p and q.

In Figure 7-21, as θ approaches 0°, cos(θ) approaches 1. Conversely, when θ approaches 90°, cos(θ) approaches 0. So the closer the vectors are in terms of orientation, the more similar they are considered by the metric. Also, note that if we change the magnitude of q, it has no impact on the similarity between p and q, since the angle θ between the two vectors remains the same.

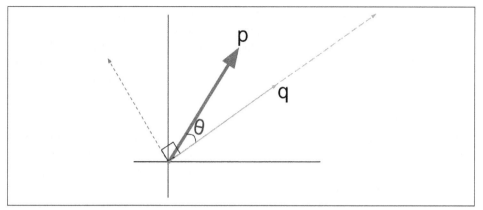

Figure 7-21. Cosine similarity

Selecting the optimal value for k is the next important step in kNN-based algorithms. Typically, lower k values will be susceptible to noisy data but will have low bias. Higher k values will have low variance (to noise) but can have a high bias. The value of k will depend on the nature of the data being processed by the algorithm. Some data scientists use simple techniques, such as setting k to the sqrt(N) where N is the number of samples in your training set. Another guideline is to use an odd number for k in case there are only two classes. This is to avoid ties. We can also use cross-validation techniques to run the algorithm using several k values and then optimize for validation error.

When using the kNN algorithm for classification, we can run into a situation where we have a tie. Consider k=5 for a classification problem with three classes. If we get a split of 2-2-1 when it comes to the five neighbors (Class A - 2, Class B - 2, Class C - 1), how do we break the tie between Class A and Class B when determining the class of a new vector? In such a scenario, a few approaches can be considered:

- Choose a different value for k that does not create a tie.
- Randomly choose a classification from the tied classes.
- Add weights to the classification so that observations closer to the unobserved value are weighted higher than those that are farther away.

kNN is known as a lazy algorithm. This is because when it comes to training, all it does at that stage is store the training data provided to it. This is different from other algorithms; for example, in the case of polynomial regression, the algorithm is figuring out the best-fit curve during training and a neural network is trying to determine the weights for each of its connections (or synapses). In kNN, all computations are done when an unobserved value is introduced into the dataset. It is at this point that the algorithm figures out the distances and the k-neighbors. Note that kNN algorithms can become quite resource-hungry as the training set grows.

The kNN algorithm is used across several vertical industries for a variety of use cases. For example, it can be used for credit ratings of individuals based on others with similar characteristics. We can also find extensive use of several variations of the kNN algorithm in building recommender systems across the ecommerce, media, and music industries. It is used in text mining and computer vision applications, as well.

kNN-based recommender systems

The *surprise* library provides a number of algorithms that can be used to build a recommender system. We will use the kNN-inspired algorithms. If you are interested in learning more about the algorithms provided by *surprise*, please refer to the *surprise* online documentation (*https://oreil.ly/bg-73*).

We begin by selecting the algorithm we want to use and defining options for the algorithm:

```
# Similarity options
sim_options = {
    "name": "cosine", # Use the cosine similarity matrix
    "user_based": False,  # Compute similarities between items
}
algo = KNNBasic(sim_options=sim_options) # The algorithm to use
```

We are using the KNNBasic algorithm, which is a kNN-inspired basic collaborative filtering algorithm. As we discussed earlier, kNN algorithms can use many different distance metrics. We are using the cosine similarity metric to calculate the similarity between our data points. Collaborative filtering solutions can work by calculating item-to-item similarity or user-to-user similarity. The user_based option helps us choose between the two. For our example, we are using item-to-item similarity as user_based is set to false. So, in a nutshell, we will be using a kNN-inspired algorithm that will use the cosine similarity metric to calculate similarities between items.

For our dataset, item refers to the movie titles. We have chosen cosine similarity for our recommendation system due to its robustness in high-dimensional data and insensitivity to vector magnitudes. It's ideal for user-based recommendations, efficiently measuring similarity between user vectors while handling sparse data effectively. Its computational efficiency and normalization properties make it suitable for real-time and large-scale systems. In sparse datasets, cosine similarity focuses on nonzero dimensions, ignoring missing ratings and ensuring reliable recommendations. Its ability to handle varying rating scales and capture relative preferences makes it a preferred metric for collaborative filtering-based recommendation engines. This collaborative filtering approach will work on a structure similar to what we discussed at the beginning of this section. However, note that implementation details may vary.

Once we have loaded the dataset, we split the data between trainset and testset, using a test size of 25%:

```
trainset, testset = train_test_split(data, test_size=0.25)
```

We then train the model using the algorithm we previously selected, by passing it the training dataset. For ease of use, we define a simple training function and then use it to fit our model:

```
def train_model(algo, trainset):
    algo.fit(trainset)
    return algo
algo = train_model(algo, trainset)
```

At this point, we have successfully trained our model. Note that when it comes to kNN-based algorithms, the training part involves just loading the data in memory, since it is a lazy model. The actual calculations happen only when we use the model to predict values.

Next, we test the model on the `testset` to understand model accuracy for the `test set`:

```
predictions = algo.test(testset)
print(accuracy.rmse(predictions), accuracy.mae(predictions) )
Computing the cosine similarity matrix...
Done computing similarity matrix.
RMSE: 1.0339
MAE:  0.8192
1.0338596265367448 0.8192292987220225
```

We observe here that our RMSE is 1.0339 while our MAE for the recommender is 0.8192. But what do these values really mean? The items being predicted by the algorithm are the missing movie ratings in the User / item (Movie) interaction matrix. The movie ratings have a scale of 1 to 5. At this stage, we have predicted the missing ratings in the test dataset. The original dataset contains user and item pairs (U_x, I_m) and their corresponding movie rating, R_{xm}, which represents the rating given by user U_x to item I_m. Note that not all movies will be rated by all users, so the user-item rating matrix would represent a sparse matrix.

The next step is to get movie recommendations for a user. For this purpose, we define the uid and the number of movies we want to predict:

```
uid = '1' #User ID to be used for the recommendations
top = 10  #Number of movies that we want to recommend
```

Next, we create a dataset that contains all the user-item pairs that are *not* in the training set. This allows us to build a dataset of user-item pairs in which the user has not yet provided the explicit movie rating for that particular movie. We will then recommend movies from this dataset. This will ensure that we are not recommending any movies that have already been recommended (and hence watched) by the user. Do note that there might be scenarios where you would want to recommend items that have already been rated. So this is just a matter of context and not a requirement.

The *surprise* library provides a built-in function to create this `testset`:

```
#Predict ratings for all pairs (u, i) that are NOT in the training set.
testset = trainset.build_anti_testset() #Build the anti-set
predictions = algo.test(testset) #Predict ratings for the anti-set
```

At this point, for each known user and each known movie in the training set, we have created a set of all (`user,movie`) pairs so that the movie is new to the user and hence the rating is a predicted rating. All that is left to do is recommend the top (predicted) rated movies to the user. We create yet another useful function to generate these predictions:

```
#Generate a list of movie name recommendations
# for a user based on user-movie (predictions)
def get_movie_names(uid,predictions,top):
    top_n = get_top_n(predictions, n=top)
```

We pass to this function the user ID (`uid`), the predictions from our `anti_set`, and the number of movies we want to recommend. This function makes use of two additional functions that are provided in the FAQ section of the *surprise* documentation. I will describe the purpose of these functions here. You are free to implement your own versions of these functions.

The first function is `get_top_n`. This function takes the predictions and the total number of movies to be predicted as input. It also utilizes the `uid`, which is defined as a global variable. It then returns a dictionary list where the `top_n[uid]` element contains a list of top *n* predicted ratings for this user against movie IDs that are represented by `iid`, where *n* represents the number of movies we want to recommend. We then convert this dictionary to a Pandas DataFrame:

```
top_n_pd = pd.DataFrame(top_n)
```

Next, we parse the DataFrame element to get the list of all the recommended movie IDs for this user:

```
recommendation_ids = top_n_pd[uid].apply(lambda x: x[0])
```

At this step, we use the second function provided in the FAQ section of the *surprise* documentation: `read_item_names`. This function fetches all the movie names from the raw dataset files and returns a couple of mappings that map movie IDs to movie names, and another mapping that maps movie names to movie IDs:

```
iid_to_name, name_to_iid = read_item_names()
```

Now, we create a list of the `top_n` movie names using our `recommendation_ids` by mapping these IDs to their respective movie names. The function returns the list of top *n* recommended movies:

```
recommendations = (iid_to_name[iid] for iid in recommendation_ids)
    return recommendations
recommendations = get_movie_names(uid,predictions,top)
```

The last part of this code prints the recommended movie names:

```
print("\nTop 10 Movie recommendations for uid:", uid)
for movie in recommendations:
    print(movie)
Top 10 Movie recommendations for uid: 1
Big Bang Theory, The (1994)
Further Gesture, A (1996)
Other Voices, Other Rooms (1997)
Bent (1997)
Entertaining Angels: The Dorothy Day Story (1996)
Coldblooded (1995)
Cyclo (1995)
Last Summer in the Hamptons (1995)
Chairman of the Board (1998)
King of New York (1990)
```

This is a possible set of top 10 recommendations for the user with uid=1.

Finally, we combine all the code in a function to make it more reusable:

```
def run_predictions(algo):
    data = data_loader(dataset)
    trainset, testset = train_test_split(data, test_size=0.25)
    algo = train_model(algo, trainset)
    predictions = algo.test(testset)
    print(accuracy.rmse(predictions), accuracy.mae(predictions) )
    #Predict ratings for all pairs (u, i) that are NOT in the training set.
    testset = trainset.build_anti_testset()
    predictions = algo.test(testset)
    recommendations = get_movie_names(uid,predictions,top)
    print("\nTop 10 Movie recommendations for uid:", uid)
    for movie in recommendations:
        print(movie)
```

Next, we look at another kNN-based algorithm with a slight variation:

```
#KNN - With Means - user based / cosine similarity
sim_options = {
    "name": "cosine",
    "user_based": True,  # Compute similarities between users
}
algo = KNNWithMeans(sim_options=sim_options)
```

Here we are using the KNNWithMeans algorithm, which takes into account the mean rating of each user when deriving similarity and predicting ratings. Additionally, we are using the cosine similarity matrix and basing our collaborative filtering on user-to-user similarity (versus item-to-item similarity in the previous example). We utilize our reusable function to run this model and generate recommendations:

```
run_predictions(algo)

Computing the cosine similarity matrix...
```

```
Done computing similarity matrix.
RMSE: 0.9603
MAE:  0.7578
0.9603486632253324 0.757812749935527

Top 10 Movie recommendations for uid: 1
Safe Passage (1994)
Boys, Les (1997)
Santa with Muscles (1996)
Saint of Fort Washington, The (1993)
Aiqing wansui (1994)
Some Mother's Son (1996)
Great Day in Harlem, A (1994)
Anna (1996)
Crossfire (1947)
Hugo Pool (1997)
```

This model produces slightly better RMSE and MAE values and a list of top 10 recommendations for uid. We also run cross-validation on our model to further understand how it performs across multiple splits of data:

```
data = data_loader(dataset)
# Run fivefold cross validation and print results
cross_validate(algo, data, measures=["RMSE", "MAE"], cv=5, verbose=True)

Computing the cosine similarity matrix...
Done computing similarity matrix.
Computing the cosine similarity matrix...
Done computing similarity matrix.
Computing the cosine similarity matrix...
Done computing similarity matrix.
Computing the cosine similarity matrix...
Done computing similarity matrix.
Computing the cosine similarity matrix...
Done computing similarity matrix.
Evaluating RMSE, MAE of algorithm KNNWithMeans on 5 split(s).
```

	Fold 1	Fold 2	Fold 3	Fold 4	Fold 5	Mean	Std
RMSE (testset)	0.9556	0.9523	0.9526	0.9566	0.9618	0.9558	0.0035
MAE (testset)	0.7537	0.7529	0.7528	0.7536	0.7598	0.7546	0.0026
Fit time	0.37	0.37	0.41	0.38	0.40	0.39	0.01
Test time	2.38	2.47	2.44	2.35	2.54	2.44	0.07

The cross-validation in *surprise* is inspired from the scikit-learn library. Therefore, we can observe the similarity between this and what we discussed in Chapter 5 with regard to cross-validation using scikit-learn. Cross validation can help us with model selection when building our recommender system. The model shown here performs quite consistently across five different folds.

We can also run a cross-validation with varying values for k. Up until this point, we have been running with a default value of 40 for k in the kNN algorithms. However, you can experiment with different values of k to improve your model accuracy and recommendations. The value of k can be customized using sim_options for kNN-based algorithms in *surprise*.

This was a simple approach to building a recommender system. This approach involved the following:

1. Loading a dataset
2. Splitting the dataset into test and training sets
3. Defining a kNN-based algorithm
   a. Selecting the similarity metric
   b. Defining whether the similarity is user based or item based
4. Testing model accuracy
5. Creating the `anti_testset`
6. Using the model to predict ratings for the `anti_testset`
7. Using the predicted ratings to recommend the top 10 movies to the user

Two-stage recommender system

Another approach that is quite prevalent while building recommendation engines is to use a two-stage recommender system. A two-stage recommender system is sometimes referred to as the retriever-ranker model. The retriever stage is responsible for finding the first-cut relevant items for the user. Think of these as coarse recommendations. Some of them might be irrelevant, or some might be items that the user has already consumed (or rated). The details can vary across implementations.

The two-stage recommender system allows us to address a few important aspects:

- With a very large catalog of items, recommendations can get more generalized. Having a user-focused first stage that uses reliable feedback (e.g., explicit ratings or user purchase history) improves the accuracy of the final result.
- The model can easily scale for large datasets. As we will observe shortly, a retriever-based model can cut the ranking (or rating) dataset by 50 to 100 times.
- The retrieval stage can quickly identify relevant items to the user, thus making the ranking task more efficient without the need for ranking (rating) the entire catalog for each recommendation.
- Since the model is modular, it allows for better flexibility and interoperability, where we can customize each stage independently in terms of both the algorithm and the implementation, so long as both stages can communicate with each other.

Let's look at an example of a two-stage recommender system. If you plan to follow along, you can continue to use the same *Chapter7-Surprise-RecommendationEngine-PAFME.ipynb* as before (available on the book's GitHub repository (*https://oreil.ly/lirVi*)). The code imports for this section are the same as for the previous section. We will reuse some parts of the previous code and then use additional code for our new model.

Retriever stage. We begin by defining our retriever stage for the model. As before, we start by importing the MovieLens 100K dataset. We then use a helper function from the *surprise* package to build a training set based on the complete dataset:

```
#Step 1 - Load the full dataset (100k movies)
data = data_loader(dataset) #Load the dataset
#Build the training set based on complete data
trainset = data.build_full_trainset()
```

We are working to get recommendations for a specific user. So we define a variable uid to point to a specific user:

```
uid = '1' #User to get recommendations for
```

We continue by retrieving all explicit ratings by the user in our training dataset. Next, we sort all the entries by ratings to get a list of the 10 movies that were rated the highest by this user:

```
#Get all movies rated by the user - uid
user_items = trainset.ur[int(uid)]
#Get the top 10 user rated movies
user_top_rated = sorted(user_items, key=lambda x: x[1], reverse=True)[:10]
```

Next, we will define our retrieval model using the KNNWithMeans algorithm. We will define the collaboration model with the item-to-item-based similarity calculation and choose cosine similarity as our similarity metric.

We fit the model with our training set, which is the complete MovieLens 100K dataset:

```
#Build the retriever model - item based cosine similarity
sim_options = {'name': 'cosine', 'user_based': False}
item_model = KNNWithMeans(sim_options=sim_options)
item_model.fit(trainset)
```

What we want to do next is get movies similar to the ones the user has already watched. We use our model to get the nearest neighbors for each of the 10 movies. For this purpose, we define a new function, get_neighbours:

```
def get_neighbours(algo, mrid):
    # Convert Movie RawID to innerID
    movie_inner_id = algo.trainset.to_inner_iid(mrid)
    # Retrieve inner IDs of the nearest neighbors of the movie mrid
    movie_neighbors = algo.get_neighbors(movie_inner_id, k=10)
```

```
# Convert inner IDs to raw IDs
movie_neighbors = (
    algo.trainset.to_raw_iid(inner_id) for inner_id in movie_neighbors
)
return movie_neighbors
```

The preceding code block includes a bit of boilerplate code, but let's look at the important aspects of it. The function takes an algorithm and a `movie_id` and returns the `movie_ids` of the 10 nearest neighbors of that movie. It does this based on the algorithm (which is kNN item based in this case). We are calling the built-in function `get_neighbors` that is available with kNN-based algorithms in *surprise*. What you have to understand is that *surprise* uses `raw_ids` for movies in certain functions, and another mapping, called `inner_id`, in other functions. This is to improve processing of the IDs by the package. Therefore, we need to perform these conversions as we had been working with `raw_id(s)`, however the `get_neighbors` built-in function uses `inner_id(s)`.

Next, we call our `get_neighbours` function for each of the 10 movies in our top-rated-movies list:

```
#Get nearest neighbors for all 10 top_rated_movies
all_neighbors = 0
for movie_rid in user_top_rated:
    neighbors = get_neighbours(item_model,str(movie_rid[0]))
    if(all_neighbors!=0):
        all_neighbors= it.chain(all_neighbors,neighbors)
    else:
        all_neighbors = neighbors
#Convert the all_neighbors iterator to a list
mylist = list(all_neighbors)
print(len(mylist))
100
```

We merge all the nearest neighbors into a single list. At this point, we have a list of 100 movies that are similar to the top 10 movies rated by this user. Note that the similarity is based on a cosine similarity user-item matrix. So, while we are looking at the similarity between movies, this similarity is based on how the different users have rated these movies.

This concludes Stage 1. The output of Stage 1 is a set of 100 recommendation candidates for our user. Before we move on to Stage 2, let's consider the following:

- This stage works with the complete dataset and calculates neighbors based on cosine similarity. However, it does not need to calculate any predicted ratings, because the nearest neighbors are calculated based on cosine similarity and not ratings.

- This stage has a cold-start problem. If a new user is added to the system, they would not have any movie ratings, so the top 10 movies list would be empty. In such a scenario, a new user can be started off with popularity-based recommendations. So the top 10 movies list could be the top 10 rated movies across all users instead of our individual user. We can start the user on this list, and as their interaction with the content grows, we can move them to the specific user-based stage one that we discussed earlier.

Ranker stage. The ranker stage is responsible for producing the recommendations for our user. Let's analyze the following code:

```
#Build a new dataset with nearest neighbors of top_rated_movies
data = data_loader(dataset)
my_trainset = data.build_full_trainset()
my_data = my_trainset.build_testset() #Take full dataset
```

We start by loading the dataset. You can use the dataset from the retriever stage if you want. We use the dataset to build a `testset` on the complete data. This `testset` will have 100K Dataset ratings for the movies from various users:

```
#Filter only data where the movie is in the top neighbors
filtered_data = [d for d in my_data if d[1] in mylist]
```

Next, we filter out all the ratings that are related to our candidate movies from the previous stage:

```
#Add an entry from the existing set
#just in case there is no movie rated by this user in the neighbours
for d in my_data:
    if d[0] == uid:
        filtered_data.append(d)
        break
```

We add some boilerplate code to handle the edge case where we end up with a set of candidates that have not been rated by our user. In this case, we end up with a dataset that does not produce any recommendations for our user, as the user is not part of the filtered data:

```
filtered_data = pd.DataFrame(filtered_data) #Create a DataFrame for filtered data
filtered_data.columns = ["userID", "itemID", "rating"]

reader = Reader(rating_scale=(1, 5))
#Read data back in to create a testset
my_data = Dataset.load_from_df(filtered_data
                    [["userID", "itemID", "rating"]],
                    reader)

new_trainset = my_data.build_full_trainset() #Create filtered training set
```

The preceding code creates a DataFrame from our filtered data and then uses it as input to create a new dataset based on the filtered ratings only. You could use another method to create a filtered training set, so long as it only contains the ratings for the candidate movies from the previous stage. We can check how many ratings are in our filtered training set as follows:

```
print(new_trainset.n_ratings)
3034
```

 The training set for our model that will be used for predictions is reduced to a focused set of 3,034 ratings from 100,000 ratings. This allows the two-stage recommender system to efficiently handle very large datasets. We will be calculating ratings on a much smaller user-item matrix than what we would have in a single-stage recommender system.

Next, we define the user_model we will be using for our ranking (ratings). This is using the KNNWithMeans algorithm provided by *surprise*. We define the collaboration model with a user-to-user-based similarity calculation and choose cosine similarity as our similarity metric. We fit the model using our curated training set:

```
#Train user model with the new dataset
sim_options = {'name': 'cosine', 'user_based': True}
user_model = KNNWithMeans(sim_options=sim_options)
user_model.fit(new_trainset)
```

We build an anti_testset using a built-in function provided by *surprise*. This allows us to build a test set consisting of all the users and all the movies from our training set where the rating is not known for the user-item pair. This means we are going to be recommending movies that the user has not rated yet. We run a test on our user_model using this testset and save the predicted ratings:

```
#Build an anti_testset for all known movies and users
#in the testset where the ratings are unknown for (u, i) pair
testset = new_trainset.build_anti_testset()
predictions = user_model.test(testset)
```

The last step of the ranker stage is to get the top 10 predictions for the user:

```
#Print top 10 movie recommendations for user(uid)
recommendations = get_movie_names(uid,predictions,10)
print("\nTop 10 Movie recommendations for user with uid:", uid)
print("-------------------------------------------------\n")
for movie in recommendations:
    print(movie)


Top 10 Movie recommendations for user with uid: 1
-------------------------------------------------

Hearts and Minds (1996)
So Dear to My Heart (1949)
Beautiful Thing (1996)
Jackie Brown (1997)
```

```
City of Lost Children, The (1995)
North by Northwest (1959)
Thieves (Voleurs, Les) (1996)
Ghost in the Shell (Kokaku kidotai) (1995)
Ninotchka (1939)
In the Name of the Father (1993)
```

We use the `get_movie_names` function that we defined earlier to get the top 10 recommendations for the user. These are based on the `top_n` predicted movie ratings for this user based on the `user_model`.

Our two-stage recommender system consists of the following stages:

Stage 1: Retriever

1. Create a `top_n` list of the top-rated items for our user.

2. For each item in the `top_n` list, find the best `item` candidates that can be used for recommendations to our user using `item_model`. In our case, this was based on the kNN algorithm finding the nearest neighbors.

3. Curate a list of all recommendation candidates by combining the individual candidates for each `top_n` item.

Stage 2: Ranker

1. Create a dataset based on the list of recommendation candidates received from Stage 1.

2. Train a `user_model` using the new dataset.

3. Create a training set for the full data and a testing `anti_set` to get recommendations based on items that have not been rated by the user yet.

4. Use the `user_model` to run predictions for the `anti_set`.

5. Get the `top_n` recommendations based on the rating predictions for the user.

Recommender systems are a vast topic. A bunch of technologies and methodologies are available, and there is no one solution that fits all use cases. The business context is as important (if not more so) as the technology itself. This section of the chapter aimed to introduce you to recommender systems, get you started with a good understanding of the foundations, and share some implementation ideas that you can adopt and build upon. For further reading on recommender systems, see *Building Recommender Systems with Machine Learning and AI* by Frank Kane (O'Reilly, 2021).

We will switch gears now and move to the financial industry, where we will discover the use of predictive analytics to solve a common problem: identifying fraudulent credit card transactions.

Credit Card Fraud Classification

It is likely that credit card is the default mode of payment for your day-to-day dealings. From grocery shopping to buying movie tickets and ordering printer ink from Amazon, credit cards are used everywhere. Cash has been displaced in many parts of the world by credit and debit cards in physical or virtual forms. Checks are another payment method in circulation. However, card-based payments form the lion's share when it comes to global payments.[1] Users are leaning more toward credit cards than debit cards due to benefits such as delayed payments, lifestyle benefits, and better fraud protection.

Banks provide several fraud protection services that allow users to control their credit card payments. One-time passwords (OTP) via email/SMS, protection against repeat transactions within a few minutes, daily spending limits, and restrictions on the geographic locations where the cards can be used are among the many mechanisms provided to credit card consumers. In spite of all the different methodologies, fraudulent credit card transactions are a reality with a real cost associated with them. While users can inform banks about fraudulent transactions and the charges are mostly reversed, unfortunately these charges need to be borne by someone in the payment chain. Depending on the specifics, this could be the bank itself, an insurance company, the merchant, or some intermediary in the payment workflow. With the ever-increasing volume of credit card transactions worldwide, credit card fraud detection and prevention has been an area of acute focus for the financial industry.

Comprehensive credit card fraud protection is a multilayered approach that includes user confirmation for transactions, rule-based fraud detection for known policies and patterns, rule-based transaction scoring, and ML-based transaction classification, to name a few. Let's look at a few categories of credit card fraud and how the different credit card fraud protection layers can help us:

Stolen or lost cards
> A fraudster will attempt to use a stolen or lost card as quickly as possible. Typically, users can tell banks to block the card if they are aware that the card is no longer with them. Techniques such as the use of PINs and OTP confirmations for transactions can also help prevent the use of a stolen card. However, social engineering and fishing are common techniques used to obtain a user's PIN and OTP illegally. While rule-based engines can help, ML-based classification and anomaly detection can be effective in identifying fraudulent transactions based on trained models and consumer transaction history.

---

1 Becky Pokora, "Credit Card Statistics and Trends 2024" (*https://oreil.ly/NrBCS*), *Forbes Advisor*, March 9, 2023.

Card details stolen/counterfeit cards

When credit card information is stolen, the spending usually occurs online, by phone, or through email. Anomaly detection based on outlier models and predictive modeling to identify patterns between legitimate and fraudulent transactions can help identify such transactions so that the banks or merchants can take corrective action. Note that the stolen information might not be used for a long time after the theft, which makes it difficult to identify exactly when/where the information was stolen.

Other scenarios

Intercepting a legitimate new card before it reaches the consumer or getting a card issued on someone else's behalf is another fraud pattern observed in the industry. Identifying interception fraud is more a matter of process in terms of card delivery and activation confirmation, among other things. Also, fraudulent applications can be identified before they are processed using background checks to confirm the true identity of the applicant.

Credit card fraud detection can be considered a binary classification problem: we want to know whether a credit card transaction is legitimate or fraudulent. Therefore, we can use ML classifier algorithms to attack the problem. Some potential candidates could be logistic regression, random forest classifiers, or even a neural network with a sigmoid function on the output layer for binary classification. However, note that we will mostly be dealing with a few fraudulent transactions among a large number of legitimate transactions. This will give us imbalanced data, and we will look at a few things that we can do to handle this imbalance. For this reason, fraud detection can also be considered an anomaly detection problem, where the fraudulent transactions are the anomaly among the legitimate transactions. Algorithms such as isolation forests can be used to perform anomaly detection on credit card fraud datasets.

Credit Card Fraud Baseline Analysis Using Artificial Neural Networks

We will begin by using TensorFlow to build a neural network that can be used to detect credit card fraud. The dataset we will be using in this section is provided by Machine Learning Group (*https://oreil.ly/nOJwG*).

Real public financial transaction data is hard to come by due to privacy and security concerns. The dataset we are using in this section provides credit card transactions by European consumers in September 2013. All the fields except for the Time and Class fields are numeric in nature and are the result of principal component analysis (PCA) on the original data. No further information about the original data is available.

If you want to follow along, you can find the code in *Chapter7-CrediCard-FraudAnalytics-Tflow-PAFME.ipynb*, located on the book's GitHub repository (*https://oreil.ly/KT6VL*). You can run the code in the Jupyter Notebook environment or use any other compatible Python environment. You can also download a copy of the dataset from the book's GitHub repository (*https://oreil.ly/zN1ea*).

We begin by importing the required packages for data processing, TensorFlow, visualization, and some other utilities:

```
#Data processing imports
import numpy as np
import pandas as pd
import sklearn
from sklearn.model_selection import train_test_split
from sklearn.preprocessing import StandardScaler
#Tensorflow imports
import tensorflow as tflow
from tensorflow import keras
from tensorflow.keras import layers
#Visualization imports
from sklearn.metrics import confusion_matrix
import seaborn as sns
import matplotlib as mpl
import matplotlib.pyplot as plt
import plotly.express as px
#Utilities
import os, tempfile, datetime
```

We run an import on the locally downloaded dataset:

```
#import the Credit Card Dataset
#Change this to the location where you downloaded and unzipped the dataset
url = "./Datasets/creditcard.csv"
data_df = pd.read_csv(url) #load data in a dataframe
data_df
```

The source dataset sample is shown in Figure 7-22.

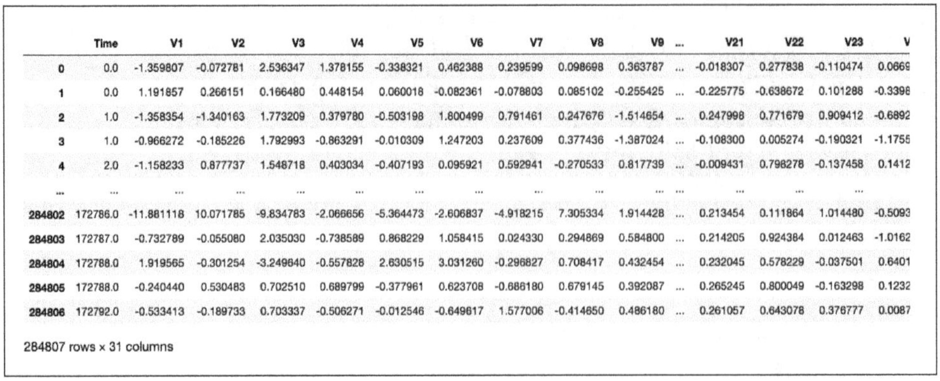

	Time	V1	V2	V3	V4	V5	V6	V7	V8	V9	...	V21	V22	V23	V
0	0.0	-1.359807	-0.072781	2.536347	1.378155	-0.338321	0.462388	0.239599	0.098698	0.363787	...	-0.018307	0.277838	-0.110474	0.0669
1	0.0	1.191857	0.266151	0.166480	0.448154	0.060018	-0.082361	-0.078803	0.085102	-0.255425	...	-0.225775	-0.638672	0.101288	-0.3398
2	1.0	-1.358354	-1.340163	1.773209	0.379780	-0.503198	1.800499	0.791461	0.247676	-1.514654	...	0.247998	0.771679	0.909412	-0.6892
3	1.0	-0.966272	-0.185226	1.792993	-0.863291	-0.010309	1.247203	0.237609	0.377436	-1.387024	...	-0.108300	0.005274	-0.190321	-1.1755
4	2.0	-1.158233	0.877737	1.548718	0.403034	-0.407193	0.095921	0.592941	-0.270533	0.817739	...	-0.009431	0.798278	-0.137458	0.1412
...	...	...	...	...	...	...	...	...	...	...		...	...	...	...
284802	172786.0	-11.881118	10.071785	-9.834783	-2.066656	-5.364473	-2.606837	-4.918215	7.305334	1.914428	...	0.213454	0.111864	1.014480	-0.5093
284803	172787.0	-0.732789	-0.055080	2.035030	-0.738589	0.868229	1.058415	0.024330	0.294869	0.584800	...	0.214205	0.924384	0.012463	-1.0162
284804	172788.0	1.919565	-0.301254	-3.249640	-0.557828	2.630515	3.031260	-0.296827	0.708417	0.432454	...	0.232045	0.578229	-0.037501	0.6401
284805	172788.0	-0.240440	0.530483	0.702510	0.689799	-0.377961	0.623708	-0.686180	0.679145	0.392087	...	0.265245	0.800049	-0.163298	0.1232
284806	172792.0	-0.533413	-0.189733	0.703337	-0.506271	-0.012546	-0.649617	1.577006	-0.414650	0.486180	...	0.261057	0.643078	0.376777	0.0087

284807 rows × 31 columns

Figure 7-22. Credit card fraud dataset

Table 7-6 provides the descriptions for the various fields that form this dataset.

Table 7-6. Credit card fraud dataset fields

Serial #	Column name	Description
1	Time	The total time in seconds that has elapsed between the first transaction and this particular transaction
2	Amount	The transaction amount
3	Class	(0,1) 0 = legitimate transaction; 1 = fraudulent transaction
4	V1–V28	Numerical input values driven from a PCA on the original input data
	Total transactions	284,807

Normally, time would be a useful feature for identifying fraudulent transactions. However, time in this dataset is the elapsed time in seconds between the first transaction and the one we are interested in. It does not tell us anything about the time of day or day of the week. Since we have no user, merchant, or account information, we cannot even use this time to group together transactions for the same user or same merchant in a short span of time.

Because there isn't much we can do with the Time column without additional information, we drop it from our dataset:

```
#Drop Time - It is relevant in the context of the user or the terminal
#however we don't know much about the columns and hence their
#relationship with time is not relevant
data_cc = data_df.copy()
data_cc.drop(['Time'], axis=1, inplace=True)
```

It would be interesting to understand the distribution of fraudulent and legitimate transactions across the different features. We use the following code to generate feature-wise distributions for legitimate and fraudulent transactions:

```
#Use this code if you want to explore the features.
#The loop will be CPU heavy for the machine running the notebook.

features = data_cc.iloc[:,0:28].columns #Get all the features

for f in features: #Loop through the features and for each

    graph = pd.DataFrame(
        #Create a data frame with the feature and the corresponding label
        {str(f): data_cc[f], "Class": data_cc['Class'], }
    )

    #Plot the feature distribution
    fig = px.histogram(
        graph,
        x=f,
        title="Feature " + str(f) + " Distribution",
        color="Class",
        marginal="box",
        labels={"0": "Legitimate", "1": "Fraudulent"},
    )

    fig.update_traces(opacity=0.75)
    fig.show()
```

Figure 7-23 depicts a few of the resulting plots.

Histograms in scikit-learn provide a visual representation of the distribution of a feature across different classes. The horizontal bars superimposed on the histograms in Figure 7-23 offer key statistical information including the median, first quartile, third quartile, minimum, and maximum values.

By examining the histograms and their associated statistics, we can discern how the data is spread out and where the majority of data points lie within each class. The range between the first and third quartiles, known as the *interquartile range*, is particularly informative.

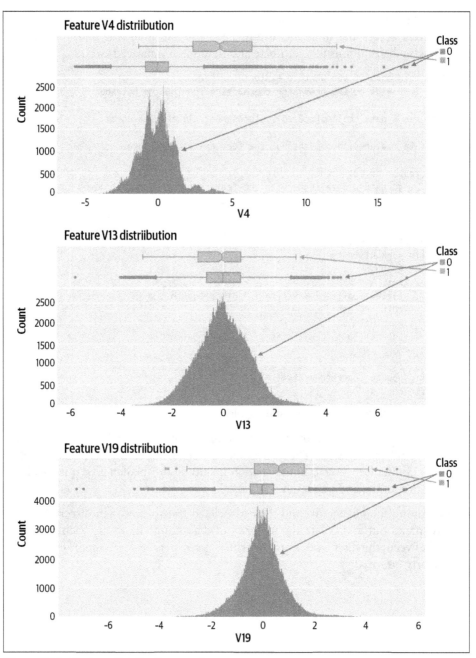

Figure 7-23. Feature distribution graphs

For instance, if we compare features V4, V19, and V13, we observe distinct characteristics:

- V4 exhibits entirely separate interquartile ranges between the legitimate and fraudulent transactions, indicating clear distinctions in the feature's values for each class.
- V19 displays a partial overlap of interquartile ranges between the two classes. While there is some distinction, there are also shared regions where the values of the feature overlap between the classes.
- V13 showcases completely overlapping interquartile ranges between the legitimate and fraudulent transactions, suggesting minimal discrimination between the two classes based on this feature alone.

Understanding the interquartile range helps us gauge the variability of a feature and its potential contribution to classification tasks. Features with distinct interquartile ranges across classes are more likely to provide meaningful discrimination and contribute significantly to the prediction process. Conversely, features with overlapping interquartile ranges may have less discriminatory power and may not contribute as effectively to classification tasks. Therefore, analyzing histograms and interquartile ranges aids in identifying which features are most informative for prediction tasks and in understanding the variability within the dataset.

Next, we separate the features and labels and create our training, validation, and testing datasets:

```
labels = pd.DataFrame(data_cc['Class'])
features = data_cc.drop(['Class'], axis = 1)

#Create Training, Validation and Test sets
train_features,test_features,train_label,test_label = train_test_split(
    features,labels,test_size=0.20, random_state=110)
train_features,val_features,train_label,val_label = train_test_split(
    train_features,train_label,test_size=0.20, random_state=110)
```

We create the test set as 20% of the total set and the validation set as 20% of the training set. We use a `random_state` so that we can produce repeatable datasets across multiple iterations of our testing.

From our earlier discussion, we understand that credit card fraud data will usually have an imbalance in terms of the number of fraudulent versus legitimate transactions, where the latter will usually be the dominant class. Let's calculate this data imbalance for our dataset:

```
#Calculate the imbalance in the data
fraud = len(data_cc[data_cc['Class']==1].index)
legit = len(data_cc[data_cc['Class']==0].index)
total = len(data_cc)
```

```
print("Total fraudulent transactions: ", str(fraud))
print("Total legitimate transactions: ", str(legit))
print("Total transactions: ", str(total))

Total fraudulent transactions:  492
Total legitimate transactions:  284315
Total transactions:  284807
```

Since this is a binary classification problem, we are going to use a sigmoid function in our final layer. However, our data is imbalanced, as we can see in the preceding code, and a neural network would commonly spend a long time learning this imbalance. If we want to speed up the learning process, we can introduce a bias to our final layer. The formula for calculating the bias is as follows:

$$InitialBias = \log_e\left(\frac{NumOfFraudTransactions}{NumOfLegitTransactions}\right)$$

Information on how this formula was derived is available on the TensorFlow website (*https://oreil.ly/u81U0*).

As we build the model, we want to monitor certain metrics during training and testing to understand how well the model is trained and how it performs on unseen data. Let's look at some of the metrics that will be relevant to our discussion:

True positives
    Number of transactions that were correctly classified as fraudulent.

True negatives
    Number of transactions that were correctly classified as legitimate.

False positives
    Number of transactions that were incorrectly classified as fraudulent. Think of these as legitimate transactions that were flagged as fraudulent.

False negatives
    Number of transactions that were incorrectly classified as legitimate. Think of these as fraudulent transactions that were missed by the model.

Accuracy
    Measure of how many correct classifications the model was able to perform versus the total number of transactions processed. The formula for such a calculation would look like the following:

$$Accuracy = (TruePositives + TrueNegatives) / TotalTransactionsProcessed$$

Precision

Measure of how many true positive classifications were made versus the total number of positive classifications. In this case, a positive classification refers to a fraudulent classification. The formula for precision is as follows:

$$Precision = TruePositives/(TruePositives + FalsePositives)$$

Recall

Measure of how many true positive classifications were made versus the total number of positive (fraudulent) transactions. We can think of this as the ratio of identified fraudulent transactions versus actual fraudulent transactions. The formula for recall is as follows:

$$Recall = TruePositives/(TruePositives + FalseNegatives)$$

AUPRC

Stands for "area under the precision-recall curve." This is a popular evaluation metric for binary classification problems, especially when the data is imbalanced, such as the data we are dealing with right now.

The *precision-recall curve* represents the trade-off between precision and recall, where precision is the fraction of true positives among all predicted positives and recall is the fraction of true positives among all actual positives. The curve shows how the precision and recall values change as the decision threshold for classification is varied. A decision threshold value is what decides the classification. Most classification algorithms don't output a binary 0 or 1 when it comes to classification of data. They output a probability between 0 and 1. For example, if we set a threshold of 0.5, everything above 0.5 will be classified as a fraudulent transaction and everything below as a legitimate transaction.

In an imbalanced dataset, the AUPRC is preferred over other metrics such as accuracy and AUC-ROC (area under the curve receiver operating characteristics) because it focuses on the performance of the classifier on the minority class. A high AUPRC indicates that the classifier is able to identify a high percentage of positive examples while maintaining high precision. A perfect model will not make any mistakes, so the false positives will always be zero. The model is able to achieve 100% recall without any false positives.

The *random classifier baseline* is the score that represents the performance of a random classifier, which assigns labels randomly without using any information from the input data. The baseline score depends on the class distribution; that is, the proportion of positive and negative examples in the dataset. For a problem with a class distribution of p% positive and (100-p)% negative examples, the random classifier baseline for the AUPRC score is p, the proportion of positive examples in the dataset.

It is important to compare the classifier's performance with the random classifier baseline when evaluating its performance on an imbalanced dataset. In doing so, we can determine whether the classifier is able to learn from input data and provide better results when compared to random classification.

Our next step is to define the initial bias and the metric that should be monitored by our model:

```
#Calculate initial bias to improve training speed
initial_bias = np.log([fraud/legit])
#Define bias as a Keras constant
bias = tflow.keras.initializers.Constant(initial_bias)
#Define how we want to measure the performance of the model
MON = [
      keras.metrics.AUC(name='prc', curve='PR'),
      keras.metrics.Precision(name='precision'),
      keras.metrics.Recall(name='recall'),
      keras.metrics.BinaryAccuracy(name='accuracy')
]
```

We define and adopt a normalizer to bring all our features to the same scale. The layer works by scaling inputs in a distribution of around 0 with a standard deviation of 1:

```
#Define a normalizer
#A preprocessing layer which normalizes continuous features
normalizer = tflow.keras.layers.Normalization(axis=1)
normalizer.adapt(np.array(train_features))
```

Next, we build our model using the sequential model class in Keras:

```
#Build the model
cc_model = tflow.keras.Sequential()
```

The first thing we do is add the normalizer layer to the model:

```
cc_model.add(normalizer) #Add a preprocessing layer
```

Then we add a dense layer to the model:

```
cc_model.add(layers.Dense(
    16, activation='relu',input_shape=(train_features.shape[-1],)))
```

Note the following:

- The activation function used by this layer is the ReLU. This introduced nonlinearity in the model by outputting the input directly if it is positive, and outputting zero otherwise.

- The input shape for the layer is based on the shape of the training features.

- We have 16 units (neurons) in our dense layer.

The purpose of the densely connected hidden layer is to learn complex patterns and relationships in data.

This is followed by a dropout layer:

```
cc_model.add(layers.Dropout(0.5))
```

The dropout layer sets input to 0 using the rate parameter (0.5). During training, a fraction of randomly selected neurons (in this case, 50% or 0.5) are temporarily dropped out. This helps prevent the network from relying too heavily on any particular set of neurons and encourages the network to learn more robust features. The dropout layer improves the generalization and performance of the neural network by reducing overfitting.

The last layer of the model is a linear layer that outputs the probability of the transaction classification:

```
cc_model.add(keras.layers.Dense(1, activation='sigmoid',bias_initializer=bias))
```

Note the following:

- It uses the sigmoid activation function for binary classification.
- It has only one unit (neuron), as it needs to output a single value. Sigmoid activation squashes the output to the range [0, 1], which is interpreted as the probability of the input belonging to the positive class.
- We are using the bias that we calculated earlier to speed up the model training.

The purpose of the linear layer is to provide a probability estimate of the positive class for binary classification tasks.

We follow this up by compiling the model and defining some additional hyperparameters. Hyperparameters in a neural network are preset configuration settings crucial for guiding the learning process and the network's architecture. Unlike model parameters such as weights and biases, which are learned from data during training, hyperparameters are predetermined by the ML practitioner. They play a vital role in tuning the model's performance and generalization ability, but they remain fixed throughout the training process. Fine-tuning hyperparameters stands as an indispensable aspect of building a potent neural network, often entailing thorough experimentation to identify the optimal combination that maximizes performance for a specific task and dataset.

We discussed the considerations for architecting the number of layers and nodes in a neural network in Chapter 6. In our example here, we are following the same principle of starting with a few layers to keep our architecture simple. Later in this chapter, we will iterate over this architecture and compare the results. We will also discuss some additional hyperparameters.

For this example, we are using the hyperparameters provided on the TensorFlow website (*https://oreil.ly/u81U0*) as a baseline:

```
# Define the learning rate
learning_rate = 0.001

# Compile the model
cc_model.compile(
    optimizer=optimizers.Adam(learning_rate=learning_rate),
    loss=losses.BinaryCrossentropy(),
    metrics=MON
)

# Setting up parameters
CYCLES = 100
BATCH = 2048

# Defining Early Stopping callback
early_stopping = EarlyStopping(
    monitor='val_prc',  # Monitoring validation precision-recall curve
    verbose=1,  # Verbosity level
    patience=10,  # Number of epochs with no improvement
    mode='max',  # Monitoring mode, maximizing precision-recall curve
    restore_best_weights=True  # Restoring the best model weights
)
```

We will start with the compile method, about which we note the following:

- The code uses the Adam optimizer with a learning rate of 0.001, which signifies the step size at which the weights of the neural network are updated during training. A smaller learning rate generally leads to slower but more stable training. The Adam optimizer enhances gradient descent by adapting learning rates based on moment estimates. "Adam: A Method for Stochastic Optimization (*https://oreil.ly/_MiFU*)" (Kingma & Ba, 2017) provides more information on this topic.

- Loss is defined as `BinaryCrossEntropy`, which is commonly used in binary classification problems. It works by calculating the difference between the predictions and the labels and penalizes the model for incorrect predictions.

- We pass the metrics we defined earlier to be monitored by the model.

The next parameters that are defined are `CYCLES` (epoch cycles) and `BATCH`. The cycles define the number of epochs for which the model will be trained. For our imbalanced dataset, we want to ensure that the batch has a good chance of having some positive samples. The batch size represents the number of samples processed before the model is updated during training. Using smaller batches speeds up training and allows for more efficient use of computational resources.

We also define `earlystopping` using `tf.keras.callbacks.EarlyStopping`, imported earlier in the code. Early stopping is a regularization technique to stop the training of a model before it has run for its full set of cycles if a defined metric does not improve across multiple epoch cycles, thereby preventing overfitting by stopping the training when the performance on the validation set starts to degrade. In our case, it is a metric set to `val_prc`, which is the AUPRC (precision recall curve) we discussed earlier.

Following this we have `patience=10`, which means the model training process waits for 10 epochs with no improvement in the monitored metric before stopping training. In our case, if the precision-recall curve does not improve for 10 consecutive epochs, training will stop.

The `mode='max'` parameter specifies whether to maximize or minimize the monitored metric. Since the precision-recall curve is a performance metric, setting mode to `'max'` means the training will continue until the precision-recall curve stops increasing.

With `restore_best_weights=True`, when the training stops due to early stopping, the model weights will be set to those that achieved the highest precision-recall curve on the validation set.

Following is a summary of the model:

```
#Model summary
cc_model.summary()
Model: "sequential_1"
```

Layer (type)	Output Shape	Param #
normalization_1 (Normalizat ion)	(None, 29)	59
dense_1 (Dense)	(None, 16)	480
dropout_1 (Dropout)	(None, 16)	0
dense_2 (Dense)	(None, 1)	17

```
Total params: 556
Trainable params: 497
Non-trainable params: 59
```

We save the initial weights of the model so that we can restore them when needed. In our case, they can be used to compare multiple runs of a model with different initialization parameters. In other instances, we might want to save the weights of a trained model before performing further fine-tuning:

```
#Save the model's initial weights
init_weights = os.path.join(tempfile.mkdtemp(), 'iw')
cc_model.save_weights(init_weights)
```

We initialize the `tensorboard` for visualizing our metrics, followed by fitting the model.

Note the following:

- We are saving the model-fitting history for visualization.
- The BATCH and CYCLES parameters are passed as before.
- Callbacks include `early_stopping` (based on AUPRC monitoring) and `tensorboard_callback` (for visualization).

```
cc_model.load_weights(init_weights) #Use this on a second run

#Initialize tensorboard callback
log_dir = "logs/pafme/" + datetime.datetime.now().strftime("%Y%m%d-%H%M%S")
tensorboard_callback = tflow.keras.callbacks.TensorBoard(
    log_dir=log_dir, histogram_freq=1)

#Fit the model on the training data
history = cc_model.fit(
    train_features,
    train_label,
    batch_size=BATCH,
    epochs=CYCLES,
    callbacks=[early_stopping, tensorboard_callback],
    validation_data=(val_features, val_label))
Epoch 1/100
90/90 [==] - 2s 9ms/step - loss: 0.0098 - prc: 0.3966 - precision: 0.6104 -
recall: 0.4393 - accuracy: 0.9985 - val_loss: 0.0059 - val_prc: 0.7278 -
val_precision: 0.9000 - val_recall: 0.4235 - val_accuracy: 0.9988
Epoch 2/100
90/90 [==] - 0s 3ms/step - loss: 0.0079 - prc: 0.5059 - precision: 0.7407 -
recall: 0.4361 - accuracy: 0.9987 - val_loss: 0.0055 - val_prc: 0.7302 -
val_precision: 0.9048 - val_recall: 0.4471 - val_accuracy: 0.9989
    .
    .
    .
Epoch 39/100
89/90 [==>.] - ETA: 0s - loss: 0.0049 - prc: 0.6717 - precision: 0.8058 -
recall: 0.5171 - accuracy: 0.9989Restoring model weights from the end of
the best epoch: 29.
90/90 [==] - 0s 3ms/step - loss: 0.0049 - prc: 0.6717 - precision: 0.8058 -
recall: 0.5171 - accuracy: 0.9989 - val_loss: 0.0032 - val_prc: 0.8086 -
val_precision: 0.9310 - val_recall: 0.6353 - val_accuracy: 0.9992
Epoch 39: early stopping
```

The training does an early stop at 39. We can use TensorBoard to look at the training and validation metrics (see Figures 7-24 to 7-27).

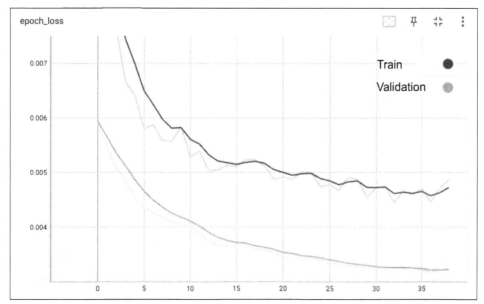

Figure 7-24. Loss metric

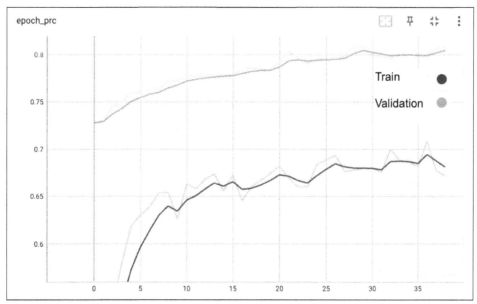

Figure 7-25. AUPRC metric

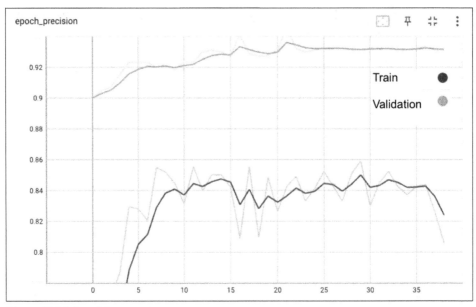

Figure 7-26. Precision metric

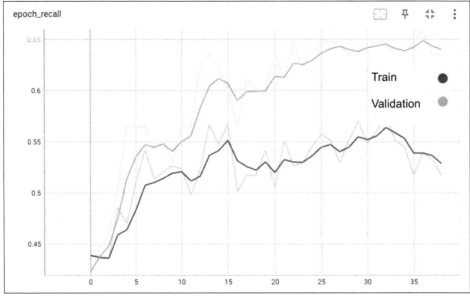

Figure 7-27. Recall metric

Note the following:

- AUPRC maximizes at under 0.7 for this model.
- While the model is precise at around 0.83, the recall is low at 0.525.
  - The ratio of true positives versus false positives is good.
  - The ratio of true positives versus actual positives can be improved. Our model is missing fraudulent transactions.

We further analyze this using a confusion matrix and test summary:

```
#Generate predictions for test dataset
test_predictions_baseline = cc_model.predict(test_features, batch_size=BATCH)
#Function to create a confusion matrix and test summary
def plot_matrix(actual, predictions, threshold=0.5):
    matrix = confusion_matrix(actual, predictions > threshold)
    sns.set(font_scale=1.2)
    plt.figure(figsize=(8, 6))
    sns.heatmap(matrix, annot=True, fmt="d", cmap="YlGnBu",
                xticklabels=['Legitimate', 'Fraud'],
                yticklabels=['Legitimate', 'Fraud'])
    plt.title('CC Fraud Transactions (Threshold: {:.2f})'.format(threshold))
    plt.xlabel('Predicted')
    plt.ylabel('Actual')
    plt.show()

    fraud_total, fraud_detected = matrix[1].sum(), matrix[1][1]
    legit_total, legit_detected = matrix[0].sum(), matrix[0][0]
    fraud_missed, legit_missed = matrix[1][0], matrix[0][1]

    print('\033[1m' + 'Fraud summary (actual = 1): ' '\033[0m')
    print('- Total: ', fraud_total)
    print('- Detected: ', fraud_detected)
    print('- Missed: ', fraud_missed)

    print('\033[1m' + '\nLegitimate summary (actual = 0): ' '\033[0m')
    print('- Total: ', legit_total)
    print('- Detected: ', legit_detected)
    print('- Missed: ', legit_missed)

#Plot the test summary
plot_matrix(test_label, test_predictions_baseline)
```

Figure 7-28 shows a confusion matrix to visualize how the model is performing across legitimate and fraudulent transactions.

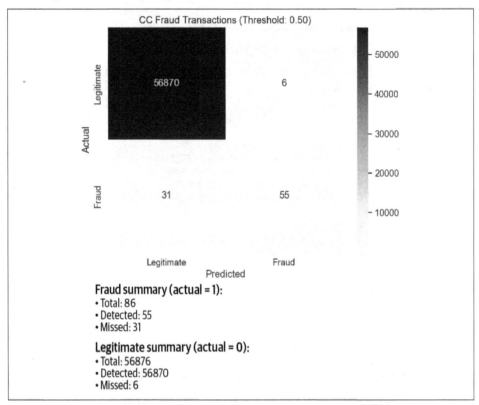

Figure 7-28. *Baseline model: confusion matrix*

As shown in Figure 7-28, although we have only misclassified six actual transactions as fraudulent, we have misclassified 31 fraudulent transactions as legitimate. At this stage, it is crucial to comprehend the business context of the problem and determine what holds greater significance for us:

- The ability to classify most fraudulent transactions correctly (an inability to do this effectively can lead to financial loss)
- The ability to classify most legitimate transactions correctly (an inability to do this effectively can lead to poor customer experience)

In an ideal world we would like to optimize both, but most times one will come at the cost of the other.

Credit Card Fraud Weighted Analysis Using Artificial Neural Networks

One way to handle class imbalance in a dataset is to assign class weights. The idea is to heavily weight the minority class in the classifier to compensate for the small sample representation. Following is the formula for calculating the class weights:

$$Call\_weight = \frac{Total\_samples}{(\#\_of\_class\_samples \times \#\_of\_classes)}$$

We calculate the weights for our two classes:

```
#Weight the classes to handle imbalance of data
#class-weight =n_samples_total / (n_classes * n_samples_class)
legit_weight = total / (legit * 2)
fraud_weight = total / (fraud * 2)
print('Weight (legit) class 0:', legit_weight)
print('Weight (fraud) class 1:', fraud_weight)
weight = {0: legit_weight, 1: fraud_weight}

Weight (legit) class 0: 0.5008652375006595
Weight (fraud) class 1: 289.4380081300813
```

Note that our minority class has a weight of almost 600 times that of the other class. If you are following along, the code in this section is very similar to the code in the previous section. I will not go through the code line by line, and instead will highlight only the outputs and the differences:

```
#Step 1 - Define initial bias
bias = tflow.keras.initializers.Constant(initial_bias)

#Step 2 - Build the model
weighted_model = tflow.keras.Sequential()
weighted_model.add(normalizer) #Add a pre-processing layer
weighted_model.add(layers.Dense(16, activation='relu',input_shape=(
    train_features.shape[-1],)))
#weighted_model.add(layers.Dense(16, activation='relu',input_shape=(
#    train_features.shape[-1],))) #Uncomment this for Multiple Hidden Layer NN
weighted_model.add(layers.Dropout(0.5))
weighted_model.add(keras.layers.Dense(1, activation='sigmoid',
                                    bias_initializer=bias))
weighted_model.load_weights(init_weights)

#Step 3 - Setup Tensorflow
#Define Tensorboard log directory
log_dir = "logs/pafme/" + datetime.datetime.now().strftime("%Y%m%d-%H%M%S")
tensorboard_callback = tflow.keras.callbacks.TensorBoard(
    log_dir=log_dir, histogram_freq=1)

#Step 4 - Compile the model
weighted_model.compile(
        optimizer=keras.optimizers.Adam(learning_rate=0.001),
```

```
        loss=keras.losses.BinaryCrossentropy(),
        metrics=MON)

weighted_model.load_weights(init_weights)

#Step - 5 Fit the model
weighted_history = weighted_model.fit(
    train_features,
    train_label,
    batch_size=BATCH,
    epochs=CYCLES,
    callbacks=[early_stopping, tensorboard_callback],
    validation_data=(val_features, val_label),
    class_weight=weight) #Class weights are passed here

Epoch 1/100
90/90 [==] - 1s 7ms/step - loss: 1.0587 - prc: 0.4230 - precision: 0.4969 -
recall: 0.5837 - accuracy: 0.9982 - val_loss: 0.0079 - val_prc: 0.6711 -
val_precision: 0.7381 - val_recall: 0.7294 - val_accuracy: 0.9990
Epoch 2/100
90/90 [==] - 0s 4ms/step - loss: 0.7417 - prc: 0.4635 - precision: 0.3900 -
recall: 0.7072 - accuracy: 0.9975 - val_loss: 0.0108 - val_prc: 0.6704 -
val_precision: 0.6542 - val_recall: 0.8235 - val_accuracy: 0.9989
.
.

.
Epoch 11/100
79/90 [==>....] - ETA: 0s - loss: 0.2947 - prc: 0.2152 - precision: 0.0433 -
recall: 0.8491 - accuracy: 0.9666          Restoring model weights from the end
of the best epoch: 1.
90/90 [==] - 0s 4ms/step - loss: 0.3170 - prc: 0.2122 - precision: 0.0427 -
recall: 0.8411 - accuracy: 0.9665 - val_loss: 0.0742 - val_prc: 0.4841 -
val_precision: 0.0919 - val_recall: 0.9176 - val_accuracy: 0.9829
Epoch 11: early stopping
```

During fitting, we are passing the class weights that we calculated in the beginning of this section. The model stops early after the 11th epoch. We load TensorBoard to review our training metrics:

```
#Load TensorBoard
%load_ext tensorboard
%tensorboard --logdir logs/pafme
```

Figures 7-29 and 7-30 depict the different training and validation metrics for our model.

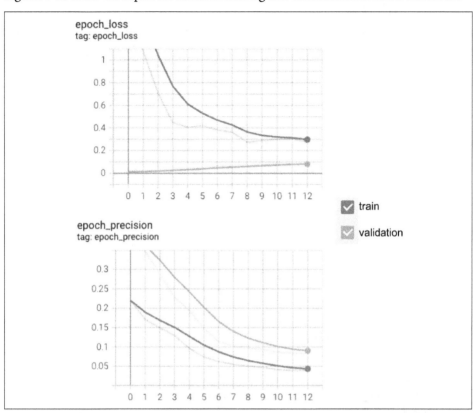

Figure 7-29. Training/validation metrics: weighted model (epoch_loss and epoch_precision)

Note the following in Figures 7-29 and 7-30:

- AUPRC for the model is low.
- While the model precision is low, recall is high:
  - The ratio of true positives versus false positives has declined.
  - The ratio of true positives versus actual positives has improved. Our model is missing fewer fraudulent transactions.

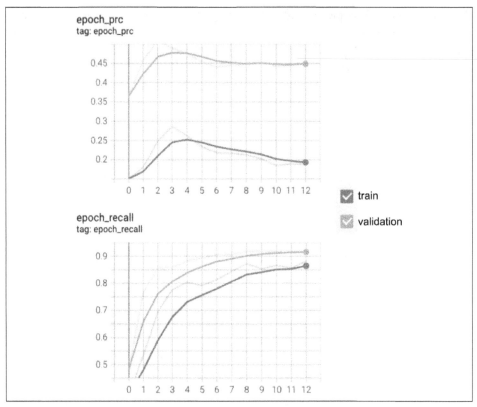

Figure 7-30. Training/validation metrics: weighted model (epoch_prc and epoch_recall)

Let's make predictions on our test set and then plot the test results (see Figure 7-31):

```
#Make predictions on test dataset
test_predictions_weighted = weighted_model.predict(test_features,
                                                   batch_size=BATCH)

#Plot test prediction
plot_matrix(test_label, test_predictions_weighted)

Fraud summary (val = 1):
- Total:   86
- Detected:  68
- Missed:   18

Legit summary (val = 0):
- Total:   56876
- Detected:   56848
- Missed:   28
```

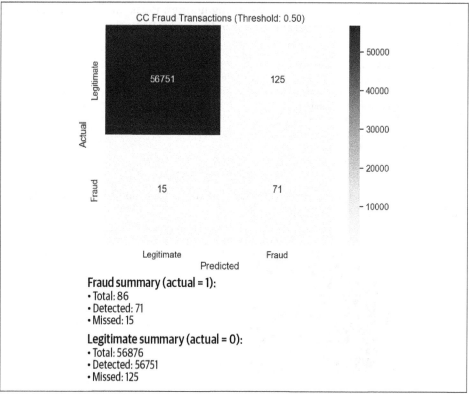

CC Fraud Transactions (Threshold: 0.50)

Fraud summary (actual = 1):
• Total: 86
• Detected: 71
• Missed: 15

Legitimate summary (actual = 0):
• Total: 56876
• Detected: 56751
• Missed: 125

Figure 7-31. Weighted model: confusion matrix

Note the following when comparing the weighted model (Figure 7-31) with the baseline model (Figure 7-28):

- The number of correctly classified fraudulent transactions has increased. This means false negatives (fraudulent transactions classified as legitimate) have been reduced. Hence, recall has increased.

- The number of false positives (legitimate transactions classified as fraudulent) has also increased. Hence, precision and AUPRC have decreased.

For this model, we have misclassified 125 actual transactions as fraudulent (increased from before) and 15 fraudulent transactions as legitimate (reduced from before).

Credit Card Analysis with Multiple Hidden Layers in the Artificial Neural Network

We can do one more variation in our two models by adding another hidden layer. The idea is to allow the neural network to be able to learn more complex patterns in the data. You can achieve this easily by changing the models in the same notebook and rerunning the notebook. Your model should now look like this:

```
#Build the model
model = tflow.keras.Sequential()
model.add(normalizer) #Add a preprocessing layer
model.add(layers.Dense(16, activation='relu',input_shape=(
    train_features.shape[-1],)))
model.add(layers.Dense(16, activation='relu',input_shape=(
    train_features.shape[-1],)))
model.add(layers.Dropout(0.5))
model.add(keras.layers.Dense(1, activation='sigmoid',
                            bias_initializer=bias))
```

Figure 7-32 shows a summary of what our baseline model is able to achieve after the addition of another hidden layer.

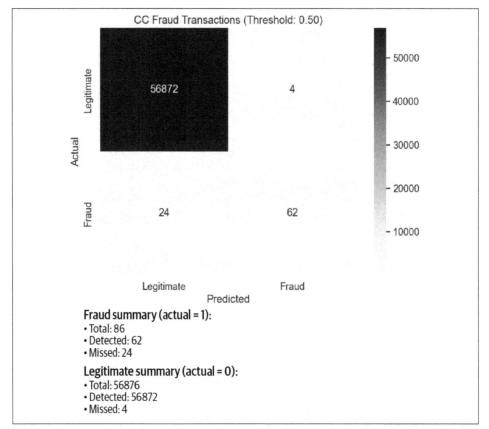

Figure 7-32. Modified baseline model: confusion matrix

Figure 7-33 shows a summary of what our weighted model is able to achieve after the addition of another hidden layer.

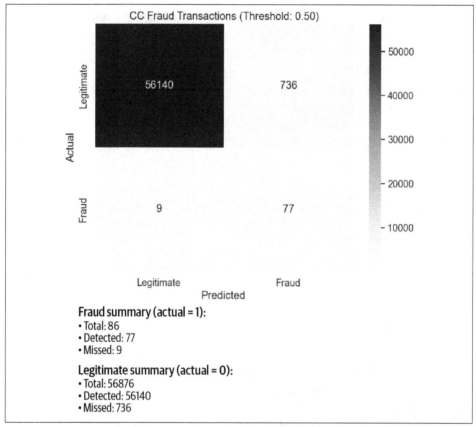

Figure 7-33. Modified weighted model: confusion matrix

Table 7-7 offers a comparison of the results of these tests.

Table 7-7. Test result comparison

	Baseline	Weighted	Modified baseline	Modified weighted
Fraud detected	55	71	62	77
Fraud missed	31	15	24	9
Legit detected	56870	56751	56872	56140
Legit missed	6	125	4	736

Comparing the various summaries in Table 7-7, we can look at a couple of metrics for our analysis:

- Our baseline model performed the worst when it came to detecting fraudulent transactions. It missed 31 fraudulent transactions. The model that performed the best on this metric was the modified weighted model, which missed only 9 fraudulent transactions.

- Similarly, when it came to missing (or misclassifying) legitimate transactions, our modified weighted model performed the worst, with 736 legitimate transactions classified as fraudulent. Our modified baseline model performed the best, with only 5 legitimate transactions being missed, while the baseline model was a close second, with 7 legitimate transactions missed.

There are many ways to model a problem and more ways to fine-tune it. Metrics are important when evaluating different model strategies, but it is important to keep the business context in mind. In this section, we dealt with imbalanced data and countered it using class weights. We also looked at how initial bias can help speed up model training and discussed several metrics to evaluate our model performance. We compared multiple models and looked at the business outcome for each to understand how improving one business metric can adversely impact another.

Conclusion

In this chapter, we looked at real-world problem-solving using predictive analytics and machine learning. We evaluated how predictive analytics can help a business decide on an optimal price to drive revenue growth. We then moved into entertainment and built a user-based recommendation system for movies. Finally, we worked with credit card fraud data to understand how we can use predictive analytics to classify a small number of fraudulent activities among a very large set of legitimate transactions. The theme was to start with a simple model and make incremental improvements to get better results. We went through the build process to better grasp the concepts through hands-on exercises. This also gave us the opportunity to discuss the business nuances behind certain problems and appreciate the fact that the best mathematical solution for a problem might not map to the optimal business outcome. I would urge you to use these as baselines for continuous building and improvement.

## CHAPTER 8

Exploring AWS Cloud Provider Services for AI/ML

There are only a handful of large public cloud providers in the world. The ones you have probably come across are Amazon Web Services (AWS), Google Cloud Platform (GCP), Microsoft Azure, and Alibaba Cloud. While there is a lot of buzz around generative AI at the time of this writing, cloud providers have been helping enterprises accelerate their AI vision for a few years now. In this chapter, we will explore some AI/ML services provided by AWS and its parent company, Amazon.

To Cloud or Not to Cloud

Prior to delving into AI/ML cloud offerings, I'd like to discuss the value of dedicating time and resources to constructing machine learning (ML) solutions using public cloud provider services. Why would one choose to use AWS services (or any other cloud provider) instead of building their solution open source or in software that is cloud agnostic? Although this question may appear theoretical, it is frequently a significant consideration for chief technology officers and other technology executives. To understand this, we need to do a quick cost-benefit analysis, with "cost" referring not just to money, but also to time and control, among other things.

An AI/ML pipeline is a composite of multiple components that come together to serve the ML needs of an enterprise. For large companies, this pipeline needs to ingest, transform, and process large amounts of data from a multitude of sources. This requires significant investment in both infrastructure and the operational skills required to manage the infrastructure. As businesses push for faster time to market for new services, the acquisition time for physical infrastructure (which is typically weeks) is unable to keep up with the development life cycle (which can be days or sometimes hours).

Ensuring that the infrastructure is available and can be scaled at speed is something cloud providers specialize in. Cloud providers also ease the pain of making these services highly available and resistant to regional disasters, something that would take months just to plan for a regular enterprise. Most cloud provider solutions are well integrated into the cloud ecosystem. This means an AI/ML platform can easily integrate with tens of hundreds of data sources out of the box. Extensive logging and telemetry are also integrated into these platforms to allow for easy debugging of AI/ML pipelines. Most cloud solutions are built for millions of consumers. Therefore, there is a huge focus on ease of adoption and ease of use, which is why most cloud provider solutions have a relatively gentle learning curve and easy-to-follow documentation. In addition, there is a plethora of third-party training material available.

From a cost perspective, most cloud services are based on a "pay for what you use" model (aka "pay as you go"). This means businesses can start building their AI/ML solutions without having to invest large sums of capital in infrastructure and other resources. In addition, it removes the barrier for startups and small enterprises to compete with well-funded organizations in the same space. Due to the large number of customers they need to serve on a shared infrastructure and the sensitive nature of some businesses, cloud providers focus heavily on security; as such, customers also reap the benefits of cloud providers' significant investments in the security space. What's more, the distributed nature of the cloud allows teams in different locations all over the world to easily collaborate on projects. Add to all of these benefits easy integration with other cloud provider services, and you can see why enterprises are adopting the cloud to manage large AI/ML pipelines (see Figure 8-1).

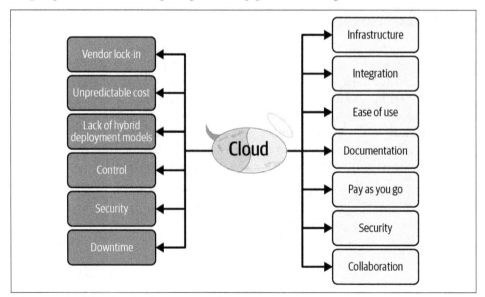

Figure 8-1. Public cloud adoption considerations

It is unlikely that an enterprise would choose its cloud strategy based purely on how it wants to run its AI/ML platform. However, as we move into the era of ML and language learning models, the importance of AI/ML platforms across organizations will only increase with time.

When moving to the cloud, there are certain considerations to keep in mind. Let's say your organization decides to use AWS. It's one thing to move to a cloud platform and another to build business solutions based on managed services provided by the cloud platform. Consider a scale from a self-managed environment at one end to a fully managed environment at the other. In a cloud environment, as we move toward the fully managed side of the scale we are increasing our likelihood of reaping all the benefits stated earlier. However, we are also locking ourselves into a specific cloud provider.

This is why enterprises have begun considering a multicloud strategy. Such a strategy enables businesses to be resilient to cloud provider outages and ensures that the service is available across multiple providers at the same time. Along these lines, there are certain organizations that are looking for hybrid deployment models supporting both the public and private cloud, and while there are a few services that help enable this, not all cloud provider services can be run in a private setup.

Another item to consider, especially when it comes to the pay-as-you-go model, is the predictability of the cost to the business over a period of time. More often than not, enterprises are surprised by how much they are paying and struggle to understand how these costs can be reduced. Finally, with a shared infrastructure (even with advanced security measures and service-level agreements), enterprises are committing to a shared security and control model, which can potentially expose them to risk, especially in terms of sensitive information.

In this chapter, we will take an exploratory approach to AWS AI/ML services, focusing on the different features available and how they can speed up and ease the process of building our AI/ML pipelines. This is different from our approach in Chapter 6, which was more comprehensive and had a specific end goal in mind. We are changing our approach for two reasons. First, cloud providers provide excellent documentation that is detailed enough to make it easy to follow along. Second, these services change fairly rapidly, so a step-by-step guide would probably be out of date before this book is published.

Exploring AWS SageMaker

AWS SageMaker is a fully managed service that allows you to build an end-to-end ML pipeline. A multitude of services are available within the SageMaker environment, and it would be impossible to explore all of them in the context of this chapter. Therefore, I will give you a good starting point. First, we will focus on data ingestion, exploration, and data preprocessing. Then, we will perform different data transformations, encodings, and other changes to make our data suitable for training. We'll use the data to train multiple models and let the platform choose the best model for our delivery. Finally, we will use the model to perform a few simple predictions (Figure 8-2).

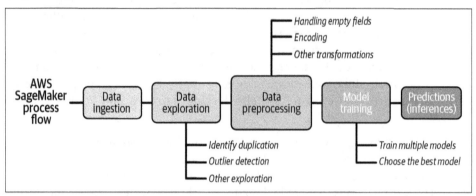

Figure 8-2. AWS SageMaker: high-level process flow

Prerequisites

The text assumes the following prerequisites, if you want to try the features on your own:

- A working knowledge of AWS Cloud and its basic services.
- An operational AWS account (some of the services can be charged, so the account might need AWS credits or the equivalent).
- Access to the SageMaker service in AWS. If this is the first time you are using AWS SageMaker, you will need to sign in to the AWS service (*https://oreil.ly/ YUe36*) and create the following:

  — A SageMaker domain

  — A user with the required roles to follow along

- An S3 bucket in the same cloud region as the one you are operating in. We will use this for data ingestion.

 Do not use a bucket name that has a period (.). This can cause processing issues at a later stage.

A final note before we begin: if you are new to the cloud, be vigilant when working with cloud provider services. Many cloud providers charge for these services on a pay-as-you-go basis, which means you could end up with a significant bill if you are not careful about cleaning up the services you have used in your deployment. To help you with this, I end the discussion of each service with a section on cleanup.

Data Ingest and Exploration

Now that the prerequisites are in place, we can start exploring SageMaker. Go to the AWS SageMaker service page and open SageMaker Studio using the credentials you provided when you initially signed in to the service. Once SageMaker Studio has loaded (be patient, as this can take a bit of time), you'll have access to the environment that can help you create and execute ML pipelines.

We'll begin by importing some data into our environment that we can use for training our models. We do this inside a component known as Data Wrangler. At the time of this writing, SageMaker Studio supported more than 60 data source types, some of which are shown in Figure 8-3.

Figure 8-3. Data Wrangler data sources

I would urge you to explore the data sources that are relevant to you at this point. Think about the problem you are trying to address. Identify the main data source you have access to and then see whether you can use the built-in connectors to import data into SageMaker. Consider the effort required to ingest data from this source without the connector, and compare it to how easy (or difficult) it is in this particular case.

For the purposes of this discussion, we will use a modified version of a dataset, available in the file *melb_data.csv*, located on the book's GitHub repository (*https://oreil.ly/ymuYS*). The dataset (*https://oreil.ly/1Xfid*) represents the prices of different properties in Melbourne, Australia. To import this data, we need to upload it to our S3 bucket:

1. Log in to the AWS Management Console (*https://oreil.ly/YUe36*) and navigate to the Amazon S3 console.

2. On the left side of the navigation pane, select Buckets.

3. Locate and click the name of the bucket where you wish to upload your files or folders.

4. Click Upload.

5. In the Upload window, either drag and drop or select Add file or Add folder to choose the items you want to upload. Then, click Open.

6. To proceed with the upload using the default settings, simply click Upload at the bottom of the page. Amazon S3 will start uploading your files and folders. Once the upload is complete, you will receive a success message on the Upload status page.

Once you have ensured that the data is uploaded, you can import the data by using S3 as a data source and selecting your uploaded data, as depicted in Figure 8-4.

At this point, we can start exploring the data. As we import the data, we notice that SageMaker has already started building a pipeline. It might not look like much, but as we progress, the pipeline will continue to grow. If you want to look at a visual representation of the pipeline, you can locate it under "dataflow."

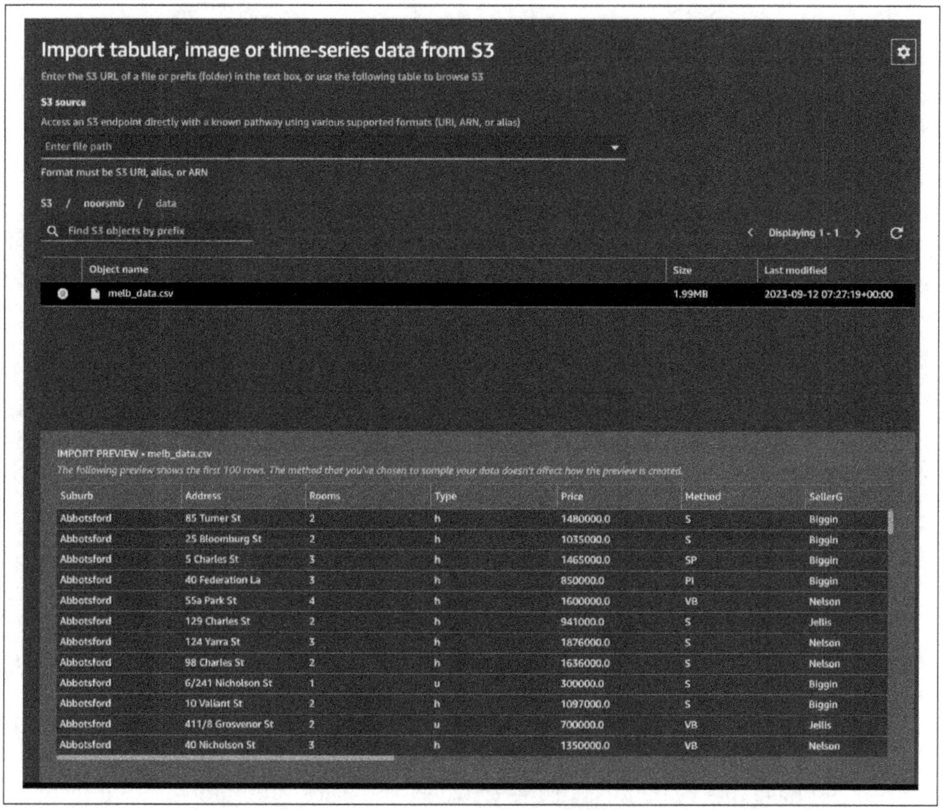

Figure 8-4. Importing data from S3

The first thing we want to do is analyze our dataset to determine the preprocessing and transformations required to train our model. We can do this using the Data Quality and Insights report. This is a very detailed report that looks at the various aspects of the data quality so that we can identify any issues with our dataset and address them at the data preprocessing stage. For our example, our target column (the one we would eventually like to predict) is "price," reflecting the property price. To access the report, follow these steps:

1. Select + next to the last node in the dataflow.

2. Choose Get data insights.

3. Specify a name for the insights report.

    a. As discussed, the target column is price.

    b. The Problem type is Regression.

4. For Data size, specify a subset of the entire data.

5. Choose Create.

As this is a detailed report, it takes a while to generate.

Let's look at some of the components in the report. The report starts with a summary that identifies key elements, such as number of features, percentage of missing data, and data duplication, among others. It also provides a categorization of the different datatypes we have in our dataset. As we continue to scroll through the report, we realize that several warnings with varying priorities are provided to us.

Let's start with the high-priority warning depicted in Figure 8-5.

The bar chart in the warning screen plots the predictive power of each feature on its own for our target label, Property Price. One thing that stands out is that the Municipalityfee feature can predict the price on its own 100% of the time.

This gives us an opportunity to look at a concept we have not discussed yet: target leakage. *Target leakage* represents a scenario where our dataset contains features that can individually predict our target without the need for additional features. When we see something like this in the dataset, we need to be more critical in terms of our analysis to understand the lineage of this feature. The question we need to ask here is: Will this attribute (feature) be available when we make our predictions? More often than not, we will realize this column is either a duplicate or a derivative of the target column. In our case, the Municipalityfee is 5% of the Property Price, and it is unlikely that we will have this value for a property where the price is unknown. Such features are often generated as part of postprocessing and should not be used for training, because they would not be available when the target value is unknown.

Because this report helps you identify *potential* problems, it's up to you as a data professional to determine whether you agree with the assessment and whether any action is needed in this regard. You could have a legitimate feature with high predictive power; in that case, you should leave it as is. Note that the warning provides us with information on how to fix the problem using data transformations, which we will explore shortly.

The bar chart in Figure 8-5 also helps us identify which features would be useful from a prediction perspective. This can be helpful for determining features we want to drop from the original dataset because we feel they don't contribute as much to the final result.

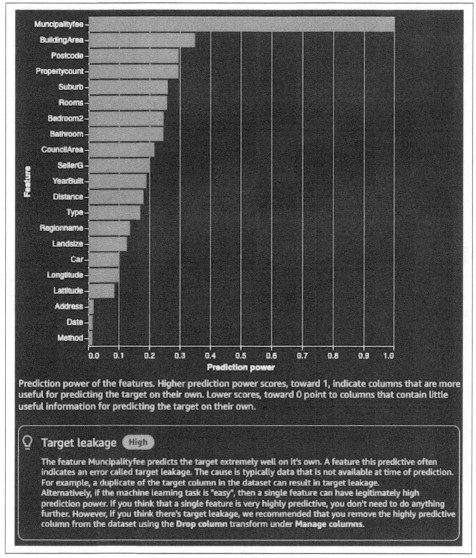

Prediction power of the features. Higher prediction power scores, toward 1, indicate columns that are more useful for predicting the target on their own. Lower scores, toward 0 point to columns that contain little useful information for predicting the target on their own.

Q **Target leakage** `High`

The feature Muncipalityfee predicts the target extremely well on it's own. A feature this predictive often indicates an error called target leakage. The cause is typically data that is not available at time of prediction. For example, a duplicate of the target column in the dataset can result in target leakage.
Alternatively, if the machine learning task is "easy", then a single feature can have legitimately high prediction power. If you think that a single feature is very highly predictive, you don't need to do anything further. However, if you think there's target leakage, we recommended that you remove the highly predictive column from the dataset using the **Drop column** transform under **Manage columns**.

Figure 8-5. Target leakage warning

At the bottom of Figure 8-5, we can see a data duplication warning (see Figure 8-6). The first step is to identify whether these duplicates are valid. If they aren't, they could point to data collection problems, such as duplicate data originating from different data sources or our data sources sending out data more than once. This is yet another item for us to look into during the data transformation phase.

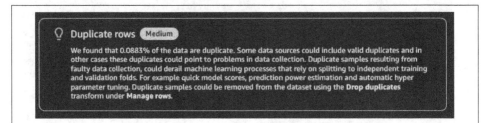

Figure 8-6. Duplicate data warning

We can also see a warning about outliers. Outliers can be values of the target label that fall outside the regular data distribution. Certain algorithms are good at handling outliers and certain use cases warrant having them in the dataset. So, depending on the use case, we can decide whether or not to address these outliers. However, note that the system is automatically able to detect them and bring them to our attention, as seen in Figure 8-7.

We can continue to explore the report and look at the attributes of some of the features to assist us in building our ML pipeline. For example, we can look for ill-formatted data, which does not follow a regular pattern in terms of values and which certain ML algorithms struggle with during training. We can also look for and drop records containing disguised missing values, which are values that may be set to 0 as a default but are actually missing. In addition, we can identify imbalanced data and address any biases that exist by going through each feature to understand how the values are distributed, and we can identify categorical features that need to be encoded. As you can see, AWS SageMaker generates an extensive report, and it might be worthwhile to spend some time on it so that we can better understand our data, identify issues, and see how different features can impact our end result.

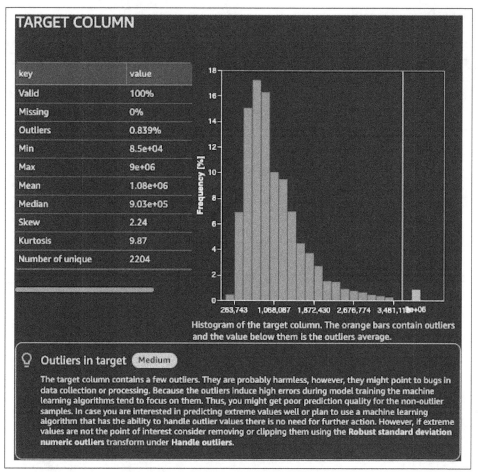

TARGET COLUMN

key	value
Valid	100%
Missing	0%
Outliers	0.839%
Min	8.5e+04
Max	9e+06
Mean	1.08e+06
Median	9.03e+05
Skew	2.24
Kurtosis	9.87
Number of unique	2204

Histogram of the target column. The orange bars contain outliers and the value below them is the outliers average.

💡 **Outliers in target** `Medium`

The target column contains a few outliers. They are probably harmless, however, they might point to bugs in data collection or processing. Because the outliers induce high errors during model training the machine learning algorithms tend to focus on them. Thus, you might get poor prediction quality for the non-outlier samples. In case you are interested in predicting extreme values well or plan to use a machine learning algorithm that has the ability to handle outlier values there is no need for further action. However, if extreme values are not the point of interest consider removing or clipping them using the **Robust standard deviation numeric outliers** transform under **Handle outliers**.

Figure 8-7. Outliers in the target

At this point, your dataflow in SageMaker should look similar to Figure 8-8. In the next section, we will use SageMaker data transformations to address some of what we've learned from our data analysis.

Figure 8-8. Data ingest and data quality exploration

Data Transformation

Before performing the transformations, it can be helpful to create a map similar to the one shown in Figure 8-9. This map lists the different ways we want to manipulate our data before using it for model training. You can use your own format to document your findings from your data analysis and the specific fields that you want to transform. Such documentation makes the transformation process more streamlined.

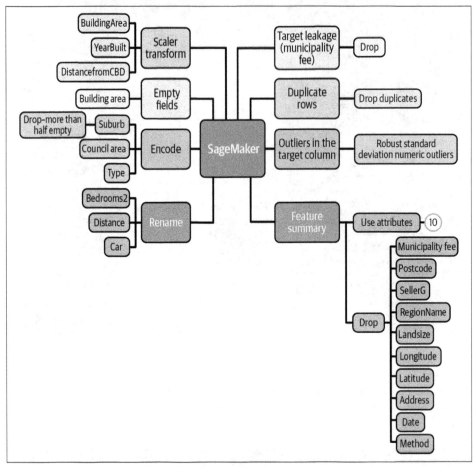

Figure 8-9. Data ingest and data quality exploration

We'll be covering most of the transformations mentioned in Figure 8-9. In real-world scenarios, you should expect to spend a significant amount of time getting your data to a stage where it can be used for machine learning. Therefore, I would highly encourage you to explore additional data transformation options in AWS beyond what is discussed here.

We start by adding a transformation step to drop the features we don't need (see Figure 8-10). We will keep the features that do not significantly impact the prediction of the target label, and we will keep "municipality fee," which was identified to cause target leakage. Follow these steps to drop a column:

1. Select the last block in the flowchart.

2. Click the plus sign (+).

3. Click the Add Transform menu option.

4. Search for Manage columns.

5. Select Drop column.

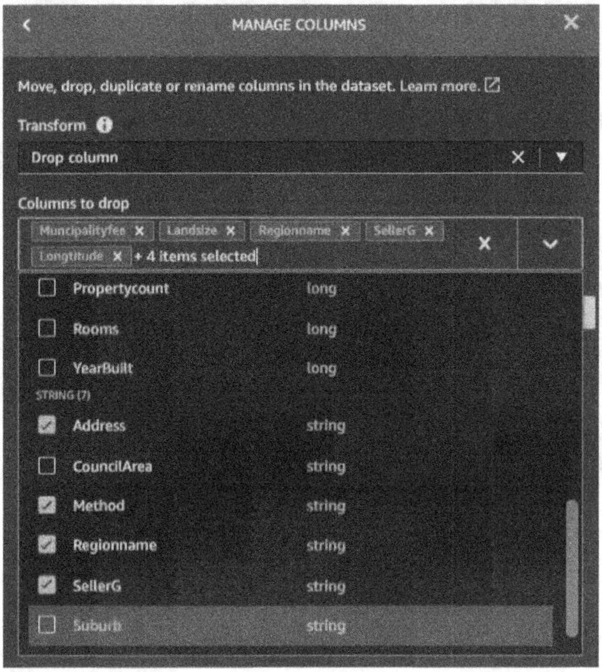

Figure 8-10. Dropping columns

Now we'll look at how to drop duplicate data. You can easily achieve this by adding a transformation step under Manage rows and using the Drop duplicates option, as shown in Figure 8-11.

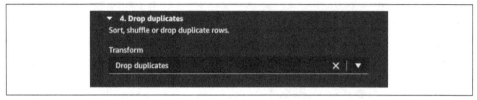

Figure 8-11. Dropping duplicates

The next step is to manage the outliers. Our Data Quality and Insights report tells us how to handle outliers using the Standard deviation numeric outliers option. We can use this transformation to trim the outliers for our target label, as shown in Figure 8-12.

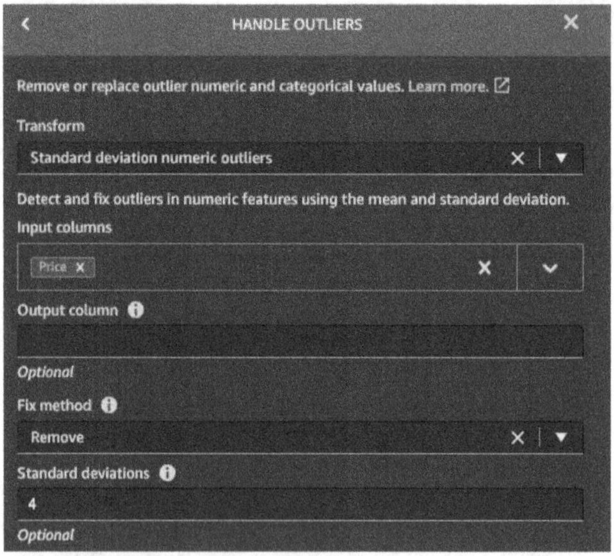

Figure 8-12. Managing outliers

We can continue our transformation by renaming some of the columns for better readability. Note that this step does not really have an impact on the model training. But it does improve our comprehension of the data and makes it easy for others to work with it in the future. Figure 8-13 shows a transformation step configuration for the three attributes being renamed.

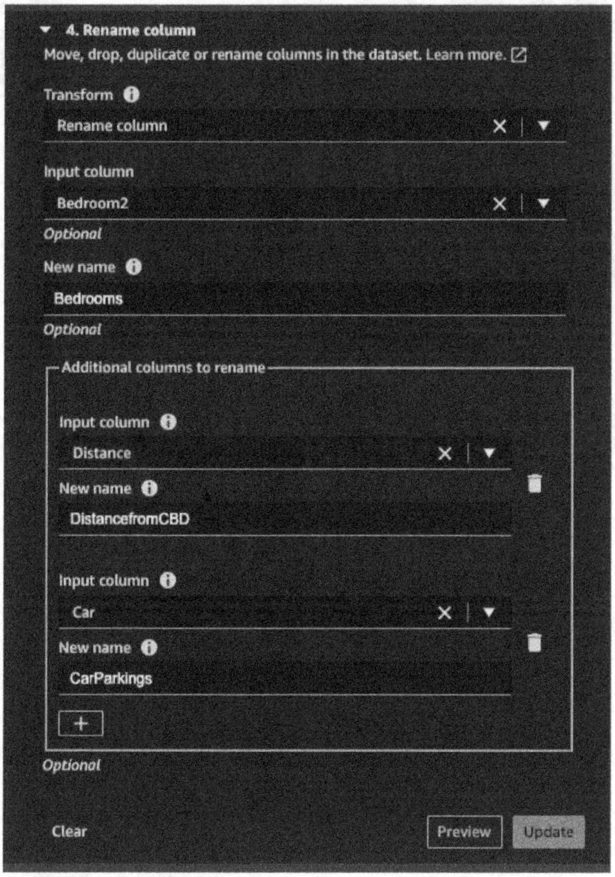

Figure 8-13. Renaming attributes

As per our initial report, the BuildingArea feature had missing values. The next step helps us drop records with missing values for particular features. We use the Drop missing transformation for this purpose, as shown in Figure 8-14.

Figure 8-14. Handling missing values

During this step, if you do not provide any value for Input columns, all rows with one or more missing values for any column will be removed from the dataset.

The next step is to scale values using a scaler. We will use the Standard scaler option, as shown in Figure 8-15. However, you can also explore the min-max scaler and other scalers depending on your dataset requirements.

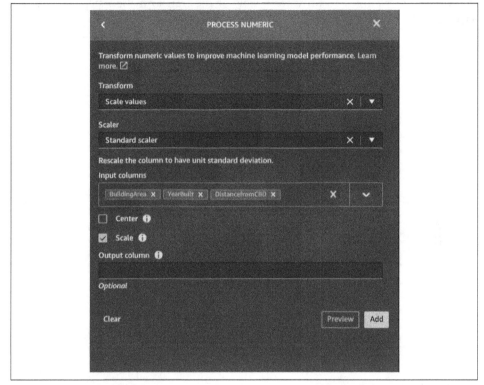

Figure 8-15. Scaling values

Similarly, we can perform one-hot encoding of categorical attributes. Note that certain ML algorithms can handle categorical data without the need to encode them. So, depending on which algorithm you are trying to use, you can choose to perform this step or skip it. Figure 8-16 provides a view of the transformation step for one-hot encoding.

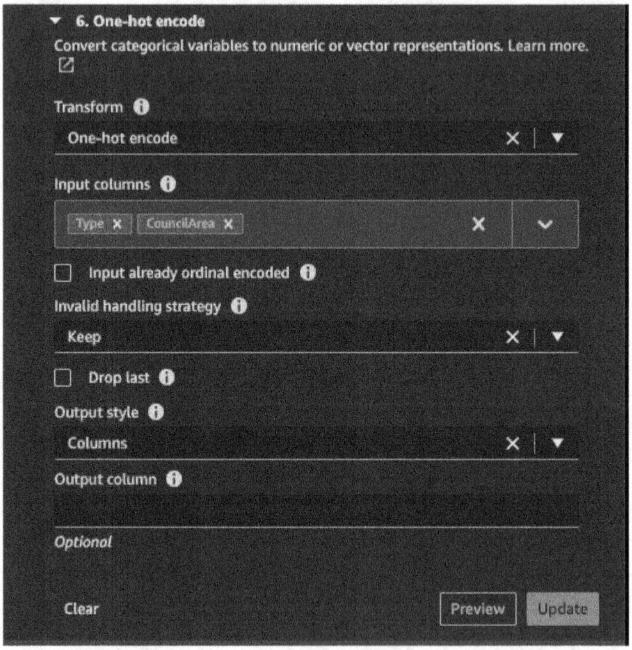

Figure 8-16. One-hot encoding

At this point, we have completed the required transformations. We can now export the transformed dataset to a destination from which it can be consumed later for training:

1. Click the + next to the last step in the dataflow.

2. Select Add Destination and choose Amazon S3.

3. Fill in the dialog box, as shown in Figure 8-17:

    a. Make sure to provide a target dataset name.

    b. Keep the type as CSV.

    c. Point to your S3 location. Ensure that the S3 location exists.

Your dataflow should now look similar to Figure 8-18. Note that we have defined everything so far, but nothing has been executed in terms of the data transformations. You can further analyze the data using additional reports and take further remediation steps as needed. However, a discussion of these reports is beyond the scope of this book.

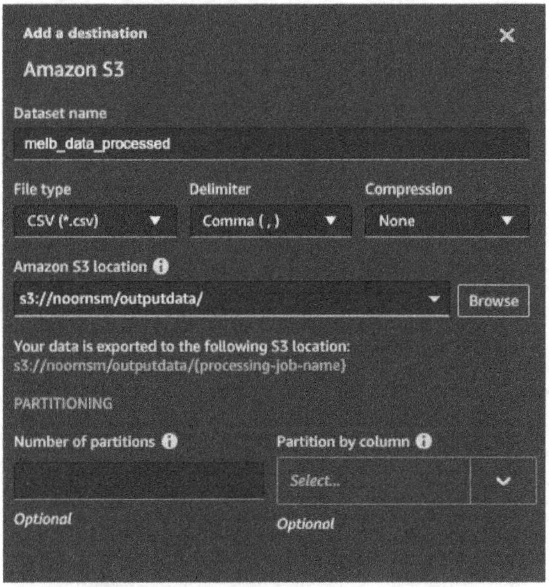

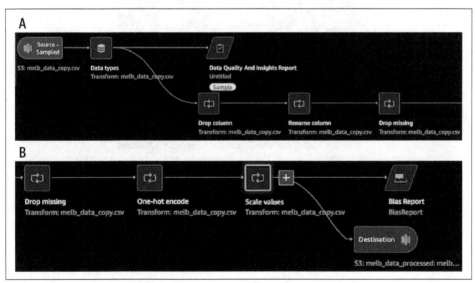

Figure 8-17. Exporting the transformed data to S3

Figure 8-18. Final dataflow (a, start; and b, end)

We will now execute our pipeline:

1. Click Run validation to ensure that there are no errors.
2. Click Create job.
   a. This will open a dialog box for Job Creation. Follow the steps shown in Figures 8-19 and 8-20 and do the following:
      i. Give the job a name.
      ii. Ensure that the S3 location is correctly specified. It needs to point to an existing S3 location that your user has access to.

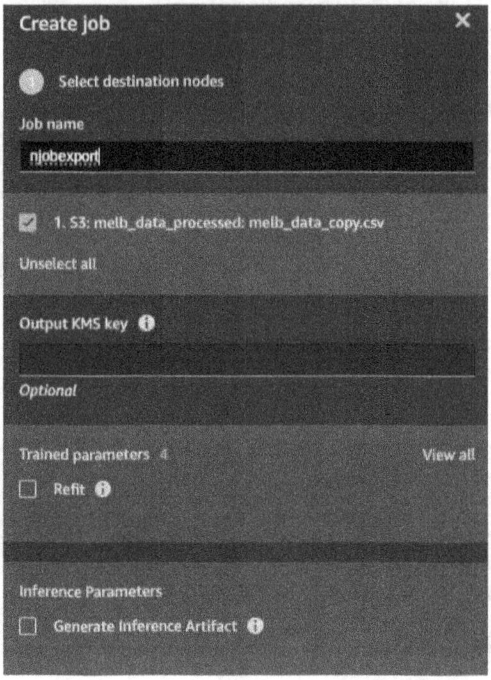

Figure 8-19. Naming the job

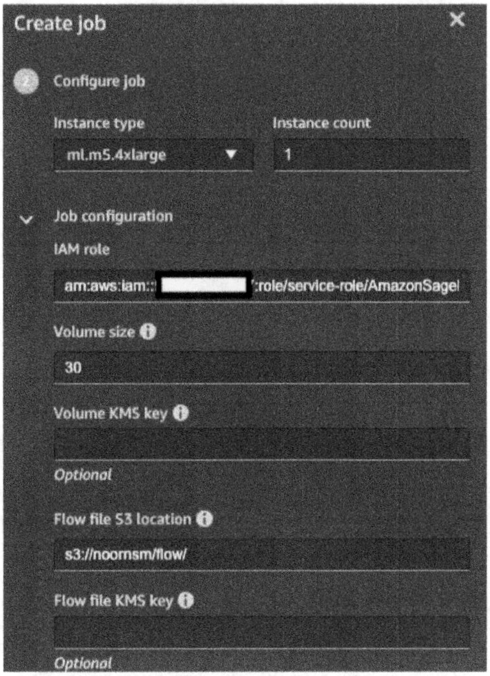

Figure 8-20. Checking the job configuration

Click Create on the Create Job task, and you should receive confirmation that the job was created successfully. You can follow the progress of job execution by clicking the provided link. This should lead you to a job status link, as shown in Figure 8-21.

Once the status for the job is complete, you can explore your S3 location to ensure that the transformed data is now available in the destination file you configured previously.

This completes our exploration of the data transformation phase. Next, we will train a few models using the transformed data and then use the models to make predictions.

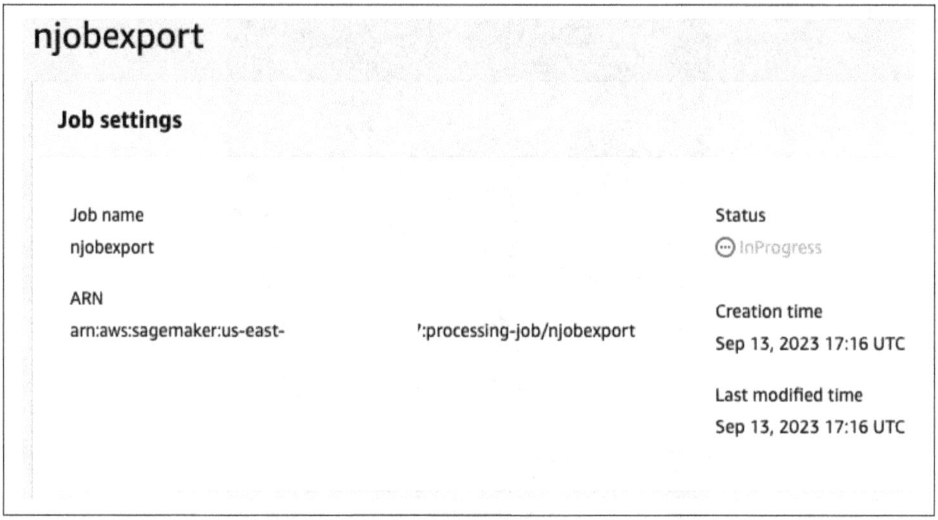

njobexport

Job settings

Job name
njobexport

ARN
arn:aws:sagemaker:us-east-   ':processing-job/njobexport

Status
⊙ InProgress

Creation time
Sep 13, 2023 17:16 UTC

Last modified time
Sep 13, 2023 17:16 UTC

Figure 8-21. Job execution status

Model Training and Prediction

Let's explore how to export our transformation and model training to a SageMaker Inference pipeline in the Jupyter Notebook environment. On the last node of the dataflow:

1. Select the +.

2. Select Export to and then choose SageMaker Inference Pipeline (via Jupyter Notebook).

This will open a Jupyter Notebook with all the steps needed to perform transformations, model training, and predictions. You can go through each step individually to understand the execution of the step and analyze the corresponding output. If you encounter errors, you can always go back and rerun the step or the entire notebook.

When you open the notebook for the first time, SageMaker will take a while to launch the notebook kernel. Once the launch is complete, you can start executing the corresponding steps. Note the following steps in the notebook:

1. Install dependencies:
   a. Install all the notebook dependencies needed for import, pipeline creation, transformation, training, and inference.

2. Define inputs and outputs:

   a. Define the original data source.

   b. Define the S3 output location:

      i. "Define the bucket" = "<*Your Bucket Name*>" (make sure you point this to a bucket that you have access to for output).

   c. Define the flow location (the notebook uses this flow file from Data Wrangler to apply the needed transformations).

   d. Create the processor for the pipeline.

3. Create the SageMaker pipeline:

   a. Define the pipeline:

      i. Define `target_attribute_name = "Price"`. This is where we are setting our target label. In our example, we used `use_automl_step = automl_enabled`. This is because otherwise, the notebook will use `XG_boost`, which uses the first column in the dataset as the target column, which is *not* `Price` in our case. This step will train many supported models in Sage-Maker and then select the best model for prediction.

   b. Execute the pipeline:

      i. This will combine different steps into a single pipeline, submit it for execution, and then follow the execution to monitor the status of the pipeline. You can follow the execution of the pipeline using the Pipeline menu option in the leftmost pane of SageMaker Studio.

4. Create the SageMaker inference pipeline:

   a. Define the `target_column_name = "Price"`.

   b. Define the model locations (unless you want to add your models, you can run this as is).

   c. Create the SageMaker models.

   d. Create the inference pipeline:

      i. Create a pipeline model.

      ii. Deploy the model to an endpoint for inference (predictions). The deployment phase can take some time to finish.

5. Make predictions:

   a. Use the Make a Sample Inference Request option to perform predictions. Currently, it provides a sample data point that you can use to perform predictions. You can use the data point and then make some changes to it to perform multiple predictions, as shown in Figure 8-22.

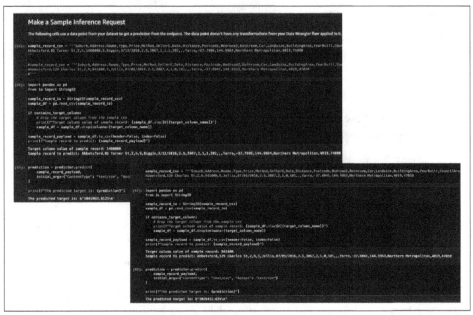

Figure 8-22. Making predictions

This is just the tip of the iceberg for AWS SageMaker, which is a huge platform with many options at each step to design, build, and execute ML pipelines. Refer to the AWS SageMaker Developer Guide (*https://oreil.ly/mdiDn*) for a list of SageMaker features.

Cleanup

As we discussed earlier, cloud provider charges can get out of control if left unchecked, so it is important to ensure that all services are shut down and the corresponding resources are decommissioned. This section provides guidelines on how to perform a cleanup.

 Please note that cloud provider services are constantly evolving, and while I am providing best-effort guidelines here, it is the sole responsibility of the reader to ensure that they understand all the services they have deployed and that they decommission these services accordingly. When in doubt, always refer to the AWS official documentation for the latest updates.

Here are the steps to follow to perform a cleanup:

1. Clean the S3 bucket:

   a. Go to your Amazon S3 console. Choose Buckets, then click the bucket you created and select the checkbox next to the name of the item(s) you want to delete. Choose Delete. Ensure that you permanently deleted the object.

   b. Once the bucket is empty, you can delete your bucket by following the same procedure.

2. Delete the SageMaker Studio apps:

   a. Go to the SageMaker Studio console, select studio-user, and under Apps, click Delete app to delete all the apps listed.

   b. Wait for the Status to update to Deleted before proceeding. For additional information, please refer to the AWS documentation (*https://oreil.ly/Om-Zt*).

3. Clean the SageMaker Studio domain:

   a. Access the CloudFormation console by typing `CloudFormation` into the AWS console search bar and selecting it from the search results.

   b. Within the CloudFormation pane, navigate to Stacks.

   c. From the status drop-down menu, choose Active.

   d. Locate the stack named CFN-SM-IM-Lambda-catalog under Stack name and click it to view the stack details page.

   e. On the CFN-SM-IM-Lambda-catalog stack details page, click Delete to remove the stack along with the resources it generated in step 1.

 As a reminder, please refer to the latest documentation from AWS about working with SageMaker to keep up with the latest changes to the service and to ensure that you can decommission all the resources you don't need, to avoid any unnecessary charges.

Exploring Amazon Forecast

The second service we will explore from the AWS AI/ML stack is Amazon Forecast. This service provides forecasting capabilities on time series data. *Time series data* is data created by taking repeated measurements of the same thing at regular intervals over a period of time. A few examples of time series data are:

- Heartbeat readings from a smartwatch every 10 minutes
- Periodic temperature readings from a weather sensor for 24 hours
- Stock ticker values over the past three months
- Number of items sold per day recorded over the past year

The common element among time series data is a timestamp associated with each reading. Also note the interval between two consecutive readings. This interval can be in microseconds, days, or even months, but in most cases it remains constant across a time series recording. This helps make the data predictable and allows for performing grouping, aggregations, and other analytics on top of the data.

Now that you understand what a time series is, let's look at what it means to forecast a time series. Consider the time series plot in Figure 8-23.

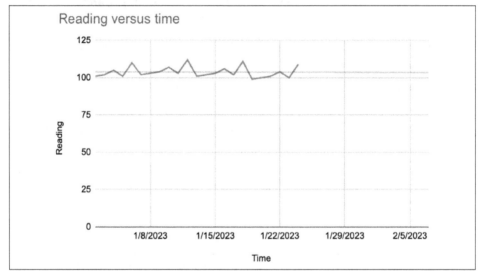

Figure 8-23. Time series plot

The jagged line represents actual readings for the time series data, which ends at around January 24, 2023. The straight line is a linear trend line mapped on top of the time series data. We could also do a trend line using other statistical functions, such as exponential or moving averages. While this time series plot gives us a fair idea of the trend of the time series, it is not nearly accurate enough to predict or forecast daily readings beyond the data we have available. This is where Amazon Forecast comes in. We will go through an example to see whether we can generate more accurate forecasts on our time series data using this service.

For this discussion, we will use a sample time series dataset that is a modification of an original dataset (*https://oreil.ly/o37ON*) of synthetic time series data. The modified dataset, *sales_inventory_3.csv*, can be downloaded from the book's GitHub repository (*https://oreil.ly/T-VR_*). The dataset describes the demand for different items on a particular day. The following columns exist in the data:

timestamp
> The day on which the item demand was recorded

item_id
> A unique ID that represents a particular item

demand
> The demand for that particular item on the given day

The time series data in this dataset contains data up to November 30, 2018. We call this our *historical time series*. Amazon Forecast can also consider other data that complements our historical data. In our case, we can consider the historical data containing the key, which is the item_id, and the target for the forecast, which is the demand. Another time series dataset can contain additional information, such as the item's price; AWS calls such a dataset a *related time series*.

While the historical data only contains data points up to the point where the forecasting window starts, related time series data can contain data points inside the forecasting window. When this is the case, the time series is known as a *forward-looking related time series*. In our examples, we will use a forward-looking related time series dataset that contains the item price as well. This related dataset is a modification of the original dataset. The related dataset, *sales_inventory_supp_3.csv*, can be downloaded from the book's GitHub repository (*https://oreil.ly/fJnsV*).

Amazon Forecast can use related time series data to further improve the accuracy of the forecast and help perform "what-if" analyses. As a prerequisite, import both the historical dataset and the forward-looking related dataset into an S3 bucket in the same region where you plan to use Amazon Forecast.

Import Data

The first step is to import our data into Amazon Forecast. Navigate to the Amazon Forecast Console (*https://oreil.ly/zSGPU*), open it, and create a dataset group, as shown in Figure 8-24.

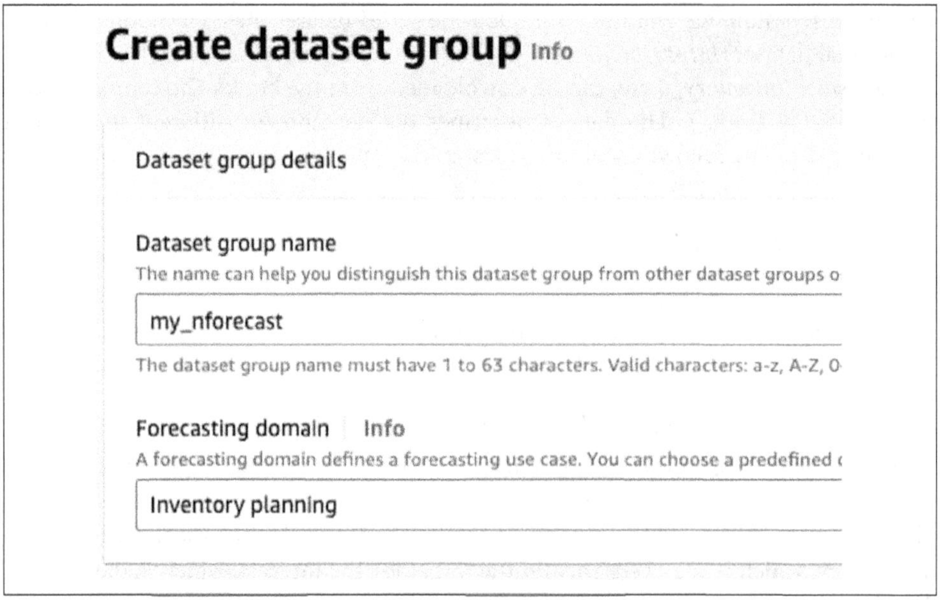

Figure 8-24. Creating a dataset group

Amazon provides a set of predefined forecasting domains, as well as the option to use a custom domain if the use case does not fit in any of the predefined domains. We will use the inventory planning domain. The idea is that based on historical data, we want to predict the demand for particular items to plan our inventory accordingly. You can also consider the retail domain and contrast it with the results you get from the inventory planning domain.

Once we select the domain, the wizard allows us to import our historical data into the dataset group. Consider the following items:

Frequency of data

Set this interval to the reading in your time series data. In our case, we are taking daily readings, so we will set it to one day.

Data schema

This defines how the data is represented in our dataset. Since we are using the inventory planning domain, we will have item_id, timestamp, and demand as prepopulated columns. Ensure that the order of the attributes matches the order in which the columns occur in the historical data. You can use the graphical Schema Builder on the JSON-based schema definition. You would want to change the timestamp format to yyyy-mm-dd as this is what is being used in our dataset. Here is my JSON schema for reference:

```
{
    "Attributes": [
        {
            "AttributeName": "timestamp",
            "AttributeType": "timestamp"
        },
        {
            "AttributeName": "item_id",
            "AttributeType": "string"
        },
        {
            "AttributeName": "demand",
            "AttributeType": "float"
        }
    ]
}
```

Data import details

Here we need to provide the information about the historical data that we want to import into our dataset:

1. Select CSV as the import type and point the S3 location to the historical dataset imported into S3 as part of the prerequisites.

2. We do not need to use a time zone in our dataset, so leave it as is.

3. If this is the first time you are using Amazon Forecast, select the option to create a new role under "IAM role." As part of this creation, select your S3 bucket where the datasets are placed to make sure Amazon Forecast can access your datasets for import.

It should not take too long for the data to import. You will be routed to a dashboard where you can monitor the progress of the import. Once the import is complete, use the Import option under Related time series data to import the forward-looking related dataset to the dataset group.

Train the Predictor

Once the data is imported, we can move to the second step, which is training a predictor. This can be achieved from the dashboard itself. As part of the training definition, we need to consider the following parameters:

Forecast frequency

This will be set to the frequency of the data, which is one day in our case.

Forecast horizon

This tells the model to determine the forecast window. We will use 30. This number multiplied by the forecast frequency provides the total length of our forecast window. In our case, it will be 30 days.

Forecast quantiles
> This measures the percentage fraction of the forecasted values that will be higher than the observed values. So, let's say we are using 0.90; this means the observed value will be either equal to or lower than the forecasted value 90% of the time.

Optimization metric
> The predictor works by minimizing average losses for forecasts. You can further optimize the predictor by selecting an additional accuracy metric. We will leave this at its default.

Other parameters
> We will leave the other parameters at their defaults, as well.

At this point, the training for the predictor should begin. It took me a little over three hours to train my predictor with the preceding configuration.

Create a Forecast

To create a forecast, we just need to select the predictor we trained in the previous step and then select All items. Once the forecast is created, we can query it from the dashboard. Depending on the dataset and the forecast horizon, the start and end date parameters will need to be specified within a range. Figure 8-25 shows how a forecast is generated for a specific item_id. You can vary the item_id and generate different forecasts as needed.

The shaded area on the left represents the historical data from our initial dataset. The lines on the right represent the P10 and P90 demand forecast for the next 30 days for item_id 39.

As an example use case, with Amazon Forecast a retail store chain can use its existing sales data to train a demand model and then use the model to predict the demand for each of its products. This would feed into its inventory management, which would use this information to determine how much inventory to maintain in different locations based on the demand forecasts. Accurately predicting demand can have the following benefits:

- Improve customer satisfaction in terms of stock availability.
- Avoid overstocking, which can be expensive and lead to losses in the case of perishable items.
- Optimize inventory distribution.
- Streamline manufacturing or sourcing of products.

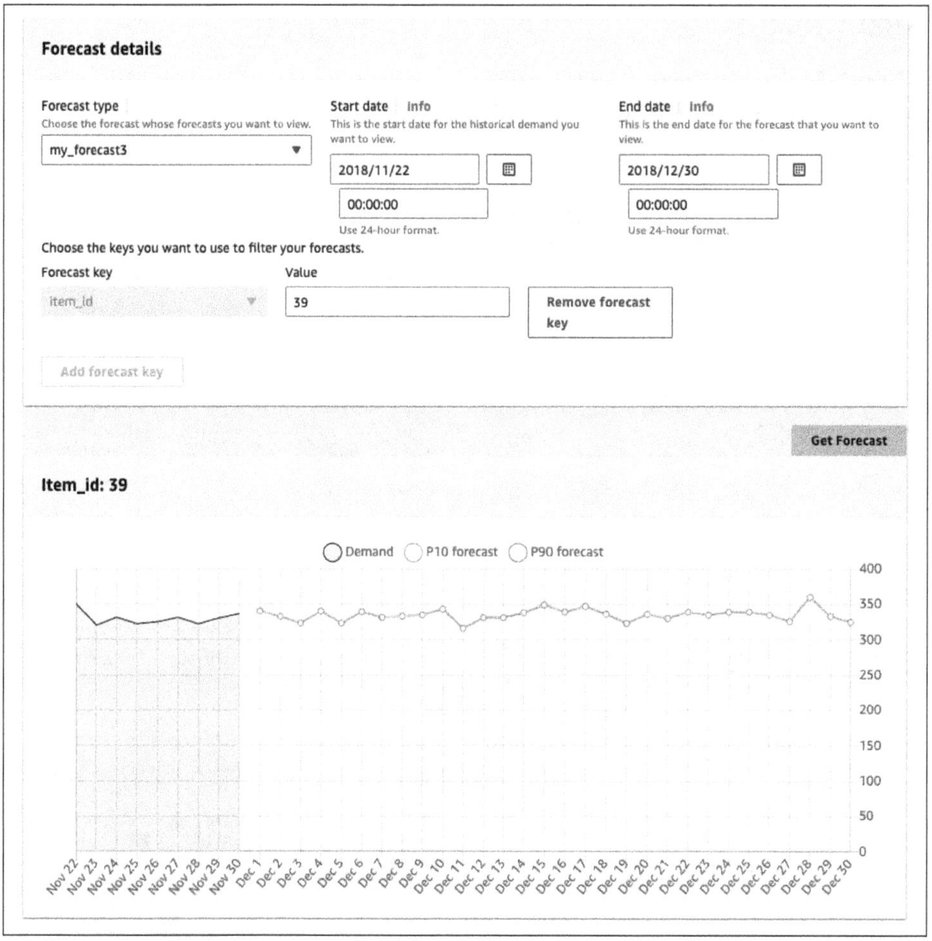

Figure 8-25. Generating a forecast

Besides the dashboard, the forecast can be consumed using the following methods:

- Export the forecast to S3 and then consume from there.
- Query the forecast using the Amazon Forecast Query Service API.

Note that as additional data becomes available, it can be imported into the dataset group, and the model can then be retrained over the new data.

What-If Analysis

Another interesting use of Amazon Forecast is creating "what-if" analyses. These can help organizations understand how their forecast would be impacted if certain parameters in their dataset were changed.

 You need a forward-looking related time series dataset in your dataset group for a what-if analysis to work.

In our case, our related dataset contains price information. The questions we want to ask are as follows:

- How would my forecast vary if I were to increase my product price by a factor of 1.5?
- What would be the impact on my forecast if I were to discount my product price by 50%?

To answer these questions, we create a what-if analysis using the dashboard. Select the Explore what-if analysis option and create a what-if analysis.

Next, we need to create a couple of what-if forecasts. A what-if forecast provides a means to alter the original related time series data and see how it impacts the original forecast. There are currently two methods to alter the data:

1. Define transformations on the data.

2. Use a replacement dataset.

Let's use option 1 to create two what-if forecasts (see Figure 8-26).

| Increase price by 1.5 | Multiply ▼ | price ▼ | by | 1.5 ↕ |
| Discount price by 50% | Divide ▼ | price ▼ | by | 2 |

Figure 8-26. What-if forecasts

Once the forecasts are created, we compare them by selecting them and then generating a comparison. I generated the comparison shown in Figure 8-27 using an `item_id` value of 39.

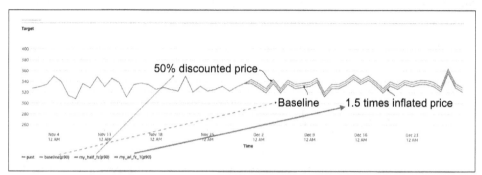

Figure 8-27. What-if analysis #1

A quick analysis of the comparison in Figure 8-27 reveals that as we discount the item, the demand for that item increases when compared to the baseline; likewise, when we increase the price of the item, the demand decreases. We can do further analysis to look at the impact of increasing the price of the product by a factor of 5.

Create another what-if forecast using a transformation to multiply the price by 5. Figure 8-28 shows the impact of the price increase.

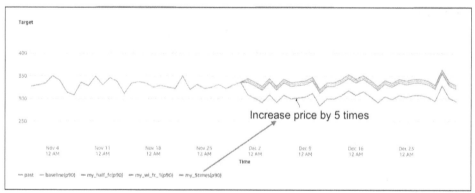

Figure 8-28. What-if analysis #2

Further increasing the price negatively impacts product demand as the what-if comparison shows a significantly lower demand graph.

Cleanup

As we discussed earlier, it is important to ensure that all services are shut down and the corresponding resources are decommissioned. This section provides guidance on how to perform a cleanup after finishing the preceding exercise.

 Please note that cloud provider services are constantly evolving, and while I am providing best-effort guidelines here, it is the sole responsibility of the reader to ensure that they understand all the services they have deployed and that they decommission these services accordingly. When in doubt, always refer to the AWS official documentation for the latest updates.

Amazon Forecast uses the concept of resource trees, so some resources are nested inside trees. When you delete a parent resource the corresponding children of that tree are automatically deleted. You can choose to delete individual resources or resource trees to perform a cleanup. Please refer to the Amazon Forecast documentation (*https://oreil.ly/FGO9r*) to learn more about managing and deleting Amazon Forecast resources.

We have deployed the following resources:

- Dataset group
- Predictor
- Forecast
- What-if analysis
- What-if forecast

Here are the steps to follow to perform the cleanup:

1. Clean up Amazon Forecast resources:
   a. Log in to the AWS Management Console (*https://oreil.ly/zSGPU*) and access the Amazon Forecast console.
   b. Go to the navigation pane and select the resource type of the parent resource or the individual resource that you want to delete.
   c. Select the specific resource you intend to remove, then click Delete.
   d. In the confirmation field, enter **delete**.
   e. Finally, click Delete to confirm the removal process.

2. Clean the S3 bucket:

   a. Go to your Amazon S3 console. Choose Buckets, then click the bucket you created and select the checkbox next to the name of your bucket. Choose Delete. Ensure that you permanently deleted the object.

   b. Once the bucket is empty, you can delete your bucket by following the same procedure.

3. Clean the IAM role (if you created a new IAM role):

   a. Access the AWS Management Console (*https://oreil.ly/09JWw*) and launch the IAM console.

   b. Use the navigation pane and select Roles. Then, tick the checkbox next to the role name you wish to remove.

   c. Click Delete, located at the top of the page, to initiate the deletion process.

 Please refer to the latest documentation from AWS about working with Amazon Forecast to keep up with the latest changes to the service and to ensure that you can decommission all the resources you don't need, to avoid any unnecessary charges.

Conclusion

In this chapter, we discussed the pros and cons of building ML systems using cloud provider services. We explored a couple of important AI/ML services from AWS that can assist us with predictive analytics. We started with AWS SageMaker, which helps us build and execute end-to-end ML pipelines, and then looked at Amazon Forecast, which makes it tremendously simple for organizations to perform predictive forecasts on their existing time series data.

AWS has a ton of services in the AI/ML space, and this number is ever increasing. If you're interested in exploring more services, I suggest trying Amazon Personalize (*https://oreil.ly/WeZQw*). This AWS service allows enterprises to add personalized recommendations in their applications and effectively perform user segmentation. Another related service that could be of interest is Amazon Lookout for Metrics (*https://oreil.ly/nT44z*), which helps with use cases that depend on anomaly detection.

## CHAPTER 9

Food for Thought

In order to predict the future, we must understand the past.

Let's recap what we explored in this book. We started with a background of predictive analytics. Chapter 1 assumed minimal prior knowledge of the subject and painted a picture in terms of everyday life. We discussed the use of predictive analytics versus other forms of analytics, and we took a walk down memory lane to understand the origins of data analytics and how it has evolved over the past century. The chapter then introduced the tools and frameworks available for data professionals to start implementing predictive analytics in their enterprises. What I enjoyed most about writing this chapter was the conceptualization of the magic store and the data analytics timeline. Since this is a rapidly evolving industry, I see the list of tools and frameworks changing over the course of future edits to the book.

Chapter 2 built on the discussion in Chapter 1, covering how organizations have moved from data producing to data driven. We explored the significance of data within organizations and strategies for maximizing the potential of this frequently underestimated organizational resource. Then, we dove into common challenges faced by enterprises when they are trying to build a predictive analytics practice, highlighting a few successful implementations of predictive analytics across vertical industries. The part I had the most fun writing was the detailed account of the use of predictive analytics in the entertainment industry. I see more detailed predictive analytics use cases being added in the future. My inclination is toward something being used in conjunction with generative AI, but only time will tell.

Chapter 3 delved deeper into the mathematics. It covered topics for statistics and linear algebra and then built on that knowledge to talk about how various ML algorithms work. Some algorithm discussions were more in-depth than others. That is not to be interpreted as one being more pertinent, but only a matter of choice when it comes to figuring out the best way to build this knowledge from the ground up.

While the linear algebra discussion took me back to my favorite university courses, the part I enjoyed most was the discussion about support vector machines. I see an obvious evolution in terms of the algorithms and see more being added to this list. I also feel that in time, more details on existing commentary can be added.

In Chapter 4, we discussed the nuances of working with data. I wanted to focus on data processing for higher-quality predictive modeling, a topic not discussed enough in the field. The chapter then zoomed out and covered the end-to-end predictive analytics pipeline so that we could put all the Lego bricks together and understand the placement of different components within the pipeline.

Chapter 5 is where the fun began, especially if you enjoy hands-on learning. The chapter talked about the three foundational components for predictive analytics and machine learning in Python: NumPy, Pandas, and scikit-learn. I thought it would be useful to start with how to set things up and then to talk about how NumPy and Pandas can help when working with data in Python. Finally, we dove into a few simple examples of using the scikit-learn Python library to do some basic predictive modeling and predictions. This chapter might feel elementary for some readers, but I found myself going back to it from time to time as a reference, to sort out individual steps in a long sequence of modeling and training.

Chapter 6 discussed TensorFlow fundamentals and its use in predictive analytics. We used linear regression as our baseline to understand the steps involved when using TensorBoard for an ML pipeline. The chapter then dove into a deep neural network example using the framework. Anyone who has worked with TensorFlow knows it can be complex to navigate. The idea for this chapter was to help readers navigate this complexity while focusing on explaining the code where needed and getting to the finish line in a predictable manner.

Chapter 7 is where we started industrializing things. The chapter gave examples of using predictive analytics in three vertical industries: retail, entertainment, and finance. The retail use case looked at optimal retail price recommendations for maximizing sales for individual items. The entertainment use case discussed a recommendation engine for a streaming service, but it could be applied to any form of media in the entertainment industry. The finance case looked at identifying fraudulent credit card transactions based on historical data. What I enjoyed most in this chapter was the retail use case for optimal price recommendations. It allowed me to discuss the process of working with data and getting to predictive insights in an evolutionary fashion, without overcomplicating things.

Chapter 8 looked at the AI/ML services provided by public cloud providers and discussed a couple of them to get you started. It began by asking the question every chief technology officer wants to address for the next five years: Should the organization move to a cloud-only strategy or is there wisdom in keeping things hybrid (or even self-managed in some cases)? We then discussed AWS SageMaker and Amazon

Forecast, which allow us to build ML pipelines and make forecasts on time series data, respectively. My favorite parts of this chapter were the cloud strategy discussion in the beginning and the what-if analysis when discussing Amazon Forecast.

A Few More Use Cases

Before we conclude, let's discuss some forward-looking use cases and see whether predictive analytics can be used to improve their operational accuracy.

Navigation and Traffic Management

Anyone who drives a car these days uses some form of navigation. Before the advent of smartphones, we had companies dedicated to GPS-based navigation and maps. Now, most people rely on their smartphones for this. Both Google and Apple have navigation applications that help us move around daily.

When we are looking for directions, these applications can predict arrival times to a particular destination with a fair amount of accuracy. These calculations consider factors such as distance and average driving speed. However, they also can incorporate traffic conditions and compare different days of the week to come up with better time estimates.

For the sake of simplicity, let's consider a model that uses the following parameters:

- Distance
- Time of day
- Day of the week
- Traffic conditions
- Accidents
- Road speed limit

Here are other factors that can impact traveling speeds and therefore arrival estimates:

- Car make and model
- Driver's age (we might be able to figure out a common pattern among drivers from similar age groups)
- Weather conditions
- User's travel history
- Known versus unknown terrain

Some or even all of these items might already be used by navigation applications. Some of them might not be relevant, some might be redundant, and for some the data might be too scarce. The feasibility of using them would require a bit of analysis and research. However, the idea is to look at potential areas of improvement for applications we already use regularly.

In the transportation industry, traffic systems use programmable traffic lights that run according to preexisting timers, certain simulations, or existing traffic conditions. The idea is to ease traffic congestion and avoid bottlenecks. Traffic lights work as a tool to manage the flow of vehicles. Typically, navigation software is targeted at optimizing the travel journey of an individual, but it could potentially be used as a tool to manage traffic flow. In simple terms, the directions given to individuals could also consider the impact of their travel on overall traffic. From a service perspective, this could mean the application might prioritize traffic conditions over an individual consumer's preference to reach their destination as efficiently as possible. Figure 9-1 provides a rough representation of this.

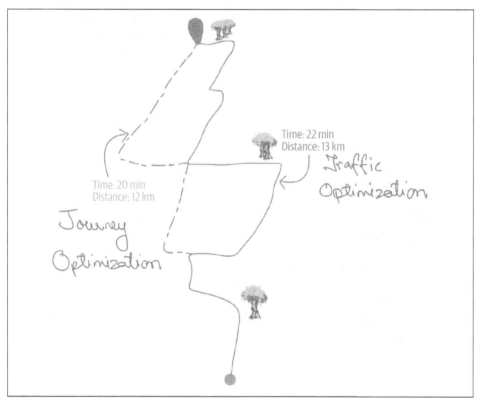

Figure 9-1. City traffic versus individual journey optimization

Would this be acceptable by consumers?

Credit Scoring

Let's talk about another use case: credit scoring. Typically used by financial institutions, credit scoring is the process of rating an individual to determine whether they should be approved for a loan and what the amount of that loan should be. Some considerations when calculating an individual's credit score could be their annual income, existing loans, credit history, and assets. The point is to figure out, with a certain level of accuracy, the likelihood of an individual paying back a loan.

While credit scoring started with financial loans, its use has become widespread among other industries. For example, in my city, if I would like to be put on a payment plan by my cell phone service provider so that I can pay for a new device, the service provider would check my credit score to decide what (and how many) devices I'm eligible to put on the payment plan. Due to the increased usage of credit scoring, many developed economies have centralized bodies as part of their government to maintain the credit history and scoring of their citizens.

Another implementation of this idea considered by several governments and law enforcement agencies is social scoring systems. The concept for such systems is to score citizens based on their everyday lives. Theoretically, a person's food preferences, exercise habits, salary, spending habits, and how they conduct themselves as a citizen, among other things, could act as input. Someone who exercises, eats healthily, and does social work could be rated higher than someone who has an unhealthy lifestyle and has been racking up fines for social disruptions. With everything going digital, it is now easier than ever to create a digital twin of an individual, monitor the twin, and then predict social behavior based on these inputs.

It is not far-fetched to imagine that such systems have the potential to go from observing to surveillance and from surveillance to control, as depicted in Figure 9-2. As we continue to give up our digital freedoms, there is an ethical debate to be had on where we draw the line regarding sharing every single aspect of our lives and how that information can potentially be used.

While we have discussed several enterprise use cases, note that predictive analytics has applications in other vertical industries, including healthcare, education, insurance, the stock market, fundraising, and manufacturing.

Figure 9-2. Theoretical representation of a social scoring system

The Social Impact of Predictions

There is an ongoing debate taking place within social and scientific circles regarding the impact of content personalization. An ecommerce platform can suggest items to us based on our user profile, purchase history, and similarity to other users on the platform. The idea is to show us products we are more likely to buy. However, nothing stops the platform from suggesting content it wants to place in the market strategically. Also, paid sponsorships can boost product visibility on the platform. While this does not mean there is anything sinister going on when it comes to predictive analytics, when content is personalized it is not necessary that the parameters behind that personalization are all related to the person themselves.

We can do a similar analysis of other online platforms that depend on content personalization. The media content an online streaming platform recommends is prone to the same level of manipulation. Among the thousands of titles for movies and TV shows, what we end up watching is most frequently dependent on either what we are shown by the platform or what is recommended to us by someone we know.

Social media platforms are another example. While the promise is that the content we are shown depends on our interests and activities on the platform, commercial content is very well embedded into what we see. This question with regard to the ethics of the content shown to us existed long before the advent of the internet. Before social media we had television, and before television we had radio. Admittedly, social media platforms do provide more control to the user. The content we consume can have an impact on our thought process. It is hard to distinguish between what is being shown out of an individual's interest versus what is being shown to influence that interest.

Predictions make it easy for a platform to determine what a person might be interested in. Identifying individual interests on a mass scale can allow a platform access to the minds of millions of individuals susceptible to exploitation. Are these "predictive suggestions" based on our preferences and interaction with the system, or are they "suggestive predictions" that influence and sometimes alter our thought process (see Figure 9-3)?

Figure 9-3. The influence of media platforms

It is the responsibility of civic societies, policymakers, and enterprises to regulate the rules governing content distribution to the masses. Such a regulation should be driven by:

- Transparency:
  - The individual user should be able to clearly decipher interest-driven content from sponsored content.
  - There should be a documented balance between these content categories.
- Organic distribution of content:
  - Enterprises should work to ensure that predictive algorithms are used to identify and not to influence.
  - Enterprises should ensure that this distribution cannot be manipulated and should continuously monitor and crack down on such manipulation.
- Vigorous controls:
  - Content should be better regulated to ensure the protection of younger minds.
  - Content should be better regulated to ensure respect for different cultures.
- Who has access to what data:
  - Content providers should ensure that when predictive analytics is being used, the data lands in the right hands. Correct predictions in the wrong hands can be detrimental to individuals and societies.

Consider an algorithm that helps identify individuals who are prone to heart disease. In the right hands, this data can be used to help these individuals early on, ideally before the onset of the disease, to promote longevity and health. However, what if the same data was made available to their place of work and was used to discriminate against them?

A number of these policies are implemented across various global platforms. Some do a better job at it than others. Centralized (or distributed) governance is an area of improvement for the industry.

Conclusion

Predictive analytics is an area in science that has far-reaching impact beyond just the scientific realm. We have seen its use across enterprises as a helpful tool for decision making. With the recent advancements in machine learning and generative AI, a lot of this decision making will be automated. This means human intervention in the process will be further reduced. Considering the advanced processing capabilities and increased autonomy of distributed systems, we are laying the foundation for self-learning, data-driven decision making. We should carefully consider the ethical and moral boundaries we would want to teach in a system that might have a crucial role in the future of our species.

Index

price recommendations (see retail price recommendations)
principal component analysis (PCA), 119
product-based content filtering, 247
pruning, 83
Python, 129-166
    Anaconda, 129-131
    basics, 17-18
    exploring a business example using Pandas, 142-146
    in TensorFlow, 186-192
    installing, 130-131
    Jupyter Notebooks, 129-131
    NumPy, 132-146
    Pandas, 146-166
    scikit-learn, 167-183

R

R-squared (coefficient of determination), 67-70, 173-175
random classifier baseline, 275
random forests, 84
recommender systems, 246-266
    kNN algorithm for, 252-256
    kNN-based, 256-261
    surprise library for, 250-266
    two-stage systems, 261-266
rectified linear unit (ReLU) activation function, 88, 206
rectifier function, 88
regression analysis, 53-72
    defined, 56-59
    for retail price recommendations
        multivariate regression, 233-246
        polynomial regression, 221-232
        simple linear regression, 216-221
    model selection, 70-72
    R-squared and p-value, 67-70
    techniques, 59-67
regression trees, 80-82
reinforcement learning, 14, 108
related time series, 319
relational databases, 5
ReLU (rectified linear unit) activation function, 88, 206
retail price recommendations, 213-246
    multivariate regression model, 233-246
    polynomial regression model, 221-232
    simple linear regression model, 216-221

RMSE (root mean squared error), 58, 174

S

SageMaker, 18, 295-317
    cleanup, 316
    data ingest and exploration, 297-303
    data transformation, 304-313
    model training and prediction, 314-316
    prerequisites, 296
scikit-learn, 167-183
    clustering, 182
    random forest classifier, 175-177
    training and predicting with a linear regression model, 168-175
    training decision trees, 177-182
semi-supervised learning, 14
sigmoid function, 88
soft margin classification, 96
softmax, 92
SQL (Structured Query Language), 5
statistics, 46-53
supervised learning, 14, 106-108
surprise library, building recommender systems with, 250-266
    kNN algorithm, 252-256
    kNN-based systems, 256-261
    two-stage recommender systems, 261-266
SVM (support vector machines), 93-98
synapses, 87

T

target leakage, 300
TensorFlow, 185-210
    basics, 18
    deep neural networks, 202-210
    fundamentals, 186-192
    linear regression, 193-201
        data preparation, 194-196
        model creation and training, 196-199
        predictions and model evaluation, 200-201
tensors, 186
threshold function, 88
time series data, 317
Timeseries Insights API, 20
two-stage recommender systems, 261-266
    ranker stage, 264-266
    retriever stage, 262-264

About the Author

Nooruddin Abbas Ali is a global leader for ecosystem and AI partner Solutions Architects at MongoDB. This select global team works with innovative customers and partners looking to disrupt their respective industries. It is the team's belief that data is the key to unlocking business potential and bringing about the sustainable disruption that moves the human race forward. Nooruddin has been in the tech and service management industry for over 20 years, where he has held several positions in development, professional services, management, pre-sales, and thought leadership. He has worked for 0-1 startups, large public cloud providers (Alibaba Cloud), hyper-growth data platform companies (MongoDB), and end-to-end large system integrators.

Nooruddin has been working with distributed data systems and cloud technologies for over a decade. He has experience and credentials in multiple cloud technologies, architecture best practices, AI, and application data platforms. This unique combination of data and cloud skills, coupled with his experience at various levels of the enterprise spectrum, has allowed him to amass the knowledge and field experience required to make this book multifaceted while having depth on core foundations of predictive analytics.

Colophon

The animal on the cover of *Predictive Analytics for the Modern Enterprise* is a black dwarf honeybee (*Apis andreniformis*). In general, honeybees are important for the pollination of flowers and plants, and the black dwarf honeybee specifically provides useful products such as wax and honey.

This insect has dark black coloration and is the smallest of the honeybee species, usually being 6.5 to 10 mm in length. All honeybees are social insects, and the black dwarf honeybee is no exception. The insects live together in nests or hives and perform vertical waggle dancelike movements to communicate with each other.

The black dwarf honeybee is a relatively rare species, and its natural habitat is the tropical and subtropical regions of Southeast Asia. Although the honeybee is not particularly defensive, the insect is hard to relocate and will swarm to a new location if it is moved. Many of the animals on O'Reilly covers are endangered; all of them are important to the world.

The cover illustration is by Karen Montgomery, based on a black-and-white engraving from *Mysteries of Bee-Keeping*. The series design is by Edie Freedman, Ellie Volckhausen, and Karen Montgomery. The cover fonts are Gilroy Semibold and Guardian Sans. The text font is Adobe Minion Pro; the heading font is Adobe Myriad Condensed; and the code font is Dalton Maag's Ubuntu Mono.

O'REILLY®

Learn from experts.
Become one yourself.

Books | Live online courses
Instant answers | Virtual events
Videos | Interactive learning

Get started at oreilly.com.

©2023 O'Reilly Media, Inc. O'Reilly is a registered trademark of O'Reilly Media, Inc. | 175

Printed in the USA
CPSIA information can be obtained
at www.ICGtesting.com
JSHW051431260524
63707JS00005B/18